Study Guide
for Sigelman and Shaffer's

LIFE-SPAN HUMAN DEVELOPMENT

Prepared by
ELIZABETH RIDER
ELIZABETHTOWN COLLEGE

BROOKS/COLE PUBLISHING COMPANY
PACIFIC GROVE, CALIFORNIA

Brooks/Cole Publishing Company
A division of Wadsworth, Inc.

Printed in the United States of America

10 9 8 7 6 5 4 3 2 1

ISBN 0-534-12284-1

Contents

To the Student

This Study Guide was written to help you better understand and remember the material presented in <u>Life-Span Human Development</u> by Carol Sigelman and David Shaffer. Note that the Study Guide is a supplement to, not a substitute for, the textbook--You still need to read the textbook! The combination of carefully reading the textbook and working through the Study Guide will enhance your understanding of life-span human development. Each chapter in the Study Guide corresponds to a chapter in the textbook and contains the following sections:

<u>Learning Objectives</u> state what you should know once you have read and studied a chapter. Read these first before you begin a chapter so that you have an idea of what is in the chapter. After you have finished reading and studying a chapter, try rephrasing the objectives as questions and testing your knowledge.

<u>Summary and Guided Review</u>, when completed, provides an overview of the main points in each chapter of the text. As you read through the summary, fill-in the blanks with the terms that appropriately complete a sentence. You will notice that there are questions in parentheses scattered throughout the summary. These are meant to encourage you to think actively as you are reading and connect this summary to the more detailed information provided in the text. You can answer these questions as you are filling in the blanks or you can fill-in all the blanks, then go back and reread the entire summary, addressing the questions in order to provide greater depth of understanding. Although blank spaces are provided, you may want to write your answers on a separate piece of paper, which will make it easier to compare your answers to the correct answers. Whether you write in the spaces provided or use a separate piece of paper for your answers, don't forget to answer the questions in parentheses!

<u>Review of Key Terms and Concepts</u> is a matching exercise designed to facilitate review of important terms, which are in bold type in the textbook. Match each listed term with its appropriate definition. You might also want to try writing definitions in your own words and then checking your definitions with those here in the Study Guide or in the text.

<u>Research Summary and Review</u> is included to help you gain a better understanding of research and its contribution to what we know about life-span development. You should not worry too much about remembering names, dates, and minuscule details of research reports. But it is important in psychology and other fields to be able to concisely summarize research and understand what contribution that research makes. For each research article cited in this section, you should summarize the <u>main point(s)</u> of the research and also indicate its contribution or its importance. The research articles were selected on the basis of how much coverage they received in the text and how important they are to the field.

Self Test consists of multiple choice questions that you can use to check your understanding of key concepts in a chapter. Remember, when completing multiple choice tests, always read all the possible answers before selecting the one that best answers the question.

Application asks you to go beyond information that is directly presented in the textbook. It requires you to apply the material to a problem of current interest, or to synthesize and integrate several concepts to arrive at a new understanding of some problem. There is often no single answer to these application questions. Use the text to check that your basic facts are correct and get together with other students in the class to receive some feedback on your application of the facts and to hear other ways to answer the question.

Answers are provided for the Summary and Guided Review, Key Terms, and the Self Test. Whenever you miss a question or term, go back to the textbook and reread that section so that you understand why an answer is correct or incorrect.

A few final words of advice--Take some time at the end of each chapter to reflect on what was interesting, relevant, or important to you from the chapter material. Don't get so caught up in learning and memorizing facts that you forget to enjoy the material!

Elizabeth Rider

Chapter One
Understanding Life-Span Human Development

After reading and studying the material in this chapter, you should be able to do the following:

1. Describe the concepts of development, growth, and aging.

2. Name and describe two processes that underlie developmental change.

3. Explain how our understanding of life-span development has changed historically.

4. Describe the goals of life-span developmental psychology.

5. Discuss the five assumptions of the life-span perspective on human development.

6. Explain the scientific method and indicate its importance.

7. Describe the following data collection techniques: Interviews, questionnaires, psychological tests, naturalistic observation, and case studies.

8. Describe, and then compare and contrast, the cross-sectional design, the longitudinal design, and the sequential design. What are the advantages and disadvantages of each design?

9. Describe the experimental method, including concepts of independent variable, dependent variable, control, and random assignment.

10. Describe the correlational method and indicate how it differs from the experimental method.

11. Explain the value of cross-cultural comparisons.

12. Explain the importance of research ethics in conducting developmental research.

The following summary provides an overview of the main points contained in this chapter of the text. Fill-in the blanks with terms that appropriately complete the sentence. Although blank spaces are provided, you may want to write your answers on a separate piece of paper, which will make it easier to compare your answers to the correct answers provided at the end of this chapter.

Scattered throughout the summary are questions in parentheses. These are meant to encourage you to think actively as you are reading and connect this summary to the more detailed information provided in the text. You can answer these questions as you are filling in the blanks or you can fill-in all the blanks, then go back and reread the entire summary, addressing the questions in order to provide more depth of understanding.

Systematic changes that occur in an individual between conception and death are called (1) _____. Developmentalists are concerned with three general areas of change, including (2) _____, (3) _____, and (4) _____ changes. Biologists define (5) _____ as physical changes occurring from conception to maturity and (6) _____ as the deterioration of an individual. Developmentalists, however, argue that both positive and negative changes occur throughout the (7) _____, and that (8) _____ refers to losses, gains and changes in the individual. Developmental change results from both (9) _____, which refers to the genetically programmed biological unfolding of traits and behaviors, and (10) _____, which refers to changes resulting from experience.

The life-span is typically divided into several phases which are defined differently by different cultures. The (11) _____ _____ to which a person belongs will in part determine the privileges and responsibilities that person will be granted, but age is only a rough guideline of a person's level of (12) _____.

Historically, our conceptions of life-span development have changed significantly. Children in premodern times were viewed as family (13) _____ and treated harshly. Toward the end of the 19th century, (14) _____ emerged as a period of life distinct from adulthood. (What events led to this development?) Conceptions of adulthood have also changed, in part because of increased (15) _____ _____, which has focused attention on middle age.

The study of life-span development is considered a (16) _____ enterprise. (What does this mean, or why is this important?) (17) _____ _____ is that branch of psychology, which studies the changes within individuals and between individuals across the lifespan. The goals of developmental psychology

include (18) _____, (19) _____, and
(20) _____ of development. (Can you provide an explanation
of what each of these goals involves?)

     The study of development began with observations that were recorded
in (21) _____ _____ and (22) _____,
which were used to collect more objective information from larger
numbers of children. (23) _____ _____ is
credited as the "founder" of developmental psychology and with drawing
attention to (24) _____ as a distinct period of development
characterized by storm and stress. Today, the study of life-span
development rests of five assumptions: 1) Development is a
(25) _____ process. 2) Development must be viewed in its
(26) _____ _____. (Can you provide an example of
this?) 3) Development can take (27) _____ directions. (What
does this mean?) 4) Development is influenced by (28) _____
factors. 5) Development during any one period of life can best be
understood in the context of the whole (29) _____.

     Understanding development is best accomplished through the
(30) _____ _____ which stresses that conclusions
should be based on systematic, unbiased observations (data).
(31) _____ are often developed to describe or explain a set
of observations or facts. To test the validity of a theory, specific
predictions, or (32) _____, can be generated and should hold
true if the theory is in fact valid.

     Any good measure of behavior should be both (33) _____ and
(34) _____. If a measure yields consistent information each
time it is administered to the same person(s), it is considered
(35) _____. If a measure actually measures what it is
supposed to measure, it is considered (36) _____.

     There are a number of ways to measure behavior. People can be
asked questions about their behavior, either orally using an
(37) _____ or in writing using a (38) _____. To
measure a person's abilities, aptitudes, or personality traits, a
(39) _____ _____ is often used. Rather than
asking people questions about their behavior, researchers might use
(40) _____, or naturalistic, observation to directly observe
behavior as it naturally occurs. Finally, any or all of these measures
can be used to construct a detailed (41) _____ _____
 of a single person's development. (What are the advantages and
disadvantages of each of these measurement techniques?)

     There are three main research designs used to describe
developmental change across the lifespan. The performances of different
age groups of people are compared in a (42) _____ design,
which yields information about age (43) _____. Since people
of different ages are studied, findings from this design may reflect
(44) _____ differences in addition to age differences. The
performance of the same group of people is measured repeatedly over

time in a (45) _____ design, yielding information about age (46) _____. Since people are repeatedly tested at different times, findings from this design may reflect changes due to (47) _____ __ _____ in addition to age changes. The (48) _____ design combines the cross-sectional and longitudinal designs in a single study in order to disentangle effects due to age, cohort, and time of measurement.

In an effort to explain behavior or identify causes of developmental change, researchers use the (49) _____ _____. The researcher manipulates or changes some aspect of the environment, called the (50) _____ variable, and measures the effect that this has on the (51) _____ variable. In order to determine if a particular treatment has a different effect on one age group than it has on another, researchers may use an (52) _____ by (53) _____ design. (Can you provide an example of this type of design?) To conclude that a cause-effect relationship exists between an independent variable and a dependent variable, all factors other than the independent variable must be held constant, a procedure called (54) _____ _____. Researchers must also ensure that all subjects have an equal chance of participating in any of the treatment or control groups, through a procedure called (55) _____ _____. (What are some limitations of the experimental method?)

Some developmental questions cannot be answered by experimentally manipulating the environment. In these cases, researchers may use the (56) _____ method which involves determining whether two or more variables are related. (Can you provide an example of a question studied with this method?) A major limitation of the correlational method is that it does not establish a (57) _____ and (58) _____ relationship between the variables.

Since researchers cannot typically study all members of a population in which they are interested, they select a (59) _____ from this population. Ideally, a (60) _____ sample is selected so that all members of the population have an equal chance of being selected. A random sample allows the researcher to (61) _____ to other members of the population. To find out how developmental changes in one culture compare to developmental changes in other cultures, researchers conduct (62) _____ comparisons.

Researchers studying age changes or age differences may have difficulty finding (63) _____ that are equally valid at all ages being studied, or ensuring that a measure is in fact measuring the same trait or ability across different ages. Finally, researchers need to protect their subjects from physical or psychological harm by following certain standards of (64) _____ _____.

4

Below is a list of terms and concepts from this chapter. Match each
one with its appropriate definition. You might also want to try
writing definitions in your own words and then checking your
definitions with those here in the Study Guide or in the text.

age by treatment experiment   independent variable
age grades   learning
aging   life-span perspective
baby biographies   longitudinal design
case study   maturation
cohort   naturalistic observation
correlation   questionnaire
correlational method   random assignment
cross-cultural comparison   random sample
cross-sectional design   reliability
dependent variable   research ethics
development   sample
developmental psychology   scientific method
experiment   sequential design
experimental control   storm and stress
gerontology   theory
growth   time of measurement
hypothesis   validity

_____1. Relatively permanent changes in behavior resulting
                     from experiences or practice.

_____2. Belief that systematic and objective observations
                     should determine the merits of one's thinking.

_____3. Research technique in which some aspect of the
                     subject's environment is manipulated or altered to
                     see if there is any change in the subject's behavior.

_____4. The extent to which a test measures what it is
                     supposed to measure.

_____5. A testable prediction resulting from a theoretical
                     'position.

_____6. Standards of conduct that investigators must ethically
                     follow in order to protect subjects from harm.

_____7. Research design that involves determining whether two
                     or more variables are related.

_____8. A method in which hypotheses are tested by observing
                     behaviors under naturally occurring conditions.

_____9. Systematic changes in a person occurring between conception and death.

_____10. Recorded observations of an infant's behaviors over a period of time.

_____11. Age-related change is measured by studying subjects from different age groups repeatedly over time.

_____12. Area of psychology concerned with understanding changes within and between individuals across their lifespans.

_____13. A group of people of the same age who have been exposed to similar cultural and historical events.

_____14. A technique that ensures that all subjects have an equal chance of being included in all experimental conditions.

_____15. A relationship between two variables.

_____16. Physical changes that occur from conception to maturity.

_____17. Distinctive periods of the lifespan, usually delineated by ages.

_____18. Point(s) in history when data are collected.

_____19. Measures age-related differences by simultaneously studying subjects from different age groups.

_____20. An approach to the study of development that focuses on changes occurring from conception to death of a person.

_____21. A method in which hypotheses are tested by collecting and analyzing extensive information about the life of an individual.

_____22. Research design that includes age as well as another independent variable.

_____23. Changes that occur in a mature person.

_____24. Genetically programmed biological plan of development, relatively independent of effects of the environment.

_____25. Research technique which solicits answers to written questions.

_____26. The aspect of the environment that the investigator deliberately manipulates in order to discover what effect this has on behavior.

_____27. Characterization of adolescence as a stressful and turbulent period of change.

_____28. A set of rules or principles that describe and explain some behavior.

_____29. A subset of subjects from a larger population of interest.

_____30. A study that examines and compares behavior of people from different cultural backgrounds.

_____31. A technique that ensures that all factors besides the independent variable are controlled or held constant.

_____32. The study of aging and old age.

_____33. The extent to which a measure yields consistent scores across repeated measurements.

_____34. Measures age-related changes by repeatedly studying the same individuals over time.

_____35. The aspect of the subject's behavior that is observed or measured in order to determine whether the independent variable had an effect.

_____36. A sample of subjects drawn from the larger population of interest such that all subjects in the population have an equal chance of being selected for the sample.

RESEARCH SUMMARY AND REVIEW

For each of the following studies, briefly summarize the main point(s) of the research and indicate why the research is important. Don't worry about specific details that are not central to the main points, or memorizing names of researchers. Since the focus of this chapter is on methods for studying and measuring development, questions you might ask yourself about these studies include: What type of method was used? What was the hypothesis? What were the variables? What type of conclusion can be drawn from this research?
Use the text to check your understanding.

1. Coates and Hartup's (1969) study of developmental differences in observational learning (page 22): _____

_____

_____

_____

_____

2. Singer and Singer's (1981) study of the effects of viewing
    television (page 24-5): _____

_____

_____

_____

_____

        For additional practice, pull out some other research discussed in
this chapter or research discussed in class lectures and summarize the
main points of the studies. Or, try designing your own research study
to test some developmental question of interest to you.

SELF TEST _____

For each multiple choice question, read all alternatives and then
select the best answer.

1. The biological "unfolding" of a person's traits, abilities, and
    characteristics based on a genetic plan is referred to as
    a. development
    b. learning
    c. aging
    d. maturation

2. Development results from biologically programmed changes called
    _____ and from specific environmental experiences called
    _____.
    a. aging; learning
    b. learning; growth
    c. maturation; learning
    d. age changes; age differences

3. A child growing up in medieval times was likely to be
    a. regarded as part of a special group needing protection
    b. viewed as a "miniature" adult and governed by adult standards
    c. left to die as an infant if not judged to be healthy and strong
    d. viewed as an economic liability

4. The goals of developmental psychology are BEST described by which of the following?
    a. Developmental psychologists seek to modify behavior wherever possible.
    b. Developmental psychologists seek to identify behaviors that should be changed.
    c. Developmental psychologists seek to construct a single unifying theory to explain development.
    d. Developmental psychologists seek to describe and explain behavior, and where possible, optimize behavior.

5. An increase in life expectancy during the past century has resulted in
    a. an increased awareness of, and interest in, middle adulthood
    b. more attention to adolescence as a distinct period of the lifespan
    c. changes in the way we treat our children
    d. more research on infant capabilities

6. A measure that is reliable is one that
    a. measures what it is supposed to measure.
    b. is free from cultural bias.
    c. yields consistent information when repeatedly administered to the same individual(s).
    d. shows an improvement in scores when repeatedly administered to the same individual(s).

7. Cross-sectional designs provide information about age _____, while longitudinal designs provide information about age _____.
    a. differences; changes
    b. changes; differences
    c. differences; differences
    d. changes; changes

8. Measuring different groups of individuals repeatedly over time is called a _____ design.
    a. longitudinal
    b. cross-sectional
    c. sequential
    d. cross-cultural

9. Cross-sectional designs confound age with _____, while longitudinal designs confound age with _____.
    a. cohort; cohort
    b. time of measurement; cohort
    c. cohort; type of measurement
    d. cohort; time of measurement

10. If you wanted to show that a cause and effect relationship existed between teaching style and academic performance, you would use
    a. naturalistic observations of children in different classrooms
    b. questionnaires given to large numbers of children from different teaching situations
    c. an experimental study of children randomly assigned to different classes
    d. any of the above

11. Suppose you have one group of children role play (children assume the role of someone else) while another group of children does not role play. You then observe the level of empathy in children from both groups as they interact with other children. The dependent variable would be
    a. whether children role played or not
    b. children's level of empathy
    c. the relationship between role playing and level of empathy
    d. children's ability to role play

12. Theories generate specific _____ which can be tested to determine the validity of the theory.
    a. methods
    b. variables
    c. case studies
    d. hypotheses

13. Ensuring that all subjects have an equal chance of participating in any of the experimental treatments is accomplished
    a. through experimental control
    b. by selecting a random sample from the population
    c. through random assignment
    d. by administering a questionnaire

14. A positive correlation between viewing televised violence and aggressive behavior would indicate that
    a. children who watch less televised violence tend to be more aggressive
    b. children who watch more televised violence tend to be more aggressive
    c. increases in aggression are caused by watching more televised violence
    d. watching televised violence is not related to level of aggressive behavior

15. If you wanted to assess individual changes over time in prosocial behavior, you would need to use
    a. a longitudinal design
    b. a cross-sectional design
    c. a correlational design
    d. an experimental design

Many people in our society are interested in the possibility of "speeding up" some aspect of development, such as the ages when children can print or read. Similarly, parents are often concerned about providing appropriate learning experiences for their children to enhance their abilities. Design an experimental study to test the possibility that some specific aspect of development can be accelerated. Indicate the type of design and the variables used to test this hypothesis.

Another current concern is the effect of divorce on children of all ages. Design a study to assess whether divorce has a negative impact on children at different ages. Specify the type of design needed for this question and how you will measure the impact of divorce.

Before you leave this chapter, go back and take another look at the learning objectives presented at the beginning of the chapter. Rephrase each objective into a question and check to see whether you have mastered them. A good way to check your understanding of a concept is to see if you can teach it to someone else. Take turns doing this with a small group of people. Whenever you are unsure or unclear about a response, go back to the text and find out what information you are missing in order to provide a clear and complete response.

ANSWERS

Summary and Guided Review (Fill-in the blank)

1. development
2. physical
3. cognition
4. psychosocial
5. growth
6. aging
7. lifespan
8. aging
9. maturation
10. learning
11. age grade
12. development
13. possessions
14. adolescence
15. life expectancy
16. multidisciplinary
17. developmental psychology
18. description
19. explanation
20. optimization
21. baby biographies
22. questionnaires
23. G. Stanley Hall
24. adolescence
25. lifelong
26. historical context
27. multiple directions
28. multiple
29. lifespan
30. scientific method
31. theories
32. hypotheses
33. valid
34. reliable
35. reliable
36. valid
37. interview
38. questionnaire
39. psychological test
40. behavioral

41.	case study	53.	treatment
42.	cross-sectional	54.	experimental control
43.	differences	55.	random assignment
44.	cohort	56.	correlational
45.	longitudinal	57.	cause
46.	changes	58.	effect
47.	time of measurement	59.	sample
48.	sequential	60.	random
49.	experimental method	61.	generalize
50.	independent	62.	cross-cultural
51.	dependent	63.	measures
52.	age	64.	research ethics

Key Terms

1.	learning	19.	cross-sectional design
2.	scientific method	20.	life-span perspective
3.	experiment	21.	case study
4.	validity	22.	age by treatment experiment
5.	hypothesis	23.	aging
6.	research ethics	24.	maturation
7.	correlational method	25.	questionnaire
8.	naturalistic observation	26.	independent variable
9.	development	27.	storm and stress
10.	baby biography	28.	theory
11.	sequential design	29.	sample
12.	developmental psychology	30.	cross-cultural comparison
13.	cohort	31.	experimental control
14.	random assignment	32.	gerontology
15.	correlation	33.	reliability
16.	growth	34.	longitudinal design
17.	age grades	35.	dependent variable
18.	time of measurement	36.	random sample

Self Test

1.	D	9.	D
2.	C	10.	C
3.	B	11.	B
4.	D	12.	D
5.	A	13.	C
6.	C	14.	B
7.	A	15.	A
8.	C		

Chapter Two
Theories of Human Development

After reading and studying the material in this chapter, you should be able to do the following:

1. Name and explain the five major issues concerning developmental theorists.

2. Summarize Freud's three personality components--id, ego, and superego.

3. Describe Freud's stages of psychosexual development.

4. Discuss the major contributions of Freud's theory, as well as the strengths and weaknesses of the theory.

5. Summarize Erikson's theory of psychosocial development.

6. Discuss the strengths and weaknesses of Erikson's theory.

7. Compare and contrast Freud's and Erikson's theories.

8. Describe Piaget's basic perspective on cognitive development.

9. Define and give examples of assimilation and accommodation.

10. Name and describe Piaget's four stages of cognitive development.

11. Identify strengths and weaknesses of Piaget's theory.

12. Describe Skinner's operant learning theory.

13. Describe Bandura's cognitive social-learning theory.

14. Identify strengths and weaknesses of learning theory.

15. Explain the main points of ethological theory and describe how it relates to human development.

16. Identify strengths and weaknesses of ethological theory.

17. Describe the contextual-dialectical perspective.

18. Identify strengths and weaknesses of the contextual-dialectical perspective.

19. Discuss the importance of having a theory.

The following summary provides an overview of the main points contained in this chapter of the text. Fill-in the blanks with terms that appropriately complete the sentence. Although blank spaces are provided, you may want to write your answers on a separate piece of paper, which will make it easier to compare your answers to the correct answers provided at the end of this chapter.

Scattered throughout the summary are questions in parentheses. These are meant to encourage you to think actively as you are reading and connect this summary to the more detailed information provided in the text. You can answer these questions as you are filling in the blanks or you can fill-in all the blanks, then go back and reread the entire summary, addressing the questions in order to provide more depth of understanding.

This chapter examines basic issues and major theories of human development. One basic issue concerns whether people are inherently good or bad, or whether they are instead a (1) _____ _____, meaning they are inherently neither good or bad but develop according to their experiences. Another basic issue concerns whether development results primarily from biological forces or (2) _____, or whether development results primarily from environmental experiences or (3) _____. A third issue concerns whether people actively produce developmental change or are more (4) _____ shaped by biological and environmental forces outside of their control. A fourth issue is whether development is continuous or discontinuous. Continuity implies gradual and (5) _____ change, while discontinuity implies abrupt and (6) _____ change. Further, later developments can build upon early developments, or they can be unconnected or (7) _____ with earlier developments. A final developmental issue is whether we all follow the same (8) _____ path of development or whether we each follow different, (9) _____ paths of development. (Where do you stand on these issues and how do your views compare to the views of the major developmental theorists? See Boxes 2.1 and 2.8 in the text.)

Freud's (10) _____ theory proposes that humans have basic biological urges that must be satisfied. Freud found that the most important (11) _____, or biological force that motivates behavior, is the (12) _____ instinct.

Freud believed that there were three personality components. At birth, the personality consists of only (13) _____, which seeks to satisfy a person's instincts. During infancy, the (14) _____ begins to develop and tries to realistically satisfy the demands of the id. The third component of the personality is the (15) _____, which begins to develop during early childhood and functions as a person's internalized moral standards.

   Although we are presumably born with the sex instinct, the energy
associated with the sex instinct changes focus over development as
reflected by progression through Freud's stages of (16) _____
development. During the first stage, the sex instinct seeks pleasure
through (17) _____ activities. This focus shifts to
(18) _____ activities during the second psychosexual stage
of development. During the (19) _____ stage of
development, boys and girls become interested in their genitals and are
influenced by the presence or absence of a penis. Freud proposed that
boys experience the (20) _____ _____ during this
stage, characterized by desire for their mother and jealousy and fear of
their father. Resolution of these feelings involves
(21) _____ of boys' desire for their mother and
(22) _____ with their father. Girls experience the
(23) _____ _____ during this stage, which is
characterized by desire for their father and resentment towards their
mother. These feelings may simply fade away. (What explanation is
given for the difference in how boys and girls resolve the complexes of
this stage?) During the (24) _____ period, the psychic
energy of the sex instinct is channeled into socially appropriate
activities such as schoolwork. The (25) _____ stage is the
final psychosexual stage and occurs with the onset of puberty. It is
characterized by mature love with the goal of biological reproduction.

   Freud emphasized the influence of inborn biological drives but also
recognized that (26) _____ _____ could have a long-
term effect on personality development. During any psychosexual stage,
conflict among the personality components may create anxiety that is
alleviated by use of (27) _____ _____. One
example is (28) _____, which occurs when the psychic energy
remains tied to an early stage of development. Another example is
(29) _____, which involves returning to an earlier, less
traumatic stage of development. (What are the strengths and weaknesses
of Freud's theory?)

   Another psychoanalytic theorist, and one who was influenced by
Freud, is (30) _____. Erikson focuses less on sexual
instincts than Freud and more on societal forces. (In what other ways
are Freud's and Erikson's theories similar and different?) Erikson
proposed that maturation and society together create eight life
(31) _____, which correspond to Erikson's eight
(32) _____ stages of development. Each crisis can be
resolved positively or negatively and unresolved crises can have an
effect on later development. (Can you name and describe Erikson's eight
psychosocial stages?)

   Piaget focused on (33) _____ development and proposed
that children actively (34) _____ their understanding of the
world based on their experiences. Cognitive development results from
the interaction of maturation and environment. As children mature, they

develop more complex (35) _____ _____, which are
organized patterns of thought or action that are used to interpret
experiences. New experiences might be incorporated into existing
cognitive structures through a process called (36) _____, or
the cognitive structures might be altered to fit new experiences through
a process of (37) _____.

Piaget proposed four stages of cognitive development, which form an
(38) _____ _____, meaning that children progress
through the stages in order with no skipping. Infants are in the
(39) _____ stage because they learn about the world through
their sensory experiences and their motoric responses to these
experiences. Preschoolers are in the (40) _____ stage, which
is characterized by use of (41) _____ and lack of
(42) _____ thought. School-aged children are in the
(43) _____ _____ stage and can reason logically
about (44) _____ problems. Adolescents are in the
(45) _____ _____ stage, which is characterized by
(46) _____ testing and logical reasoning on abstract
problems. (What are the strength and weaknesses of Piaget's theory?)

John Watson believed it was not possible to study mental processes
and developed a "school" of psychology called (47) _____.
Watson believed that only (48) _____ behaviors were
appropriate for study and that (49) _____ associations
between a person's actions and external stimuli were the bases of human
development. Many of Watson's ideas have been advanced by
(50) _____, who demonstrated that existing behaviors become
more or less probable depending on the consequences of the behaviors.
This form of learning is called (51) _____ _____.
A (52) _____ is anything that increases the likelihood of
future responding and a (53) _____ is anything that decreases
the likelihood of future responding.

Another learning theorist, one who emphasized the importance of
cognition, was (54) _____. (55) _____
_____ theory makes the claim that humans are active
processors of environmental information. Consistent with this view,
Bandura also believes that development occurs through a constant give-
and-take relationship between a person and the environment, called
(56) _____ _____. In addition, Bandura believes
that (57) _____ _____ is the most important
mechanism through which development occurs. (What are the strengths and
weaknesses of learning theory and how are the views of learning
theorists similar and different to other theorists discussed in this
chapter?)

Ethological theory focuses on the evolved behavior of a species in
its (58) _____ surroundings. Konrad Lorenz has studied
(59) _____, an innate form of learning in some species which
occurs during a (60) _____ period of development. It is
unclear whether the same processes operate in humans. John Bowlby

believes that certain infant behaviors have evolved to promote attachment and that the first three years of life may be a kind of critical period for development of attachment. (What are the strengths and weaknesses of ethological theory?)

The (61) _____ _____ perspective proposes that as people change, they change their environments and changes in their environments produce changes in people. Riegel's (62) _____ theory holds that development results from a continuous interchange between a changing world and a changing person. (What are the four major dimensions of development according to Riegel? How are the lives of Ed and Erma used in the text to illustrate these four major dimensions?)

The theories presented in this chapter can be classified according to their general world view. Those theorists who assume that humans are like machines subscribe to the (63) _____ model of human development. Those theorists who compare humans to other living organisms adopt the (64) _____ model of development. (Can you identify which theorists "fit" these two world views?) The theories presented in this chapter offer very different answers to questions about human development. (What is the value of having so many different theoretical perspectives?)

REVIEW OF KEY TERMS AND CONCEPTS

Below is a list of terms and concepts from this chapter. Match each one with its appropriate definition. You might also want to try writing definitions in your own words and then checking your definitions with those here in the Study Guide or in the text.

accommodation
anal stage
assimilation
autonomy versus shame and doubt
behaviorism
concrete operations stage
contextual-dialectical theories
continuity/discontinuity issue
critical period
defense mechanisms
developmental stage
dialectical theory
eclectic
ego
Electra complex
ethology
fixation
formal operations stage
generativity versus stagnation
genital stage

integrity versus despair
intimacy versus isolation
latency period
libido
mechanistic model
nature/nurture issue
observational learning
Oedipus complex
operant conditioning
oral stage
organismic model
phallic stage
preoperational stage
psychoanalytic theory
punisher
reciprocal determinism
regression
reinforcer
repression
scheme

id
identification
identity versus role confusion
imprinting
industry versus inferiority
initiative versus guilt
instinct

sensorimotor stage
social learning theory
superego
tabula rasa
trust versus mistrust
unconscious motivation

_____1. A defense mechanism in which a person reverts to an earlier, less traumatic stage of development.

_____2. Process by which anxiety-provoking thoughts are pushed out of conscious awareness.

_____3. An organized pattern of action or thought that is used to deal with experiences. Also called a cognitive structure.

_____4. Psychosocial conflict of young adulthood that involves developing strong friendships and intimate relationships.

_____5. A school of psychology focusing on observations of overt behavior rather than unobservable mental processes.

_____6. Piaget's third stage of cognitive development when school-aged children reason logically in concrete problem-solving situations.

_____7. Belief that humans develop actively through a continuous reciprocal interaction between them and their environment, rather than being passively shaped by their environment.

_____8. Form of learning in which behaviors become more or less probable depending on the consequences they produce.

_____9. Specified period of time during which certain behaviors need to develop if they are going to develop normally.

_____10. A general philosophical assumption that views humans as similar to machines.

_____11. Concerns the question of whether development is primarily the result of biological or environmental forces.

_____12. Freud's term for the most primitive component of personality seeking immediate satisfaction of instincts.

_____13. Period of life characterized by a cohesive set of behaviors or abilities which are distinct from earlier or later periods.

_____14. The psychosexual stage during which the sex instinct seeks gratification through the mouth.

_____15. Freud's term for a young boy's desire for his mother and the accompanying feelings of rivalry with father and guilt.

_____16. Unconscious techniques used by the ego to protect itself from anxiety.

_____17. Psychosocial conflict in which toddlers must learn some independence.

_____18. Psychosocial conflict of older adulthood that involves assessing one's life and finding it meaningful.

_____19. The process of changing one's cognitive structures so that new information can be better understood.

_____20. Belief that children have no inborn tendencies, but their outcome depends entirely on the environment in which they are raised.

_____21. Piaget's first stage of cognitive development during which infants learn about the world through their sensory experiences and their actions.

_____22. Form of learning that results from observing the behavior of other people.

_____23. Any consequence that decreases the probability that a response will occur in the future.

_____24. An innate form of learning in which the young of certain species follow and become attached to a moving object, usually their mothers, early in life.

_____25. Theoretical perspectives that hold that development arises from the ongoing interrelationships between a changing organism and a changing world.

_____26. A general philosophical assumption that compares humans to other living organisms.

_____27. The question of whether development is smooth and gradual or somewhat abrupt.

_____28. Information in memory that influences thinking and behavior but is not recalled at a conscious level.

_____29. Freud's term for the sex instinct's psychic energy.

_____30. Psychosexual stage during which the sex instinct seeks gratification through anal activities such as defecation.

_____31. A defense mechanism in which development becomes arrested because part of the libido remains tied to an earlier stage of development.

_____32. Psychosocial conflict during elementary school in which children need to acquire important academic and social skills.

_____33. The process of understanding new experiences in terms of one's current cognitive structures.

_____34. Piaget's second stage of cognitive development when preschoolers are able to use symbols but lack logical reasoning.

_____35. Any consequence that increases the probability that a response will occur in the future.

_____36. A theory which proposes that development results from continuous dialogues between a changing person and a changing environment.

_____37. The study of the behavior of a species in its natural surroundings across generations.

_____38. Freud's term for the component of personality that seeks to realistically satisfy instincts.

_____39. Psychosexual stage in which preschool-aged children become focused on the presence or absence of a penis and find pleasure in genital stimulation.

_____40. Psychosexual phase in which the sex instinct is repressed and energy is directed toward socially acceptable activities.

_____41. The first psychosocial conflict in which infants must develop a basic sense of trust.

_____42. Piaget's fourth stage of cognitive development when adolescents can reason logically about abstract concepts and hypothetical ideas.

_____43. Freud's term for the component of personality that contains values and morals learned from parents and society.

_____44. The process of internalizing the attitudes and behaviors of the same-sex parent.

_____45. Psychosocial conflict of adolescence in which children must develop a sense of who they are socially, sexually, and professionally.

_____46. Freud's term for a young girl's envy and desire for her father since he has a penis and the corresponding feelings of jealousy toward her mother.

_____47. Individuals who believe that none of the major theories of human development can explain everything, but each has something to contribute to our understanding of human development.

_____48. Psychosocial conflict of middle adulthood that involves being productive in one's work and with one's family.

_____49. Psychosocial conflict in which a young child tries to accept more grown-up responsibilities which she/he may not be able to handle.

_____50. A theory which claims that humans are active, cognitive processors of information from the environment, rather than passive recipients of information from the environment.

_____51. An inborn biological force that motivates behavior.

_____52. Psychosexual stage in which the goal of the sex instinct in biological reproduction.

_____53. Theory which proposes that humans are driven by unconscious motives and emotions and shaped by early childhood experiences.

Since the focus of this chapter in the text is on theory, this section of the Study Guide is a theory summary, rather than a research summary. For each of the theories described in this chapter, briefly summarize the main point(s) of the theory and indicate its strengths and weaknesses. Questions you might ask yourself include: How does development occur according to this theorist? Where does the theorist stand on the various developmental issues? (See Box 2.8 in the text.) How is one theorist similar to other theorists? What are the differences between the theorists? What kinds of behaviors are best described or explained by the different theories?

Use the text to check your understanding.

SELF TEST

For each multiple choice question, read all alternatives and then select the best answer.

1. John Locke believed that human nature was
    a. inherently selfish and aggressive
    b. innately good
    c. determined by a person's experiences
    d. determined equally by both genetic and environmental factors

2. A theorist who believes that humans progress through developmental stages is likely to believe in
    a. discontinuous changes
    b. continuous changes
    c. quantitative changes
    d. multiple paths of development

3. According to Freud's theory, the _____ must find ways of realistically satisfying the demands of the _____.
    a. superego, ego
    b. defense mechanisms, id
    c. id, ego
    d. ego, id

4. Boys resolve their Oedipus complexes by
    a. fearing their father
    b. identifying with their father
    c. repressing their incestuous desires for their mother
    d. both b and c

5. Which of the following BEST characterizes Freud's position on the nature-nurture issue?
    a. He emphasized nurture more than nature.
    b. He emphasized nature more than nurture.
    c. He emphasized both nature and nurture equally.
    d. He did not really take a stand on this issue.

6. Regression occurs when
    a. a person reverts to an earlier stage of development
    b. a person pushes anxiety-provoking thoughts out of conscious awareness
    c. development becomes arrested because part of the libido remains tied to an earlier stage of development
    d. psychic energy is directed toward socially acceptable activities

7. Which of the following is FALSE regarding agreement between Freud's and Erikson's views?
    a. Both believe that people are born with a number of instincts.
    b. Both believe that development proceeds through stages.
    c. Both believe that the personality consists of id, ego, and superego.
    d. Both believe human nature is active and positive.

8. Which of the following BEST characterizes Erikson's position on the nature-nurture issue?
    a. He emphasized nurture more than nature.
    b. He emphasized nature more than nurture.
    c. He emphasized both nature and nurture equally.
    d. He did not really take a stand on this issue.

9. According to Erikson, the main task facing adolescents is
    a. developing a sense of identity
    b. achieving a sense of intimacy with another person
    c. mastering important academic tasks
    d. building a sense of self-confidence

10. Piaget used the term assimilation to refer to
    a. the process of understanding new experiences in terms of one's current cognitive structures
    b. the process of changing one's cognitive structures to in corporate new experiences
    c. an organized pattern of thought or action used to deal with experiences
    d. constructing a new understanding of the world based on experience

11. A child sees a car and a truck and labels both of them "car." The child is corrected and told that the one is a truck. The next time the child sees a truck, she says "truck." This new understanding illustrates the process of
    a. assimilation
    b. accommodation
    c. identification
    d. logical thought

12. A child in Piaget's preoperational stage is able to solve problems
    a. that are concrete by using logical reasoning
    b. that are abstract by using logical reasoning
    c. using symbols
    d. through their sensory experiences and their actions

13. Of the following, Piaget has been most criticized for his
    a. emphasis on sexual instincts during childhood
    b. belief that children are actively involved in their development
    c. description of cognitive development
    d. belief that cognitive development occurs through an invariant sequence of coherent stages

14. A basic premise of John Watson's behaviorism is that development is
    a. a series of qualitative behavior changes
    b. a continuous process of change dependent on learning experiences
    c. a combination of inborn tendencies and environmental experiences
    d. best understood by studying mental activities

15. Which of the following theories views humans as passively shaped by their environments?
    a. Freud's psychoanalytic theory
    b. Skinner' operant learning theory
    c. Bandura's cognitive social-learning theory
    d. Piaget's cognitive-developmental theory

16. Which two theorists believe that development occurs through the interaction of an active person with the environment?
    a. Piaget and Freud
    b. Skinner and Riegel
    c. Skinner and Bandura
    d. Piaget and Bandura

17. Ethologists focus on
    a. the consequences that shape behavior
    b. the continuous reciprocal interaction between a person and the environment
    c. instinctual drives that unconsciously motivate behavior
    d. innate behaviors that have adaptive value

18. Riegel's dialectical theory proposes that development results from
    a. the environment acting upon and shaping a person
    b. an ever-changing interaction between a changing person and a changing environment
    c. innate, instinctual behaviors
    d. assimilating and accommodating to the world

19. Which of the following theories is (are) based on an organismic world view?
    a. Piaget's cognitive-developmental theory
    b. Freud's psychoanalytic theory
    c. Skinner's operant learning theory
    d. Both a and b
    e. Both b and c

20. Riegel's dialectical theory would most likely criticize Watson's behaviorism for its
    a. lack of focus on inner dimensions of the person
    b. lack of stages of development
    c. underlying organismic model of development
    d. use of observable behaviors as a source of data

APPLICATION

Consider the problem of shyness. Many children and adults in our society are socially shy to a significant degree and express anxiety in many everyday, social situations. How would each of the theorists in this chapter interpret or explain the development of this condition?

Before you leave this chapter, go back and take another look at the learning objectives presented at the beginning of the chapter. Rephrase each objective into a question and check to see whether you have mastered them. A good way to check your understanding of a concept is to see if you can teach it to someone else. Take turns doing this with a small group of people. Whenever you are unsure or unclear about a response, go back to the text and find out what information you are missing in order to provide a clear and complete response.

ANSWERS

Summary and Guided Review (Fill-in the blank)

1. tabula rasa
2. nature
3. nurture
4. passively
5. quantitative
6. qualitative
7. discontinuous
8. universal
9. particularistic
10. psychoanalytic
11. instinct
12. sex
13. id
14. ego
15. superego
16. psychosexual

17. oral
18. anal
19. phallic
20. Oedipus complex
21. repression
22. identification
23. Electra complex
24. latency
25. genital
26. early experiences
27. defense mechanisms
28. fixation
29. regression
30. Erikson
31. crises
32. psychosocial
33. cognitive
34. construct
35. cognitive structures
36. assimilation
37. accommodation
38. invariant sequence
39. sensorimotor
40. preoperational

41. symbols
42. logical
43. concrete operations
44. concrete
45. formal operations
46. hypothesis
47. behaviorism
48. overt
49. learned
50. B.F Skinner
51. operant conditioning
52. reinforcer
53. punisher
54. Bandura
55. social learning
56. reciprocal determinism
57. observational learning
58. natural
59. imprinting
60. critical
61. contextual-dialectical
62. dialectical
63. mechanistic
64. organismic

Key Terms

1. regression
2. repression
3. scheme
4. intimacy versus isolation
5. behaviorism
6. concrete operations stage
7. reciprocal determinism
8. operant conditioning
9. critical period
10. mechanistic model
11. nature/nurture issue
12. id
13. developmental stage
14. oral stage
15. Oedipus complex
16. defense mechanisms
17. autonomy versus shame and doubt
18. integrity versus despair
19. accommodation
20. tabula rasa
21. sensorimotor stage
22. observational learning
23. punisher

24. imprinting
25. contextual-dialectical theories
26. organismic model
27. continuity/discontinuity issue
28. unconscious motivation
29. libido
30. anal stage
31. fixation
32. industry versus inferiority
33. assimilation
34. preoperational stage
35. reinforcer
36. dialectical theory
37. ethology
38. ego
39. phallic
40. latency period
41. trust versus mistrust
42. formal operations stage
43. superego
44. identification

45. identity versus role confusion
46. Electra complex
47. eclectic
48. generativity versus stagnation
49. initiative versus guilt

50. social learning theory
51. instinct
52. genital stage
53. psychoanalytic

SELF TEST

1.	C	11.	B
2.	A	12.	C
3.	D	13.	D
4.	D	14.	B
5.	B	15.	B
6.	A	16.	D
7.	D	17.	D
8.	C	18.	B
9.	A	19.	D
10.	A	20.	A

Chapter Three
The Genetics of Life-Span Development

LEARNING OBJECTIVES
_____

After reading and studying the material in this chapter, you should be able to do the following:

1. Describe species heredity and explain how both Darwin's theory of evolution and sociobiology have contributed to our understanding of species heredity.

2. Describe the basic workings of individual heredity, including definitions of genes, chromosomes, zygote, mitosis, and meiosis.

3. Distinguish between genotype and phenotype.

4. Name and describe the mechanisms by which traits are passed from parents to offspring and demonstrate understanding how single gene-pair and sex-linked inheritance work.

5. List and describe general characteristics of some chromosomal abnormalities.

6. Explain the concept of heritability.

7. Discuss the methods for assessing the influences of heredity and environment on behavioral characteristics. Identify the logic of the method, as well as advantages and disadvantages of each method.

8. Discuss what is known from twin and adoption studies regarding the contributions of heredity and environment to mental ability across the lifespan.

9. Discuss what is known from twin and adoption studies regarding the contributions of heredity and environment to personality across the lifespan.

10. Explain the relationship between genes and aging.

11. Discuss the three models of how genotypes and environments interact to create a person's phenotype.

12. Describe the techniques of amniocentesis, chorionic villus biopsy and ultrasound, and explain what we can learn from these techniques. Identify advantages and disadvantages of using techniques like these to test for prenatal problems and their role in genetic counseling.

The following summary provides an overview of the main points contained in this chapter of the text. Fill-in the blanks with terms that appropriately complete the sentence. Although blank spaces are provided, you may want to write your answers on a separate piece of paper, which will make it easier to compare your answers to the correct answers provided at the end of this chapter.

Scattered throughout the summary are questions in parentheses. These are meant to encourage you to think actively as you are reading and connect this summary to the more detailed information provided in the text. You can answer these questions as you are filling in the blanks or you can fill-in all the blanks, then go back and reread the entire summary, addressing the questions in order to provide more depth of understanding.

Although people are quite different from one another, (1) _____ ensures that all members of a species share some commonalities. (Can you provide an example of this common genetic endowment in humans?) Charles Darwin's theory of evolution argues that our common genetic makeup has evolved through (2) _____ _____ since those genes that promote adaptation to the environment are passed on to offspring more often than genes that do not promote adaptation.

(3) _____ is the systematic study of the biological basis of social behavior. This area of study has affected our current understanding of evolutionary theory by showing that the survival of (4) _____, not the survival of specific (5) _____, is more important from an evolutionary standpoint. (Can you explain why this makes sense?)

At conception, a woman's egg cell is fertilized by a man's sperm, resulting in a (6) _____. This new cell has 46 threadlike (7) _____, each made up of thousands of (8) _____, or segments of DNA molecules. The single cell begins to divide through a process called (9) _____ which results in daughter cells with the same 46 chromosomes as the mother cell. The sperm and ova result from the process of (10) _____ so that they each have only 23, or half, of the original cell's chromosomes. (Why do the sperm and ova have only half the number of chromosomes that are in all other cells?) Although biological siblings share the same parents, their genetic makeup is unique, partly due to the phenomenon of (11) _____ in which parts of chromosomes are exchanged during cell division. (12) _____ twins are exceptions because they develop from one zygote and so share 100% of their genes. On the other hand, (13) _____ twins are no more genetically similar than siblings. Siblings and fraternal twins share, on the average, (14) _____ of their genes.

Chromosomes can be seen through a powerful microscope and displayed through a photograph of this called a (15) _____. This

display will show either two X chromosomes for a (16) _____,
or one X and one Y chromosome for a (17) _____.

Some gene pairs seem to be responsible for producing certain effects
in a person, while (18) _____ genes are responsible for
"turning on" or "off" other genes at different times in the life span.
(Can you provide an example of gene effects that would be activated at
different times across the lifespan?) A person's actual genetic makeup
is called a (19) _____, while the actual characteristics a
person shows are part of their (20) _____.

There are three main mechanisms of inheritance. One is
21) _____ _____ inheritance in which a
characteristic is influenced by one pair of genes. Each gene of the
pair can be either (22) _____ or (23) _____. If
one gene in the pair is (24) _____, the characteristic
associated with this gene will express itself. In order for a
(25) _____ trait to express itself, a person would need to
receive a matched pair, one from each parent. Carriers of a recessive
disorder are (26) _____, meaning they have one dominant and
one recessive gene, and so they do not express the trait but can pass it
on to their offspring. People with matching gene pairs are
(27) _____ for a trait. Another pattern of inheritance
occurs when a dominant gene in a pair does not completely mask the
effects of the recessive gene. This pattern is called
(28) _____ _____. If neither gene dominates the
other but both influence a trait, (29) _____ is said to be
operating. (Can you provide examples of characteristics inherited
through each of these mechanisms?)

Some traits are called (30) _____ characteristics because
they are influenced by genes on the sex chromosomes, rather than on the
other 22 pairs of chromosomes. (Can you explain why males are more
likely than females to inherit a trait through this type of
inheritance?)

Many human characteristics are influenced by more than one pair of
genes and so are transmitted through the mechanism of
(31) _____ _____. (Can you provide an example of
a characteristic inherited through this mechanism?)

Occasionally, a new gene appears which was not passed from parent to
child, but results from a (32) _____. Down syndrome is an
example of a (33) _____ _____ and results from an
extra (34) _____ chromosome. Turner syndrome occurs in
(35) _____ when cell division results in a missing
(36) _____ chromosome. Males who inherit an extra X
chromosome are said to have (37) _____ syndrome.

(38) _____ _____ is the study of the extent
to which genetic and environmental differences among people are
responsible for differences in their traits. Behavior geneticists

often use (39) _____ estimates, which provide information about the amount of variability between people that can be attributed to the genetic differences among those people. Even traits which are highly heritable are still influenced by (40) _____ factors. (Can you think of how this concept might be misconstrued to represent something other than amount of variability?)

One way to study the influence of genes on animal behavior is to deliberately mate animals and see whether certain traits are more or less likely following this (41) _____ _____. Since this method cannot be used with humans, researchers use (42) _____ _____ to examine the presence or absence of characteristics in existing families. (Can you think of a disadvantage in using this type of analysis to draw conclusions about hereditary influences?) Researchers also study genetic influences with (43) _____ studies and (44) _____ studies. If heredity influences a trait, (45) _____ twins should be more similar on the trait than (46) _____ twins. If adopted children resemble their adoptive parents more than they resemble their biological parents on some trait, then the trait must be influenced more by (47) _____. (Can you identify some cautions regarding interpretation of findings from twin and adoption studies?)

Identical twins tend to become (48) _____ to one another in mental ability after 18 months of age and tend to follow the same (49) _____ of mental development. The tendency to respond in predictable ways is called (50) _____ and is considered a precursor to later personality. Individual differences in temperament during infancy seem to be related to (51) _____ differences among infants. Effects of environment and heredity, however, both become more significant during (52) _____. (What explanation was suggested in the text for this change?)

During childhood, (53) _____ twins stay more similar in mental ability while (54) _____ twins become more dissimilar. Adoption studies show that the (55) _____ has an impact on mental ability since scores of children can be (56) _____ if they are adopted from impoverished environments into (57) _____ environments. With respect to personality during childhood, sharing a common environment does not seem to contribute to (58) _____ between siblings. (Why is this the case?)

During adolescence, adopted children continue to resemble their (59) _____ parents in mental ability, but no longer resemble (60) _____ parents. Shared family environment seems to continue to contribute to (61) _____ between siblings on measures of personality during adolescence because environmental influences are (62) _____ to each child.

Differences between individuals' intelligence scores in adulthood continue to be related to genetic differences between these people. Research on the effects of genes on personality in adulthood has

31

focused on (63) _____, which is the degree to which someone is outgoing or shy, and (64) _____, which is the degree to which someone is stable or unstable and anxious. Differences among people on both characteristics are related to genetic differences and environmental influences unique to the individual. A disorder called (65) _____ involving disturbances in logical thinking and behavior is not inherited but is associated with a genetic (66) _____. Aging also seems to be related to genetic factors since identical twins (67) _____ at similar rates.

The (68) _____ _____ principle tries to explain heredity-environment interactions by suggesting that a person's (69) _____ sets limits on the range of (70) _____ that person will display in different environments. Scarr and McCartney (1983) proposed three models of genotype/environment interactions. In a (71) _____ genotype/environment interaction, the child as well as the child's (72) _____ are both influenced by the parent's (73) _____. In an (74) _____ genotype/environment interaction, a child's (75) _____ triggers certain responses from other people. In an (76) _____ genotype/environment interaction, children actively seek out (77) _____ that suit their particular (78) _____. (Can you provide examples of each type of genotype/environment interaction?) Across the lifespan, (79) _____ genotype/environment interactions tend to become less influential while (80) _____ genotype/environment interactions become more influential.

(81) _____ _____ is information provided to parents who are concerned about the possibility of genetic birth defects. Tests used to detect prenatal abnormalities include (82) _____ in which a needle is inserted into the mother's abdomen, and (83) _____ in which a catheter is inserted into the mother's vagina. Both extract fetal cells that can be (84) _____. An (85) _____ scans the womb with sound waves and provides a (86) _____ image of the fetus. A recessive disorder called (87) _____ results in the inability to matabolize phenylalanine, causing it to accumulate in toxic levels in the body. Left untreated, PKU results in (88) _____ _____. However, if treated with a special (89) _____, the worst damage can be avoided, which illustrates the interaction between (90) _____ and (91) _____.

REVIEW OF KEY TERMS AND CONCEPTS

Below is a list of terms and concepts from this chapter. Match each one with its appropriate definition. You might also want to try writing definitions in your own words and then checking your definitions with those here in the Study Guide or in the text.

amniocentesis
behavior genetics
carriers
chorionic villus biopsy
chromosomes
chromosome abnormalities
codominance
conception
concordance rate
correlation coefficient
crossing over
dominant gene
Down syndrome
extraversion/introversion
fraternal twins
genes
genetic counseling
genotype
heritability
heterozygous
homozygous
Huntington's disease
identical twins
incomplete dominance
karyotype
kinship

Klinefelter syndrome
meiosis
mitosis
mutation
natural selection
neuroticism
phenotype
phenylketonuria (PKU)
polygenic trait
progeria
range of reaction
recessive gene
schizophrenia
selective breeding
sex-linked characteristic
sickle cell disease
single gene-pair inheritance
sociobiology
species heredity
temperament
Turner syndrome
ultrasound
X chromosome
Y chromosome
zygote

_____1. One's genetic makeup.

_____2. Threadlike structures containing genetic material.

_____3. A fertilized egg cell.

_____4. Genetic endowment common to all members of a
                   particular species.

_____5. Two individuals who developed as a result of one
                   fertilized egg splitting in two.

_____6. Occurs when a child receives too many or too few
                   chromosomes at conception.

_____7. The gene in a dissimilar pair which usually does not
                   express itself in that person's phenotype.

_____8. The presence of this sex chromosome determines
                   whether child will be male or female.

_____9. A disorder involving premature aging starting in
                   infancy.

_____10. Each genotype sets limits on the range of phenotypes that can develop in response to different environments.

_____11. Systematic study of the biological basis of social behavior.

_____12. Two individuals who developed at the same time but from two different fertilized eggs.

_____13. The gene in a dissimilar pair that usually expresses itself phenotypically.

_____14. Process of cell division resulting in two cells identical to the one original cell.

_____15. One's expressed characteristics.

_____16. Genes that promote adaptation to one's environment will be passed to offspring more often than genes that do not promote adaptation.

_____17. Moment when a woman's egg is fertilized by a man's sperm.

_____18. A disorder involving disturbances in logical thinking, emotional expression and social behavior.

_____19. The removal of fetal cells from the amniotic sac by inserting a needle through the mother's abdomen in order to test chromosomal makeup.

_____20. Basic units of heredity.

_____21. Chromosome disorder resulting from an extra 21st chromosome.

_____22. A female who receives only one X chromosome.

_____23. Indicates the degree and direction of relationship between two variables.

_____24. Provides information to people regarding the likelihood of genetically based problems in their unborn children.

_____25. A disorder resulting in dementia, emotional problems, loss of motor control, and premature death.

_____26. Process of cell division resulting in four cells each with half the number of chromosomes as in the one original cell.

_____27. The process and outcome of photographing and analyzing chromosomes.

_____28. Both genes in pair are identical in their effects.

_____29. A phenomenon in which parts of chromosomes are exchanged during cell division.

_____30. Change in the structure or arrangement of one or more genes that results in a new phenotype.

_____31. A pattern of inheritance in which one pair of genes determines the presence or absence of a trait.

_____32. A disorder in which blood cells cluster together and distribute less oxygen than normal cells.

_____33. A male who receives an extra X chromosome.

_____34. The two genes in a pair are dissimilar in their effects.

_____35. The dominant gene in a pair is not able to totally mask the effects of the recessive gene.

_____36. The amount of variability in a trait within a large group of people that can be linked to genetic differences among those people.

_____37. Planned matings between animals having certain genotypes in order to determine if it is possible to produce offspring with certain characteristics.

_____38. Neither gene in a pair is able to completely dominate the other and both express themselves.

_____39. Traits influenced by single genes located on the sex chromosomes.

_____40. Characteristics that are influenced by multiple genes.

_____41. Individuals who do not express a trait but can pass the trait on to their offspring.

_____42. A disorder in which a critical enzyme needed to metabolize phenylalanine is missing.

_____43. The removal of fetal cells from the chorion by inserting a catheter through the mother's vagina in order to test chromosomal makeup.

_____44. The sex chromosome that, when matched with another like it, results in a female child.

_____45. Tendency to respond in predictable ways.

_____46. The probability that one of a pair of twins will show a given characteristic, given that the other twin has the characteristic.

_____47. Extent to which a person is outgoing or shy.

_____48. The degree of genetic relationship between two individuals.

_____49. Extent to which a person is stable or unstable, anxious, and easily upset.

_____50. A method of detecting fetal growth and characteristics by passing sound waves over the mother's abdomen.

_____51. The scientific study of the extent to which genetic and environmental differences within a species are responsible for differences in traits.

RESEARCH SUMMARY AND REVIEW

For each of the following studies, briefly summarize the main point(s) of the research and indicate why the research is important. Don't worry about specific details that are not central to the main points, or memorizing names of researchers. Questions you might ask yourself include: Does the research support or refute a theory or hypothesis presented in the text? How does it further our understanding of some concept? Does it provide an example of a point being made in the text? Use the text to check your understanding.

1. Kettlewell's (1959) research with moths (page 45): _____

_____

_____

_____

2. Tyron's (1940) study on maze-learning with rats (page 51): _____

_____

_____

_____

_____

3. Wilson and Matheny's (1986) research on infant's emotionality
    (page 52): _____

_____

_____

_____

_____

4. Wilson's (1978, 1983) longitudinal study of intelligence test scores
    of identical twins and fraternal twins (page 52-53): _____

_____

_____

_____

_____

5. Scarr and Weinberg's (1976,1983) research on black children adopted
    into white middle-class homes (page 53):_____

_____

_____

_____

_____

For additional practice, pull out some other research discussed in this
chapter or research discussed in class lectures and summarize the main
points of the studies.

For each multiple choice question, read all alternatives and then select the best answer.

1. All children tend to walk and talk at about 12 months of age. This universal pattern of development results from
   a. the crossing over phenomenon
   b. societal expectations
   c. species heredity
   d. single gene-pair inheritance

2. Sociobiologists have advanced evolutionary theory by showing that
   a. survival of genes, rather than survival of individuals, is more important to evolution
   b. survival of individuals is more important than survival of genes
   c. traits that are not adaptive are never passed from parent to child
   d. Charles Darwin's concept of natural selection was not applicable to humans

3. A zygote
   a. merges with a sperm cell at conception to form a fertilized cell
   b. is a cell that will split and develop into fraternal twins
   c. contains only the sex chromosomes
   d. is a fertilized egg cell

4. Normally, humans have _____ chromosomes in all cells, except the sex cells.
   a. 23
   b. 45
   c. 46
   d. 47

5. A person's phenotype is most accurately described as
   a. a person's genetic inheritance
   b. the outcome of the interaction between a person's genotype and a particular environment
   c. the result of the union between a sperm cell and egg cell
   d. those characteristics which do not have a genetic basis

6. Suppose two people are carriers for thin lips, which is a recessive trait. Each one of their children would have a _____ chance of expressing this trait in their phenotype.
   a. 25%
   b. 50%
   c. 75%
   d. 100%

7. Incomplete dominance results when
   a. two different genes in a pair are both expressed in a compromise of the two genes
   b. one gene in a pair cannot completely mask the effects of the other gene
   c. several gene pairs contribute to the expression of a trait
   d. both parents are carriers for a particular trait

8. Following mitosis, each daughter cell has
   a. half the number of chromosomes as the mother cell had
   b. twice the number of chromosomes as the mother cell had
   c. the same number of chromosomes as the mother cell had
   d. an undetermined number of chromosomes

9. A person is a carrier for a genetic disorder if she/he
   a. does not show the disorder and cannot pass on the disorder to offspring
   b. does not show the disorder but can pass on the disorder to offspring
   c. shows the disorder but cannot pass on the disorder to offspring
   d. shows the disorder and can pass on the disorder to offspring

10. In X-linked traits
    a. males and females are equally likely to express the trait
    b. males are carriers of the trait but do not always express the trait
    c. females can express the trait but do so much less often than males
    d. females and males typically carry but do not express the trait

11. If a person needs a matching pair of genes in order to express a characteristic carried by this pair of genes, the characteristic is considered
    a. recessive
    b. dominant
    c. a mutation
    d. polygenic

12. A researcher is looking at pairs of identical twins. One twin already has a particular disorder and the researcher wants to see if the other twin will get the disorder as well. The researcher is studying
    a. range of reaction principle
    b. sociobiology
    c. karyotypes
    d. concordance rates

13. Down syndrome occurs when
    a. a child receives too few chromosomes
    b. a male receives an extra X chromosome
    c. there is an abnormality associated with one of the sex chromosomes
    d. a child receives an extra 21st chromosome

14. Heritability refers to
    a. the amount of variability in a group's trait that is due to genetic differences between people in the group
    b. the degree to which an individual's characteristics are determined by genetics
    c. the degree of relationship between pairs of individuals
    d. a person's genetic makeup

15. Some people have criticized the logic of twin studies because
    a. identical twins are always the same biological sex while fraternal twins are not
    b. identical twins are more likely to participate in this type of study than fraternal twins
    c. identical twins are treated more similarly than fraternal twins, making it difficult to separate environmental from genetic factors
    d. it is not always possible to accurately identify twins as fraternal or identical

16. With respect to how identical twins are treated, some researchers have argued that
    a. twin studies are invalid because identical twins are treated more similarly than fraternal twins
    b. identical twins are treated more similarly by parents because they are more similar
    c. identical twins begin to act similarly because they are treated similarly
    d. identical twins are more like their parents than fraternal twins

17. Which of the following statements is FALSE regarding genetics and mental ability?
    a. Mental development in infancy is only weakly influenced by individual heredity and environment.
    b. Identical twins become more similar with age in their mental performance while fraternal twins become less similar.
    c. Both identical and fraternal twins become more similar in mental performance with increasing age.
    d. Genes influence the course of mental development.

18. The concept of an evocative genotype/environment interaction
    suggests that
    a. parents select environments for their children and their
       selection is determined by genetic factors
    b. children's genotypes trigger certain reactions from other
       people
    c. children seek out environments that suit their particular
       genotypes
    d. genotypes limit the range of possible phenotypic outcomes

19. Research shows that
    a. people directly inherit many psychological disorders
    b. people inherit predispositions to develop psychological
       disorders
    c. psychological disorders have no genetic basis
    d. having a parent with a psychological disorder means that the
       child of that person will also have the disorder

20. The goals of genetic counseling include all of the following
    EXCEPT
    a. Identify traits that parents might be carrying
    b. Calculate probabilities that a particular trait might be
       transmitted to children
    c. Make decisions for the couple about whether to terminate or
       continue a pregnancy
    d. Provide information about characteristics and treatment of
       genetic disorders

APPLICATION

Consider how the material in this chapter could be used in making a
decision about whether to adopt or not adopt a child. Based on
material in this chapter, what advice could you provide to someone
considering adoption? Would your answer differ for an older child
versus an infant?

Before you leave this chapter, go back and take another look at the
learning objectives presented at the beginning of the chapter.
Rephrase each objective into a question and check to see whether you
have mastered them. A good way to check your understanding of a
concept is to see if you can teach it to someone else. Take turns
doing this with a small group of people. Whenever you are unsure or
unclear about a response, go back to the text and find out what
information you are missing in order to provide a clear and complete
response.

Summary and Guided Review (Fill-in the blank)

1. species heredity
2. natural selection
3. sociobiology
4. genes
5. individuals
6. zygote
7. chromosomes
8. genes
9. mitosis
10. meiosis
11. crossing over
12. identical
13. fraternal
14. 50%
15. karyotype
16. female
17. male
18. regulatory
19. genotype
20. phenotype
21. single gene-pair
22. dominant
23. recessive
24. dominant
25. recessive
26. heterozygous
27. homozygous
28. incomplete dominance
29. codominance
30. sex-linked
31. polygenic inheritance
32. mutation
33. chromosome abnormality
34. 21st
35. females
36. X
37. Klinefelter
38. behavior genetics
39. heritability
40. environmental
41. selective breeding
42. family studies
43. twin
44. adoption
45. identical
46. fraternal
47. environment
48. similar
49. course
50. temperament
51. genetic
52. childhood
53. identical
54. fraternal
55. environment
56. impoverished
57. stimulating
58. similarities
59. biological
60. adoptive
61. differences
62. unique
63. extraversion/introversion
64. neuroticism
65. schizophrenia
66. predisposition
67. age
68. range of reaction
69. genotype
70. phenotypes
71. passive
72. environment
73. genotypes
74. evocative
75. genotype
76. active
77. environments
78. genotype
79. passive
80. active
81. genetic counseling
82. amniocentesis
83. chorionic villus biopsy
84. karyotyped
85. ultrasound
86. visual
87. phenylketonuria (PKU)
88. mental retardation
89. diet
90. genes
91. environment

Key Terms

1. genotype
2. chromosomes
3. zygote
4. species heredity
5. identical twins
6. chromosome abnormalities
7. recessive gene
8. Y chromosome
9. progeria
10. range of reaction
11. sociobiology
12. fraternal twins
13. dominant gene
14. mitosis
15. phenotype
16. natural selection
17. conception
18. schizophrenia
19. amniocentesis
20. genes
21. Down syndrome
22. Turner syndrome
23. correlation coefficient
24. genetic counseling
25. Huntington's disease
26. meiosis
27. karyotype
28. homozygous
29. crossing over
30. mutation
31. single gene-pair inheritance
32. sickle cell disease
33. Klinefelter syndrome
34. heterozygous
35. incomplete dominance
36. heritability
37. selective breeding
38. codominance
39. sex-linked characteristic
40. polygenic trait
41. carriers
42. phenylketonuria (PKU)
43. chorionic villus biopsy
44. X chromosome
45. temperament
46. concordance rate
47. extraversion/introversion
48. kinship
49. neuroticism
50. ultrasound
51. behavior genetics

Self Test

1. C
2. A
3. D
4. C
5. B
6. A
7. B
8. C
9. B
10. C
11. A
12. D
13. D
14. A
15. C
16. B
17. C
18. B
19. B
20. C

Chapter Four
Environment and Life-Span Development

After reading and studying the material in this chapter, you should be able to do the following:

1. Differentiate between the social and physical environment.

2. Explain the view of the environment as a series of life events or transitions.

3. Explain the ecological approach to development which views the environment as a series of interrelated systems.

4. Describe the three stages of prenatal development, outlining the major developments during each stage.

5. Discuss how mother's age, emotional state, and nutrition can affect prenatal and neonatal development.

6. Define teratogen and provide examples and several teratogens, including an indication of when they have their greatest impact and what that impact is on the developing fetus.

7. Describe the perinatal environment and possible hazards that may occur during the birth process.

8. Discuss the birth process from the mother's and father's perspectives.

9. Discuss whether the effects of the prenatal and perinatal environments are long lasting.

10. Discuss cultural variations in infant development.

11. Describe the three universal goals of parenting and how societies differ in the goals that they emphasize.

12. Explain how our understanding of development depends on the culture in which we study development.

13. Describe how an adolescent's development is influenced by culture and historical context.

14. Discuss how societal and cultural changes have affected perceptions about adult development and aging.

15. Explain ways in which to optimize development during the prenatal and perinatal periods.

SUMMARY AND GUIDED REVIEW

The following summary provides an overview of the main points contained in this chapter of the text. Fill-in the blanks with terms that appropriately complete the sentence. Although blank spaces are provided, you may want to write your answers on a separate piece of paper, which will make it easier to compare your answers to the correct answers provided at the end of this chapter.

Scattered throughout the summary are questions in parentheses. These are meant to encourage you to think actively as you are reading and connect this summary to the more detailed information provided in the text. You can answer these questions as you are filling in the blanks or you can fill-in all the blanks, then go back and reread the entire summary, addressing the questions in order to provide more depth of understanding.

Modern definitions of environment emphasize the (1) _____ relationship between person and environment. Environment includes the nonhuman or (2) _____ environment, as well as the human or (3) _____ influences. The environment can be viewed as a series of life events or (4) _____ during the life span. Some life events are experienced by most people in a society and are (5) _____ transitions. Other life events are unique to an individual or small group of people and are (6) _____ transitions. Societies also have (7) _____ _____ or expectations about how people at different points in the life span should behave.

Another view of the environment is as a series of settings in which development can take place. The (8) _____ approach emphasizes the interrelated systems that influence development, beginning with the (9) _____, which is the most immediate environment that a person experiences. Children can also be influenced by (10) _____, which are social settings that are not directly experienced but still influential. The broadest cultural context in which development occurs is the (11) _____. (Can you provide an example of each type of system?)

The physical environment of the womb is called the (12) _____ environment. Development in this environment is divided into three stages. The first is the (13) _____ period and lasts from (14) _____ until implantation of the (15) _____ in the wall of the uterus. At this point, the period of the (16) _____ begins and lasts through the eight week of prenatal development. The embryo receives nutrients and oxygen from the (17) _____, a tissue that is fed by blood vessels from the mother and embryo, and is connected to this tissue by the (18) _____ _____. Sexual differentiation begins

45

during the seventh and eighth prenatal weeks with development of male testes or female ovaries from an undifferentiated tissue. The testes will then secrete (19) _____, which will stimulate development of a male internal reproduction system, or in its absence, the internal reproduction system of a female.

The period of the (20) _____ lasts from the ninth week of pregnancy until birth. At about 24 weeks, the fetus may be able to survive outside the womb, making this the age of (21) _____. The last trimester brings rapid (22) _____ gain for the fetus and rapid multiplication of (23) _____ cells.

Mothers who are younger than 17 years or older than 40 years are more likely to experience complications. (What is one possible reason for this increased risk?) Mothers who experience prolonged and severe (24) _____ during their pregnancies increase the risk of harm to the fetus. (How does maternal stress impact on fetal development?) Maternal nutrition can also impact negatively on the developing fetus, particularly if malnutrition occurs during the (25) _____ trimester of pregnancy.

A (26) _____ is any environmental agent that can produce abnormalities in a developing fetus. (What generalizations can be made about the effects of teratogens?) A time when the developing embryo or fetus is particularly sensitive to environmental influences is called a (27) _____ _____.   (28) _____, or German measles, is a disease that is most damaging to the developing organism during the first trimester. (29) _____, a sexually transmitted disease, results in similar problems, but has its greatest impact on development during the middle and later stages of pregnancy. A mild tranquilizer called (30) _____ caused serious deformities which varied depending on when the drug was taken during pregnancy. Children whose mothers drank alcohol during pregnancy may exhibit a cluster of symptoms called (31) _____ _____ _____. There is no known amount of alcohol that is entirely safe to consume during pregnancy, although the severity of FAS symptoms depend on the amount of alcohol consumed. (What other environmental conditions or maternal conditions can adversely affect prenatal development?)

The environment surrounding birth is the (32) _____ environment and includes drugs administered to the mother, delivery practices, and the immediate social environment following birth. Birth consists of three stages that, in order of occurrence, are (33) _____, (34) _____, and (35) _____. During birth, lack of adequate oxygen or (36) _____ can result in brain damage. Another birth complication can result if the fetus is not positioned in the typical head-down position, but instead is positioned feet or buttocks first, called a (37) _____ presentation. Some fetuses are delivered by a (38) _____ _____ in which an incision is made in the mother's abdomen and uterus so that the fetus can be removed. Immediately and at five

46

minutes after birth, an infant will be assessed with the
(39) _____ test that measures general well-being of the
infant. (Can you list the five characteristics assessed by this test?)

The social environment surrounding birth can have an impact on
parent's experience of birth and their new infant. Mothers who receive
(40) _____ _____ and are prepared for the birth
generally have a more positive experience than other mothers. Early
(41) _____ between mother and infant can facilitate the
beginning of attachment between them, but is not critical for the
development of attachment. Some mothers may experience
(42) _____ _____, or feelings of sadness,
irritability, and depression following a birth. (What are possible
explanations for these feelings?) Fathers, as well as mothers, may show
(43) _____ with the new baby--intense interest and desire to
touch, hold, and interact with the baby.

Even if infants experience prenatal or perinatal complications,
studies show that they can recover. Success seems to depend on the
child's (44) _____ makeup as well as having a favorable
postnatal (45) _____. Babies may be at-risk if they are
(46) _____ _____ _____, which means
they are born close to their due dates but are small for their
gestation age. Another group of small babies are (47) _____
_____ because they are born more than three weeks before
their due dates.

Studies show that the (48) _____ in which an infant
develops has an effect on how the infant is raised. (Can you discuss
some ways in which the experience of infancy is affected by different
cultural contexts?) The process by which individuals acquire the
beliefs, values, and behaviors that are appropriate in their society is
called (49) _____. Although what is considered appropriate
varies considerably across and within cultures, all parents seem to
share three general goals of parenting, which are (50) _____,
(51) _____, and (52) _____. (Can you provide an
example of each type of goal?)

Cultural variations affect our understanding of development. For
example, culture affects the (53) _____ of development as
well as the (54) _____ of development. Culture also
affects how we interpret influences on development and the
(55) _____ shown by children of a given age. Thus, in
order to fully understand development, we must view the cultural context
in which development occurs.

The experience of adolescence varies considerably across cultures.
Adolescents in some cultures go through (56) _____ ___
_____, which mark the passage from one stage of life to
another. The period of adolescence is also shaped by
(57) _____ events. (How has the experience of adolescence
in our society changed historically?)

47

The experience of adulthood and aging has also changed. Most people have an internalized sense of appropriate age norms for when things should be done. This (58) _____ _____ influences how we live our lives. (Can you identify some of your own personal expectations of different ages?) Many traditional age norms in our society have weakened as we have become an increasingly (59) _____-_____ society. Perceptions of the elderly vary across cultures. (What factors seem to determine the status of older people?)

This chapter of the text ends with a discussion of how the prenatal and perinatal environments can be optimized. In addition to seeking prenatal care, many couples enroll in (60) _____ classes and learn to prepare for the birth of the baby through techniques such as the (61) _____ _____. Some couples decide to have their babies delivered at home or in an (62) _____ _____ center which is a hospital room that provides a homelike atmosphere. Some parents might receive training on how to interact with their infant and elicit responses from the infant using the (63) _____ Neonatal Behavioral Assessment Scale. Providing (64) _____ can be particularly beneficial for at-risk infants.

REVIEW OF KEY TERMS AND CONCEPTS

Below is a list of terms and concepts from this chapter. Match each one with its appropriate definition. You might also want to try writing definitions in your own words and then checking your definitions with those here in the Study Guide or in the text.

age-irrelevant society
age norms
age of viability
alternative birth centers
amnion
anoxia
Apgar test
blastula
breech presentation
Cesarean section
chorion
critical period
cultural relativity
culture
ecological approach
engrossment
environment
exosystem
fetal alcohol syndrome
germinal period

mesosystem
microsystem
neonate
nonnormative transition
normative transition
perinatal environment
period of the embryo
period of the fetus
placenta
prenatal environment
postpartum blues
rites of passage
rubella
short gestation baby
small for date
social clock
socialization
syphilis
teratogen
testosterone

Lamaze method   thalidomide
macrosystem   umbilical cord

_____1. The belief that human development can only be
                       understood in its larger cultural context.

_____2. A newborn infant.

_____3. A mild tranquilizer that, when taken during
                       pregnancy, results in birth defects.

_____4. A cluster of symptoms in children whose mothers drank
                       alcohol during their pregnancy.

_____5. A social setting that indirectly influences a child's
                       development.

_____6. Events that most people in society experience.

_____7. The third prenatal period, lasting from the ninth
                       week until birth.

_____8. A baby born more than three weeks before its due date
                       weighing less than 2500 grams.

_____9. Parents' interest in and desire to touch, hold,
                       caress, and talk to their newborn baby.

_____10. The process by which individuals acquire the beliefs,
                       values, and behaviors that are important in their
                       society.

_____11. Societal rituals that mark the passage from one stage
                       of life to another.

_____12. The perspective that development of a person occurs
                       within a series of environmental systems that interact
                       with one another and with the person to influence
                       development.

_____13. Information shared by a population which is
                       transmitted to future generations.

_____14. The first prenatal period, lasting from conception to
                       implantation of the blastula in the wall of the
                       uterus.

_____15. A membrane surrounding the amnion that attaches to
                       the uterine lining to gather nourishment for the
                       embryo.

_____16. The most immediate environment that a person experiences.

_____17. The point at about 24 weeks prenatal development when survival outside the uterus may be possible.

_____18. Any experience or event that can influence an individual's development or be influenced by an individual.

_____19. A society in which age norms have loosened and boundaries between periods of the life span have become less distinct.

_____20. Hospital rooms that provide a homelike atmosphere while still providing access to medical technology.

_____21. Societal expectations about how people at different points in the life span should behave.

_____22. The largest cultural context in which development occurs.

_____23. A period of time during which the developing organism is particularly sensitive to environmental influences.

_____24. A viral infection that, if contracted by the mother during the first trimester of pregnancy, can cause a number of serious birth defects.

_____25. An event that is unique to an individual or minority of people.

_____26. The primary male hormone secreted by the testes.

_____27. A hollow ball of cells formed from the repeated cell division of the zygote.

_____28. An environmental agent that can produce abnormalities in a developing embryo or fetus.

_____29. A test used to assess the newborn's heart rate, respiration, color, muscle tone, and reflexes immediately after and five minutes after birth.

_____30. Feelings of sadness, irritability, resentment, and depression that some new mothers experience shortly after a birth.

_____31. A person's sense of appropriate age norms for when things should be done.

_____32. The physical environment of the womb.

_____33. A tissue that connects the mother and embryo; provides oxygen and nutrients and eliminates waste products.

_____34. A fluid-filled, watertight membrane surrounding the embryo.

_____35. A sexually transmitted disease that is most damaging during the middle and later stages of pregnancy and can result in blindness, deafness, heart problems, or brain damage.

_____36. A delivery where the baby is born feet or buttocks first.

_____37. The environment surrounding birth, which includes influences such as delivery practices and social stimulation.

_____38. Babies born close to their due dates who are small (less than 2500 grams) for their gestation age.

_____39. Connects the embryo to the placenta; contains blood vessels that nourish the fetus and eliminate wastes.

_____40. Lack of adequate oxygen to the brain, which can result in brain damage.

_____41. The second prenatal period, lasting from implantation of the blastula to the end of the eighth week of prenatal development.

_____42. A surgical procedure in which an incision is made in the mother's abdomen and uterus so that the baby can be removed.

_____43. A method of prepared childbirth in which parents learn a set of mental exercises and relaxation techniques.

_____44. The interrelationships between microsystems.

RESEARCH SUMMARY AND REVIEW

For each of the following studies, briefly summarize the <u>main point(s)</u> of the research and indicate why the research is important. Don't worry about specific details that are not central to the main points, or memorizing names of researchers. Questions you might ask yourself include: Does the research support or refute a theory or hypothesis presented in the text? How does it further our understanding of some concept? Does it provide an example of a point being made in the text? Use the text to check your understanding.

1. Klaus and Kennell's (1976) research on early contact between mothers and their infants (p 115): _____

_____

_____

_____

_____

2. Super and Harkness' (1981) study of the relationship between temperament and child-rearing environment (p 119): _____

_____

_____

_____

_____

For additional practice, pull out some other research discussed in this chapter or research discussed in class lectures and summarize the main points of the studies.

SELF TEST

For each multiple choice question, read all alternatives and then select the best answer.

1. Normative transitions are events that
    a. build confidence in a person as she/he progresses through life
    b. are specific to individuals or a small subset of people
    c. have little long-term impact on development
    d. most people experience at some point in their lives

2. Urie Bronfenbrenner's ecological approach to development holds that
    a. development is influenced by interacting environmental systems
    b. the home environment is the only really important influence on development
    c. children have a passive role in development and are unable to shape their futures
    d. the environment has a similar effect on all children

3. According to the ecological approach to development, a person's most immediate environment is the
   a. microsystem
   b. mesosystem
   c. exosystem
   d. macrosystem

4. Parents' friends and workplaces affect children indirectly through the
   a. microsystem
   b. mesosystem
   c. exosystem
   d. macrosystem

5. The idea that human behavior can only be understood by considering the cultural surroundings is termed
   a. reciprocal influence
   b. cultural relativity
   c. cultural context
   d. the cultural exosystem

6. All major organs begin to form between the second and the eighth week after conception. This period of time is called the
   a. period of the embryo
   b. germinal period
   c. period of the fetus
   d. age of viability

7. The age of viability refers to
   a. the age at which a woman is still able to conceive
   b. the point at which a fetus has a reasonable chance of survival outside the womb
   c. the point at which the brain and respiratory system are completely formed and functional
   d. the point at which all the major organs can be identified

8. Prolonged and severe emotional strain experienced by the mother during pregnancy can result in
   a. a miscarriage
   b. painful labor
   c. a "difficult" baby
   d. all of the above

9. It is most important for mothers to consume ample amounts of protein, vitamins and calories during
   a. the first trimester
   b. the second trimester
   c. the third trimester
   d. before becoming pregnant

10. A critical period is a time when
    a. a fetus can survive outside the womb
    b. conception occurs
    c. the brain forms
    d. a developing organ is particularly sensitive to environmental
       influences

11. Mothers who contract rubella (German measles) during the first
    trimester of pregnancy often have children who have problems such
    as
    a. deafness, blindness, heart defects, and mental retardation
    b. missing or malformed limbs
    c. small head size and malformations of face, heart and limbs
    d. slow growth and low birth weight

12. The developing embryo receives nutrients and oxygen from the
    mother through the
    a. amnion
    b. placenta and umbilical cord
    c. blastula
    d. chorion

13. The presence or absence of testosterone affects the process of
    sexual differentiation in
    a. males only
    b. females only
    c. males and females
    d. neither males or females

14. Klaus and Kennell argue that emotional bonding between a mother
    and her newborn
    a. can occur at any time during the first three years of life
    b. is unlike any other developing relationship
    c. is necessary for later normal development to occur
    d. develops during a sensitive period 6-12 hours after birth

15. The process by which individuals acquire beliefs, values, and
    behavior important to adaptation to the environment is called
    a. socialization
    b. survival goal
    c. self actualization
    d. culture

16. The term "social clock" refers to
    a. our internal alarm clock that keeps us on time for our
       daily activities
    b. our personal sense of when we think various experiences
       should occur
    c. experiences that are shared by most people in society
    d. changes that occur over time

17. Parents who receive "Brazelton training"
    a. learn how to elicit various responses from their infant
    b. typically have an easier time during delivery of their infant
    c. can determine right after birth if their infant is healthy
    d. can determine their infant's level of intelligence

18. Longitudinal studies of babies "at-risk"
    a. show that most at-risk babies continue to have problems throughout their lives
    b. show that most of these children never develop any problems regardless of their experiences
    c. show that babies at greater risk have a better prognosis because they receive more medical care than babies at less risk
    d. suggest that children can "outgrow" their problems when placed in favorable environments

APPLICATION

The media have recently reported several cases where pregnant women have been charged with abusing their unborn children because they have consumed alcohol or drugs during their pregnancies. Now that research and technology have increased our understanding of how teratogens can affect prenatal development, how should this knowledge be used in considering such cases? The material in this chapter suggests several issues that should be considered in addressing this question.

Before you leave this chapter, go back and take another look at the learning objectives presented at the beginning of the chapter. Rephrase each objective into a question and check to see whether you have mastered them. A good way to check your understanding of a concept is to see if you can teach it to someone else. Take turns doing this with a small group of people. Whenever you are unsure or unclear about a response, go back to the text and find out what information you are missing in order to provide a clear and complete response.

Summary and Guided Review (Fill-in the blank)

1. reciprocal
2. physical
3. social
4. transitions
5. normative
6. nonnormative
7. age norms
8. ecological
9. microsystem
10. ectosystem
11. macrosystem
12. prenatal
13. germinal
14. conception
15. blastula
16. embryo
17. placenta
18. umbilical cord
19. testosterone
20. fetus
21. viability
22. weight
23. brain
24. stress
25. third (or last)
26. teratogen
27. critical period
28. Rubella
29. syphilis
30. thalidomide
31. fetal alcohol syndrome
32. perinatal
33. contractions
34. delivery
35. afterbirth
36. anoxia
37. breech
38. Cesarean section
39. Apgar
40. social support
41. contact
42. postpartum blues
43. engrossment
44. genetic
45. environment
46. small for date
47. short gestation
48. culture
49. socialization
50. survival
51. economic
52. self-actualization
53. rate
54. direction
55. behavior
56. rites of passage
57. historical
58. social clock
59. age-irrelevant
60. childbirth
61. Lamaze method
62. alternative birth
63. Brazelton
64. stimulation

Key Terms

1. cultural relativity
2. neonate
3. thalidomide
4. fetal alcohol syndrome
5. exosystem
6. normative transition
7. period of the fetus
8. short gestation baby
9. engrossment
10. socialization
11. rites of passage
12. ecological approach
13. culture
14. germinal period
15. chorion
16. microsystem
17. age of viability
18. environment
19. age-irrelevant society
20. alternative birth centers
21. age norms
22. macrosystem
23. critical period
24. rubella

25.	nonnormative transition	35.	syphilis
26.	testosterone	36.	breech presentation
27.	blastula	37.	perinatal environment
28.	teratogen	38.	small for date
29.	Apgar test	39.	umbilical cord
30.	postpartum blues	40.	anoxia
31.	social clock	41.	period of the embryo
32.	prenatal environment	42.	Cesarean section
33.	placenta	43.	Lamaze method
34.	amnion	44.	mesosystem

Self Test

1.	D	10.	D
2.	A	11.	A
3.	A	12.	B
4.	C	13.	C
5.	B	14.	D
6.	A	15.	A
7.	B	16.	B
8.	D	17.	A
9.	C	18.	D

Chapter Five
The Physical Self

After reading and studying the material in this chapter, you should be able to do the following:

1. Describe the workings of the endocrine system including the action of specific hormones.

2. Describe the basic structure of the nervous system.

3. Distinguish between survival and primitive reflexes and give examples of each.

4. Define infant states. List the six major infant states and indicate developmental changes in the states during infancy.

5. Distinguish between growth that is cephalocaudal and growth that is proximodistal, giving examples of each.

6. Describe changes in the brain during the first two years and how the concept of plasticity relates to brain development.

7. Describe the development of early motor skills.

8. Describe lateralization and explain how lateralization is determined.

9. Describe physical and sexual maturation for males and females during adolescence, including the psychological effects of timing of maturation.

10. Describe changes in the reproductive system of adults.

11. Discuss other physical and behavioral changes that are typically associated with aging.

12. Discuss whether mental abilities decline with age.

13. Discuss how nutrition affects growth and development across the lifespan.

The following summary provides an overview of the main points contained in this chapter of the text. Fill-in the blanks with terms that appropriately complete the sentence. Although blank spaces are provided, you may want to write your answers on a separate piece of paper, which will make it easier to compare your answers to the correct answers provided at the end of this chapter.

Scattered throughout the summary are questions in parentheses. These are meant to encourage you to think actively as you are reading and connect this summary to the more detailed information provided in the text. You can answer these questions as you are filling in the blanks or you can fill-in all the blanks, then go back and reread the entire summary, addressing the questions in order to provide more depth of understanding.

Physical growth in humans is guided by a genetic program that causes all humans to develop similar characteristics at similar rates. Growth is also affected by individual (1) _____ and (2) _____ factors. The (3) _____ glands secrete chemical substances called (4) _____ directly into the bloodstream. These substances regulate growth and development. The (5) _____ gland regulates other glands and secretes (6) _____ hormone, which stimulates rapid growth and development of body cells.

A male fetus develops male reproductive organs when a gene on his Y chromosome triggers development of (7) _____, which in turn secrete a male hormone called (8) _____. This hormone along with others called (9) _____ stimulate the adolescent growth spurt and development of male sex organs. In females, the (10) _____ glands secrete androgen-like hormones that trigger their growth spurt. In addition, the ovaries produce larger quantities of (11) _____, the primary female hormone. This hormone, along with progesterone, is responsible for development of female sex organs and for regulating menstrual cycles.

The nervous system is made-up of billions of nerve cells or (12) _____. Nerve cells have (13) _____ for sending messages and (14) _____ for receiving messages. During development axons of some neurons become covered by (15) _____, which improves transmission of neural impulses. Neurons "communicate" with other neurons through neurotransmitters that cross the (16) _____ or connective spaces between cells. The brain is organized into groups of interconnected neurons. One grouping is the (17) _____ _____, which controls motor, sensory-perceptual, and intellectual processes.

Newborns can produce a number of unlearned responses to stimuli called (18) _____. (Can you provide examples of some unlearned responses that are essential to survival?) Some (19) _____ reflexes do not seem to have functional value in our culture and typically disappear during the first year of life. (Can you provide examples of this type of reflex?)

Infants typically experience a range of different levels of consciousness, called (20) _____ _____, during a typical day. (What are the six states of consciousness described in your text?) There are individual differences in how much time infants spend in each state, although newborns spend about (21) _____ of their time asleep and only 2-3 hours a day actively taking in their environments. Half of a newborn's sleep time is spent in active, irregular sleep called (22) _____ sleep. This percentage decreases across the lifespan to about 20%. (What are possible explanations for this change across the lifespan?)

Growth occurs in a (23) _____ direction, meaning from the head to the tail. As a result, the head of a newborn is more fully developed than the trunk and legs. Growth also proceeds from the center outward, or in a (24) _____ direction. (What is an example of this principle of growth?)

The brain undergoes rapid growth prenatally and in the first two years following birth. Active neurons are developing connections with other neurons while inactive neurons disappear. An immature brain has (25) _____, which means that cells have not yet fully committed to a particular function and so they have the capacity to be shaped by experience.

Since motor behaviors develop in cephalocaudal and proximodistal directions, infants can sit before they can walk. Most infants can sit alone by (26) _____ months and can walk alone by (27) _____ months. Around 9 to 12 months, infants can use a (28) _____ _____ to pick up objects using only their thumb and one other finger.

During childhood, the left and right hemispheres of the cerebral cortex are becoming more specialized, a process called (29) _____. (What evidence is there for lateralization during infancy and childhood?)

Adolescents experience rapid growth, called the _____ _____, and _____, which is the attainment of sexual maturity. (32) _____ typically begin their growth spurt about two years before (33) _____. Puberty for girls is marked by (34) _____, their first menstruation, at about 12 or 13 years of age. For boys, the event that is typically used to mark puberty is their first ejaculation, which occurs around 13 or 14 years of age. There is great variation in the timing of physical and sexual maturation. Rate of development is largely determined by (35) _____ factors although environment also plays a role in timing of maturation, as indicated by the (36) _____ _____ or the trend in industrialized societies for earlier maturation and larger body size. (What factors contribute to this secular trend?)

The psychological impact of being an early versus a late developer is different for males and females. Early maturing (37) _____ are often found to have advantages over their later maturing peers. (What are some of these advantages and are they long-lasting?) For (38) _____, early development is not necessarily an advantage, at least not before junior high school. Late-maturers of both sexes often experience some anxiety, but late-maturing (39) _____ seem to experience the most disadvantages.

Although physical aging occurs over most of the lifespan, outward signs are often not noticed until one's (40) _____. Wrinkles, thinning and graying hair, and extra weight are common physical changes in middle age. Older adults may experience osteoarthritis or (41) _____, extreme bone loss leaving bones fragile. The functioning of the respiratory system declines with age, as evidenced by a decrease in (42) _____ _____ from about age 20 on.

Hormone levels fluctuate in both sexes across the lifespan, although hormone changes typically affect women more than men. Some women report experiencing (43) _____ _____, a cluster of symptoms including breast tenderness and irritability just before menstruation. Both premenstrual and menstrual symptoms are affected by biological factors such as hormone changes, and by (44) _____ factors. (Can you describe some of the social factors that contribute to symptoms?) The end of menstrual periods occurs sometime during midlife and is called (45) _____. The lower levels of female hormones that are produced result in (46) _____ _____ and (47) _____ _____ for many women. Some women experience psychological symptoms such as irritability and depression in connection with menopause. (How does the experience of menopause differ cross culturally?) Men also experience loss of reproductive capacity, but more gradually than women, during a period of time known as the (48) _____.

The (49) _____ model of aging associates aging with loss of neurons, a decline in levels of neurotransmitter chemicals in the brain, and reduced blood flow to the brain. The (50) _____ model of aging indicates that even an aging brain can develop new capabilities and change in response to experiences. Behavioral changes associated with aging include doing things more slowly and a decrease in amount of vigorous activity.

Apparent effects of aging could in fact result from other factors that are typically associated with aging. For example, research suggests that aging in the absence of (51) _____ has little effect on physical and psychological functioning. Mental and physical exercise also contribute to more effective functioning in old age, as does lack of abuse of the body.

Nutrition can have an impact on development and functioning across the entire lifespan. Infants and young children who have had inadequate nutrition experience a slowing of growth but typically experience (52) _____ _____ when their diets become adequate. Some children get too many calories and experience (53) _____. Heredity, overeating, and low activity levels all seem to contribute to obesity.

REVIEW OF KEY TERMS AND CONCEPTS

Below is a list of terms and concepts from this chapter. Match each one with its appropriate definition. You might also want to try writing definitions in your own words and then checking your definitions with those here in the Study Guide or in the text.

adolescent growth spurt
androgens
catch-up growth
cephalocaudal
cerebral cortex
climacteric
endocrine gland
estrogen
hot flashes
human growth hormone
infant states
lateralization
menarche
menopause
myelin

neuron
osteoporosis
pincer grasp
pituitary gland
plasticity
premenstrual syndrome (PMS)
proximodistal
puberty
reflex
REM sleep
secular trend
synapse
testosterone
vaginal atrophy

_____1. Male hormones, including testosterone, which trigger the adolescent growth spurt and development of male sex organs.

_____2. An unlearned and automatic response to a stimulus.

_____3. Different states of consciousness that infants exhibit in a typical day.

_____4. An endocrine gland located at the base of the brain that regulates other glands and produces growth hormone.

_____5. Sequence of growth that proceeds from the head to the tail.

_____6. A developmental state in which cells that have not yet been committed to a particular function have the capacity to be shaped by experience.

_____7. The specialization of the left and right hemispheres of the cerebral cortex.

_____8. The rapid increase in growth that occurs during adolescence.

_____9. A male hormone secreted by the testes.

_____10. A historical trend for earlier maturation and larger body size in industrialized societies.

_____11. A disease resulting from a loss of minerals, which causes deterioration of bone tissue.

_____12. A cluster of symptoms including breast tenderness, a bloated feeling, irritability and moodiness that occur just before menstruation.

_____13. A hormone secreted by the pituitary gland that stimulates growth and development of body cells.

_____14. A period of growth following a growth deficit that is faster than normal to regain the genetically programmed growth course.

_____15. Sudden, brief, and unpredictable sensations of warmth that may be followed by a cold shiver.

_____16. A ductless gland that secretes hormones directly into the bloodstream.

_____17. A female hormone secreted by the ovaries that stimulates development of female sex organs and regulates menstrual cycles.

_____18. The convoluted outer covering of the brain that controls motor, sensory-perceptual, and intellectual processes.

_____19. Sequence of growth that proceeds from the central portions of the body to the extremities.

_____20. Using the thumb in opposition to one other finger in order to pick up and manipulate objects.

_____21. The point when a person reaches sexual maturity and acquires secondary sexual characteristics.

63

_____22. The basic cell of the nervous system that transmits and receives signals.

_____23. Thinning, drying, and loss of elasticity of the vaginal walls.

_____24. The first menstrual period.

_____25. The period of time in which males and females lose their reproductive capacity.

_____26. The space between the axon of one neuron and the dendrites of another neuron.

_____27. Active, irregular sleep associated with rapid eye movements and brain wave activity that resembles wakefulness.

_____28. A waxy substance that covers the axon of some neurons and facilitates transmission of neural impulses.

_____29. The ending of a woman's menstrual periods in midlife.

RESEARCH SUMMARY AND REVIEW

For each of the following studies, briefly summarize the main point(s) of the research and indicate why the research is important. Don't worry about specific details that are not central to the main points, or memorizing names of researchers. Questions you might ask yourself include: Does the research support or refute a theory or hypothesis presented in the text? How does it further our understanding of some concept? Does it provide an example of a point being made in the text? Use the text to check your understanding.

1. Thelen's (1984) research on infant's emerging ability to walk (p 144):_____

_____

_____

_____

_____

2. Kinsbourne and Hiscock's (1983) findings on lateralization during infancy (p 145):_____

_____

3. Birren et al.'s (1963) study of the effects of disease on aging (pp 160-161): _____

_____

_____

_____

_____

For additional practice, pull out some other research discussed in this chapter or research discussed in class lectures and summarize the main points of the studies.

SELF TEST _____

For each multiple choice question, read all alternatives and then select the best answer.

1. Which structure is considered the "master gland" of the endocrine system?
    a. thyroid gland
    b. hypothalamus
    c. adrenal gland
    d. pituitary gland

2. Which of the following hormone(s) trigger the adolescent growth spurt?
    a. progesterone
    b. androgens
    c. activating hormones
    d. thyroxine

3. The primitive reflexes
    a. are essential to survival
    b. disappear sometime during infancy
    c. include rooting, sucking, and swallowing
    d. protect the infant from various adverse conditions

4. The reflex that involves fanning and curling the toes in response to
    a touch on the bottom of the foot is the
    a. grasping reflex
    b. Moro reflex
    c. Babinski reflex
    d. stepping reflex

5. When an infant attends to the environment and breathes fast and
    irregularly, she is said to be in a state of
    a. alert inactivity
    b. waking activity
    c. drowsiness
    d. irregular sleep

6. Cephalocaudal refers to
    a. growth and development of the brain and spinal cord
    b. growth and development of internal organs
    c. growth which proceeds from head to tail
    d. growth which proceeds from the midline to the extremities

7. The brain growth spurt, a period of rapid brain development, begins
    a. during the prenatal period
    b. during infancy
    c. at age 1
    d. at puberty

8. Because of the caphalocaudal direction of growth, infants typically
    can _____ before they can _____.
    a. stand; roll over
    b. roll over; control their arms or hands
    c. walk backward; walk up steps
    d. sit; walk

9. Lateralization is a process by which
    a. one hemisphere takes over for the other's functions after brain
        damage has occurred
    b. specialization of the functions of the left and right
        hemisphere occurs
    c. neurons in the brain develop rapidly
    d. neurons are covered by a myelin sheath

10. The secular trend refers to
    a. earlier maturation and decreased body size
    b. later maturation and decreased body size
    c. later maturation and increased body size
    d. earlier maturation and increased body size from generation to
        generation

11. The timing of maturation is important to the developing teenager and can even effect what the teenager will be like later in life. For example, by the age of 30,
    a. boys who matured early are less social, confident and responsible than those who matured later
    b. boys who matured later are more rigid and conforming than early maturers
    c. girls who matured later are more playful and innovative than early maturers
    d. girls who matured early are more self directed and better able to cope with events than late maturers

12. The apparent decline of physical performance of females by the end of adolescence
    a. is a myth not supported by any data
    b. results largely from socialization differences between males and females
    c. results from an overall decline in the proportion of muscle mass relative to fat
    d. is similar to the decline that occurs in males

13. The climacteric period in females is a period during which
    a. women experience an increase in estrogen levels
    b. women experience a decrease in estrogen levels
    c. estrogen levels remain stable in relation to previous hormone levels
    d. estrogen levels in the woman are at a peak level

14. As the body ages from childhood to adulthood, the brain
    a. develops more neurons
    b. grows slightly in weight and volume
    c. grows longer dendrites
    d. releases large quantities of neurotransmitters

15. Menopause is a time when
    a. women no longer ovulate or menstruate
    b. most women experience mood swings for extended periods of time
    c. women continue to ovulate but do not menstruate
    d. women experience an increase in hormone levels

APPLICATION

Watch some TV advertisements during a time when programming is geared toward children (e.g., Saturday mornings or weekday afternoons). What kind of nutrition is being promoted? Now consider the people who appear on television. How does their image fit with the nutrition being promoted? Are these people likely to be the ones who use or eat the products being promoted?

67

Before you leave this chapter, go back and take another look at the
learning objectives presented at the beginning of the chapter.
Rephrase each objective into a question and check to see whether you
have mastered them. A good way to check your understanding of a
concept is to see if you can teach it to someone else. Take turns
doing this with a small group of people. Whenever you are unsure or
unclear about a response, go back to the text and find out what
information you are missing in order to provide a clear and complete
response.

ANSWERS

Summary and Guided Review (Fill-in the blank)

1. heredity
2. environmental
3. endocrine
4. hormones
5. pituitary
6. growth
7. testes
8. testosterone
9. androgens
10. adrenal
11. estrogen
12. neurons
13. axons
14. dendrites
15. myelin
16. synapse
17. cerebral cortex
18. reflexes
19. primitive
20. infant states
21. 70%
22. REM
23. cephalocaudal
24. proximodistal
25. plasticity
26. seven or eight
27. fourteen

28. pincer grasp
29. lateralization
30. growth spurt
31. puberty
32. females
33. males
34. menarche
35. genetic
36. secular trend
37. males
38. females
39. males
40. 40's
41. osteoporosis
42. vital capacity
43. premenstrual syndrome
44. social
45. menopause
46. hot flashes
47. vaginal atrophy
48. climacteric
49. degeneration
50. plasticity
51. disease
52. catch-up growth
53. obesity

Key Terms

1. androgens
2. reflex
3. infant states
4. pituitary gland
5. cephalocaudal
6. plasticity

7. lateralization
8. adolescent growth spurt
9. testosterone
10. secular trend
11. osteoporosis
12. premenstrual syndrome (PMS)

13. human growth hormone
14. catch-up growth
15. hot flashes
16. endocrine gland
17. estrogen
18. cerebral cortex
19. proximodistal
20. pincer grasp
21. puberty
22. neuron
23. vaginal atrophy
24. menarche
25. climacteric
26. synapse
27. REM sleep
28. myelin
29. menopause

Self Test

1.	D	9.	B
2.	B	10.	D
3.	B	11.	D
4.	C	12.	B
5.	A	13.	B
6.	C	14.	C
7.	A	15.	A
8.	D		

Chapter Six
Perception

After reading and studying the material in this chapter, you should be able to do the following:

1. Distinguish between sensation and perception.

2. Describe the views of empiricists and nativists on the nature/nurture issue.

3. Describe enrichment theory and differentiation theory and explain the issue which these two theories address.

4. Describe the habituation method for assessing infant perception.

5. Describe infants' visual capabilities and preferences.

6. Explain how the visual cliff is used to assess depth perception and what we have learned about infants' depth perception by using the visual cliff.

7. Describe infants' auditory capabilities and explain how auditory learning has been studied.

8. Describe infants' taste and smell capabilities and their sensitivity to touch, temperature and pain.

9. Explain cross-modal perception and give an example.

10. Discuss the changes that occur in attention between infancy and adulthood.

11. Describe the changes that occur in visual capabilities and visual perception during adulthood.

12. Describe the changes in auditory capabilities and speech perception that occur during adulthood.

13. Explain the changes that occur in taste and smell and in sensitivity to touch, temperature and pain during adulthood.

14. Discuss the roles of nature and nurture in perceptual development, including information on how different cultural and societal experiences influence perception.

15. Distinguish between field-dependent and field-independent styles.

16. Discuss how hearing impaired persons can be helped with their hearing loss.

SUMMARY AND GUIDED REVIEW

The following summary provides an overview of the main points contained in this chapter of the text. Fill-in the blanks with terms that appropriately complete the sentence. Although blank spaces are provided, you may want to write your answers on a separate piece of paper, which will make it easier to compare your answers to the correct answers provided at the end of this chapter.

Scattered throughout the summary are questions in parentheses. These are meant to encourage you to think actively as you are reading and connect this summary to the more detailed information provided in the text. You can answer these questions as you are filling in the blanks or you can fill-in all the blanks, then go back and reread the entire summary, addressing the questions in order to provide more depth of understanding.

The process by which sensory receptors detect stimuli and transmit it to the brain is called (1) _____. The process of interpreting this information is called (2) _____. One issue concerning perceptual development is whether infants are born with knowledge or need to acquire all knowledge through their senses. The (3) _____ took the latter position and believed that infants began life as (4) _____ _____ or blank slates. This position represents the (5) _____ side of the nature/nurture issue. The (6) _____ argued that infants are born with knowledge and so represent the (7) _____ side of the nature/nurture issue.

A second issue in perceptual development is whether our perceptual experiences really exist in the world or are created by imposing meaning on our sensory experiences. The (8) _____ theory argues that we organize and interpret ambiguous stimulation received by the senses. The (9) _____ theory argues that all the information we need exists in the stimulation we receive and does not need to be constructed. According to this theory, understanding is in part a matter of noting (10) _____ _____ of stimuli.

Infants' perceptual capabilities are often assessed with a technique called (11) _____, which measures decreased response to a stimulus that has been presented repeatedly. (Can you explain the rationale of this approach?)

A newborn's ability to perceive visual detail, or (12) _____ _____, is poor. This may result from problems with (13) _____ _____, which refers to the changing shape of the (14) _____ of the eye to bring objects at varying distances into focus. Young infants can visually detect

71

differences in stimuli and prefer to look at (15) _____
stimuli such as faces. (Is the apparent preference for faces really a
preference for faces? Why or why not?) Young infants tend to be
attracted to patterns that have (16) _____ or light-dark
transitions, stimuli that move, and stimuli that are moderately complex.
(What developmental changes occur in preference for complexity?)

At around 2 months of age, infants begin to visually explore the
entire field of a figure or form, rather than just an exterior border
of the figure. They also begin to prefer (17) _____ faces
over scrambled facial features. This might suggest that infants are
beginning to form (18) _____ _____ for familiar
objects. (19) _____ psychologists argue that human
experience is (20) _____ and perception is guided by
principles for orderliness and wholeness. By 3 or 4 months or age,
infants seem to be able to use some of these organizational principles.

Another aspect of visual perception is perception of
(21) _____ or three-dimensional space. Infants develop
(22) _____ _____, which is the tendency to
perceive an object as its same size despite changes in the retinal image
of the object as its distance from the eyes changes. Depth perception
has been assessed using a (23) _____ _____,
which has an apparent drop-off. By (24) _____ months, most
infants demonstrate depth perception by avoiding the drop-off. A major
limitation of this assessment technique is that infants must be able to
(25) _____. (How has the visual cliff been used to test
younger infants?)

Newborns' auditory capabilities are fairly well developed. Infants
are able to discriminate many different (26) _____ sounds
including those used in languages not spoken in the home. Familiarity
with voices begins to develop (27) _____. (Can you explain
how this has been studied?)

The sense of taste and the sense of smell, or (28) _____,
are well developed at birth. Newborns are sensitive to
(29) _____ stimulation and may respond with reflexes if
touched in certain areas. Newborns are also sensitive to temperature
and to (30) _____. The intensity of a painful experience
can be communicated by the quality of an infant's (31) _____.

The ability to recognize through one sense modality an object that
is familiar through another sense modality is called
(32) _____ _____. (Can you provide an example
of this?) Some senses seem to be integrated earlier than other senses.
For example, hearing and vision seem to be linked very early, and so do
touch and vision. Cross-modal perception of all forms, however, does
not reliably occur until 4-6 months of age.

Although much of sensory and perceptual development is complete by
the end of infancy, children need to develop better

(33) _____, the selective focusing of perception and cognition on some particular aspect of the environment.
 (34) _____ _____ increases during childhood and attention becomes more (35) _____.   (What evidence is there to support this conclusion?) Visual scanning becomes more
(36) _____ or exhaustive during childhood. Learning to read depends on recognizing the (37) _____ _____ of letters so that they can be distinguished from one another. Attention span continues to increase during adolescence as those parts of the brain involved in attention become fully (38) _____.
Adolescents also become more efficient at ignoring (39) _____ information so that they can focus their attention more effectively.

      Sensory and perceptual capabilities gradually decline with age.
(40) _____ _____ increase, which means a higher level of stimulation is needed for sensory detection as we age. Older people may also have trouble processing sensory information.

      A number of changes occur within the eye as we age. Many adults experience (41) _____, which results in a loss of near vision. Older people are less sensitive to dim light and the process of adjusting to low light levels, (42) _____ _____, does not function as well for older people. The ability to clearly see details or (43) _____ _____ normally decreases with age. Significant decreases, however, are usually associated with pathological conditions. One such condition is (44) _____, in which the lens of the eye becomes opaque and limits the amount of light entering the eye. Older people may have trouble detecting the details of (45) _____ objects and typically have a smaller field of vision. (What are some implications of these changes in visual capabilities?) Older adults may experience difficulties processing visual information in (46) _____ and
(47) _____ situations, but have few problems with familiar tasks or tasks that are not too complex.

      Hearing problems associated with aging are called
(48) _____.   One common form is the decreased sensitivity to
(49) _____ sounds. Older adults seem to have more trouble with speech perception than younger adults, especially if there is a great deal of (50) _____ _____. As with visual perception, older adults perform better on auditory tasks that are familiar or meaningful to them.

      Sensory thresholds for some tastes increase with age. Taste for
(51) _____ substances does not seem to change markedly across the life span. Sensitivity to (52) _____ and the ability to discriminate between them are highest from middle childhood to middle adulthood and then decline in old age. Decreases in taste and smell can affect recognition of different foods, although losses in the sense of (53) _____ seem to contribute more to problems of food recognition. Sensitivity to touch and to changes in temperature decrease with age. It is unclear whether sensitivity to

pain decreases since the experience of pain is highly
(54) _____.

   Research with animals suggests that normal development of the
visual system requires a minimal amount of (55) _____ early
in life. Development of certain neurons in the visual areas of the
brain seems to require specific types of stimulation.
(56) _____ of one's self or of objects in the environment is
important for the development of depth perception in kittens and has
implications for human infants who do not move freely in their
environments.

   Societal and cultural experiences can influence perceptual
development. For example, exposure to two-dimensional pictures of
three-dimensional space contributes to the ability to perceive depth in
pictures. A person's (57) _____ _____, or
characteristic way of approaching problems, can also influence
perception. People who have a (58) _____ _____
style have perceptions that are strongly influenced by the surrounding
context. People who have a (59) _____ _____ style
have perceptions that are relatively independent of the surrounding
context. Children generally become more (60) _____
_____ as they move from childhood to adolescence, but may
become more (61) _____ _____ again in old age.
(What is the possible source of these differences in cognitive style?)

   Hearing (62) _____ and (63) _____ training
have been used to improve the speech perception of infants and young
children with hearing problems. In addition to hearing aids, the
(64) _____ can be structured to facilitate hearing in older
adults.

REVIEW OF KEY TERMS AND CONCEPTS

Below is a list of terms and concepts from this chapter. Match each
one with its appropriate definition. You might also want to try
writing definitions in your own words and then checking your
definitions with those here in the Study Guide or in the text.

accommodation (visual)   Gestalt psychology
attention   habituation
cataracts   olfaction
cognitive style   perception
contour   presbycusis
cross-modal perception   presbyopia
dark adaptation   sensation
differentiation theory   sensory threshold
distinctive feature   size constancy
enrichment theory   visual acuity
field dependent   visual cliff
field independent

_____1. Critical feature of people or objects that allows for differentiation between them.

_____2. Changes in the shape of the lens to bring objects at varying distances into focus.

_____3. School of psychology that holds that human experience is organized and perception is guided by principles of order and wholeness.

_____4. The tendency to perceive an object as its same size despite changes in the retinal image of the object as its distance from the eyes changes.

_____5. The detection of stimuli by the sensory receptors and the transmission of this information to the brain.

_____6. Sense of smell, which is mediated by receptors in the nasal passage.

_____7. An apparatus with an apparent drop-off that is used to assess early depth perception.

_____8. The point at which a minimum level of stimulation can be detected by a sensory system.

_____9. A characteristic way of approaching problems and processing information.

_____10. Decreased response to a stimulus that has been presented repeatedly.

_____11. A decreased ability to clearly see objects that are close to the eye.

_____12. The interpretation of sensory input.

_____13. The ability to recognize through one sensory modality an object that is familiar through another.

_____14. The dark and light boundaries or transitions of a perceptual pattern.

_____15. The theory that sensory experiences have all the information needed to understand the world and that we must learn to differentiate between available stimuli.

_____16. Selective focusing of perception and cognition on some aspect of the environment.

_____17. The sharpness of the visual system; ability to perceive detail.

_____18. The process of adjusting to lowered levels of light.

_____19. A type of cognitive style in which perceptions are relatively independent of the surrounding context.

_____20. The theory that our sensory experiences are fragmented and need to be enriched in order to be understood.

_____21. Hearing problems associated with aging, such as the decreased ability to hear high-frequency sounds.

_____22. A type of cognitive style in which perceptions are dependent on, or strongly influenced by, the surrounding context.

_____23. Opaque or cloudy area in the lens of the eye that decreases the amount of light reaching the retina.

RESEARCH SUMMARY AND REVIEW

For each of the following studies, briefly summarize the main point(s) of the research and indicate why the research is important. Don't worry about specific details that are not central to the main points, or memorizing names of researchers. Questions you might ask yourself include: Does the research support or refute a theory or hypothesis presented in the text? How does it further our understanding of some concept? Does it provide an example of a point being made in the text? Use the text to check your understanding.

1. Gibson and Walk's (1960) study of depth perception with the visual cliff (pages 173-4):_____

_____

_____

_____

_____

2. Walk's (1981) research with kittens on effects of movement (page 191): _____

_____

_____

3. DeCasper and Spence's (1986) study of auditory learning before birth (page 175):_____

_____

_____

_____

For additional practice, pull out some other research discussed in this chapter or research discussed in class lectures and summarize the main points of the studies.

_____

For each multiple choice question, read all alternatives and then select the best answer.

1. Sensation refers to _____ of stimuli while perception refers to _____ of this information.
    a. detection; interpretation
    b. sense; the value
    c. interpretation; detection
    d. recognition; the use

2. Nativists argue that a child is
    a. born knowing nothing and learns through interaction with the environment
    b. born with knowledge and is very similar to an adult in terms of perceptual ability
    c. influenced intellectually by genetics, maturation and the environment
    d. learns mainly through cultural experiences

3. The theory suggesting that stimulation received by the senses is fragmented and needs stored knowledge added in order to give that stimulus meaning is the
    a. empiricist approach
    b. differentiation theory
    c. enrichment theory
    d. Gestalt theory

4. Suppose you repeatedly present a stimulus until an infant loses interest in it. This technique is known as
   a. visual accommodation
   b. color discrimination
   c. visual acuity
   d. habituation

5. Newborns appear to have a preference for viewing human faces. This probably reflects
   a. an innate ability to recognize faces
   b. a preference for patterned stimuli with contour and some complexity
   c. the fact that infants will learn to look at what they have been reinforced for in the past
   d. the fact that infants can focus only on faces

6. At around 2 or 3 months of age, infants prefer to look at "normal" faces as opposed to faces that have been distorted in some way. This suggests that
   a. infants cannot really detect a difference between them
   b. infants have organized their perceptions according to Gestalt principles
   c. infants prefer the simplest form or pattern
   d. infants are developing mental representations of what a normal face looks like

7. Very young infants are most visually attracted to
   a. a highly complex stimulus
   b. a moderately complex stimulus
   c. a colorful stimulus
   d. a black and white stimulus

8. The visual cliff is an apparatus used to determine
   a. depth perception
   b. size constancy
   c. visual acuity
   d. visual accommodation

9. Two-month-olds tested on the visual cliff typically show a slower heart rate on the deep side than on the shallow side of the cliff. This suggests that two-month-olds
   a. are afraid of falling off the apparent cliff
   b. detect a difference between the two sides of the visual cliff
   c. perceive size constancy
   d. have learned to avoid potential drop-offs

10. Normal hearing in young infants is different from normal hearing in adults in that infants
    a. are better able to hear soft sounds and whispers
    b. have more difficulty discriminating between speech sounds
    c. are unable to localize sound
    d. can distinguish between all speech sounds, including those not used in the language of adults around them

11. The point at which a dim light can still be detected is termed
    a. dark adaptation
    b. sensory threshold
    c. presbyopia
    d. visual acuity

12. An infant who sucks on an object and then recognizes this object visually is showing evidence of
    a. selective attention
    b. habituation
    c. cross-modal perception
    d. recognition of the object's distinctive features

13. Research findings with animals suggest that, in order for normal perceptual development to occur, infants
    a. must be able to actively move through their environment
    b. must be able to watch movement in the environment
    c. must be exposed to patterned stimulation
    d. Both B and C

14. Most age related hearing problems originate in the
    a. hearing center of the brain
    b. auditory nerves and receptors
    c. structures of the middle ear
    d. outer ear membrane

15. An older person affected with presbycusis may have difficulty hearing
    a. a flute
    b. a bass drum
    c. a man's voice
    d. a bull horn

16. Someone who has trouble locating a figure embedded in a complex background probably has a(n)
    a. field-dependent style
    b. field-independent style
    c. perceptual problem
    d. astigmatism

17. When speaking to people who are hard of hearing, the speaker should
    a. elevate the voice--shout if necessary
    b. talk directly into the person's ear so they can hear better
    c. repeat what she has just said instead of rewarding the misunderstood statement
    d. make sure the hearing impaired person can see him/her

APPLICATION

Consider what it would be like if you lost one of your senses (vision, hearing, smell, taste, or touch). For each one, how would your life change after the loss?
How would _timing_ of the loss affect its impact?

Before you leave this chapter, go back and take another look at the learning objectives presented at the beginning of the chapter. Rephrase each objective into a question and check to see whether you have mastered them. A good way to check your understanding of a concept is to see if you can teach it to someone else. Take turns doing this with a small group of people. Whenever you are unsure or unclear about a response, go back to the text and find out what information you are missing in order to provide a clear and complete response.

ANSWERS

Summary and Guided Review (Fill-in the blank)

1. sensation
2. perception
3. empiricists
4. tabulae rasae
5. nurture
6. nativists
7. nature
8. enrichment
9. differentiation
10. distinctive features
11. habituation
12. visual acuity
13. visual accommodation
14. lens
15. patterned
16. contour
17. normal
18. mental representations
19. Gestalt
20. organized
21. depth
22. size constancy
23. visual cliff
24. seven
25. crawl
26. speech
27. prenatally
28. olfaction
29. tactile
30. pain
31. cries
32. cross-modal perception
33. attention
34. attention span
35. selective
36. systematic
37. distinctive features
38. myelinated

39. irrelevant
40. sensory thresholds
41. presbyopia
42. dark adaptation
43. visual acuity
44. cataracts
45. moving
46. novel
47. complex
48. presbycusis
49. high-frequency
50. background noise
51. sweet

52. odors
53. smell
54. subjective
55. stimulation
56. movement
57. cognitive style
58. field-dependent
59. field-independent
60. field-independent
61. field-dependent
62. aids
63. auditory
64. environment

Key Terms

1. distinctive feature
2. accommodation
3. Gestalt psychology
4. size constancy
5. sensation
6. olfaction
7. visual cliff
8. sensory threshold
9. cognitive style
10. habituation
11. presbyopia
12. perception

13. cross-modal perception
14. contour
15. differentiation theory
16. attention
17. visual acuity
18. dark adaptation
19. field-independent
20. enrichment theory
21. presbycusis
22. field-dependent
23. cataracts

Self Test

1. A
2. B
3. C
4. D
5. B
6. D
7. B
8. A
9. B

10. D
11. B
12. C
13. D
14. B
15. A
16. A
17. D

Chapter Seven
Cognition and Language

After reading and studying the material in this chapter, you should be able to do the following:

1. Describe what Piaget meant by "intelligence."

2. Describe how development occurs though organization and adaptation.

3. Describe and give examples of assimilation and accommodation.

4. Define the different aspects of a language--phonology, semantics, syntax, and pragmatics.

5. Describe each substage of the sensorimotor stage, indicating the developmental course of imitation, object permanence, and problem solving.

6. Describe the developmental course of early sound production--crying, cooing, and babbling.

7. Describe holophrastic speech and common characteristics or errors of this stage.

8. Describe characteristics and functions of telegraphic speech.

9. Describe Piaget's preoperational stage, including limitations of preoperational thought.

10. Describe Piaget's concrete operations stage and compare/contrast it with preoperational thought.

11. Explain what changes occur in language skills of preschool-age and school-age children.

12. Compare and contrast the learning theory and nativist theory of language acquisition. Be able to provide support for each perspective. Explain how the interactionist perspective integrates features of both learning and nativist theories.

13. Describe Piaget's formal operations stage and compare/contrast it with concrete operational thought.

14. Discuss the implications of formal operational thought.

15. Describe the limitations of adult cognitive performance.

16. Discuss the ways in which adults' thought may be more advanced than adolescents' thought and why the formal operational stage may not be the highest level of cognitive development.

17. Discuss the effect of aging on cognitive performance.

18. Discuss limitations and challenges to Piaget's theory of cognitive development. Explain ways to strengthen Piaget's theory.

19. Discuss whether cognitive functioning can be improved with training.

SUMMARY AND GUIDED REVIEW

The following summary provides an overview of the main points contained in this chapter of the text. Fill-in the blanks with terms that appropriately complete the sentence. Although blank spaces are provided, you may want to write your answers on a separate piece of paper, which will make it easier to compare your answers to the correct answers provided at the end of this chapter.
Scattered throughout the summary are questions in parentheses. These are meant to encourage you to think actively as you are reading and connect this summary to the more detailed information provided in the text. You can answer these questions as you are filling in the blanks or you can fill-in all the blanks, then go back and reread the entire summary, addressing the questions in order to provide more depth of understanding.

The act of knowing and the processes through which knowledge is acquired and problems are solved is called (1) _____. This chapter describes Piaget's approach to the development of cognition. Piaget used a question-and-answer technique called the (2) _____ _____ to determine the process of children's thinking. This method allows for (3) _____ but is not (4) _____ for all children. According to Piaget, (5) _____ is a basic life function that helps an organism adapt to its environment. Further, organisms are actively involved in their own development. As knowledge is gained, people form (6) _____ or cognitive structures, which are organized patterns or action or thought that allow us to interpret our experiences. Infants' schemes are (7) _____, or action-oriented, while preschool-age children develop (8) _____ schemes. The schemes of school-age children are characterized by (9) _____ _____ or mental activity performed on the objects of thought. (Can you provide an example of a logical operation?)

Schemes develop through two (10) _____ processes. One is (11) _____ in which children combine existing schemes into more complex schemes. (Can you provide an example of this?) The second process is (12) _____, which refers to the process of

83

adjusting to the demands of the environment. This adjustment occurs through (13) _____, by which new experiences are interpreted in terms of existing schemes, and through (14) _____, in which existing cognitive schemes are modified to account for new experiences. (Can you provide examples of each of these processes?) When we encounter new experiences, the conflict between new information and old understanding creates (15) _____, which is reduced by a combination of assimilation and accommodation.

Intertwined with cognition is (16) _____, which is a system of symbols that can be combined using agreed-on rules to produce messages. The sound system of language is (17) _____ and the basic units of sound are (18) _____. The meaning of language is its (19) _____ aspect. Children must come to understand that the symbols of a language represent things or ideas. The basic units of language that convey meaning are (20) _____. The rules specifying how to combine symbols meaningfully are the (21) _____ of language. Rules specifying how to use language appropriately in different contexts are the (22) _____ of language. (What is an example of this?)

According to Piaget, infants are in the (23) _____ stage, which has six substages and is dominated by (24) _____ schemes. The first substage lasts from birth to one month and is called (25) _____ _____. During the second substage (1 to 4 months), the infant uses (26) _____ _____ _____, which are actions centered on the infant's body and repeated for pleasure. During the third substage (4 to 8 months), infants gain pleasure by repeating actions that are centered on objects in the environment, called (27) _____ _____ _____. True intentional behavior emerges during the fourth substage (8 to 12 months) called (28) _____ of (29) _____ _____. Infants in substage five (12 to 18 months) engage in (30) _____ _____ _____, which involves inventing new ways of acting on objects to produce pleasurable results. The last substage (18 months to 2 years) is called the beginning of (31) _____, when the ability to use one thing to represent another thing emerges, and so infants can now experiment mentally.

Infants are not able to imitate novel responses until substage (32) _____, although they can imitate actions that are already familiar to them before this point. By substage six, infants are able to imitate models who are no longer present, an ability called (33) _____ _____. During the first two years, infants are also developing (34) _____ _____, the understanding that objects continue to exist even though not directly experienced. Infants in substage four will search for a concealed object if they watched while it was hidden, but if the object is then hidden in a new location, infants in this stage typically make the (35) _____ error. Not until substage six are infants capable of following (36) _____ displacements of objects.

84

Prelinguistic vocalizations begin at birth with several distinct cries. By the end of the first month, infants begin (37) _____, or repeating vowel-like sounds, and by 3 or 4 months of age, infants combine vowel and consonant sounds to produce (38) _____. Babbling is the same universally until about six months of age when babbling begins to change depending on the infant's experiences. (What evidence shows that experience has an impact on babbling?) At about one year, infants produce their first meaningful words, often called (39) _____ because when combined with gestures or intonation, these single words can convey the meaning of an entire sentence. Young children often (40) _____ the meaning of words by using fairly specific words to refer to a general class of objects. (Can you provide an example of this?) Young children may also (41) _____ the meaning of words by using a general word too narrowly. (Can you provide an example?)

Typically around 18 to 24 months, infants begin to combine two or more words into simple sentences called (42) _____ _____. These early sentences may be best described in terms of a (43) _____ _____, which focuses on the semantic relations between words.

According to Piaget, preschool-age children are in the (44) _____ stage of cognitive development where children use symbolic reasoning but not logical reasoning. Children in this stage lack (45) _____, the understanding that certain properties of a substance or object remain the same despite superficial changes in appearance. There are several reasons for this. They lack the cognition operation called (46) _____, which means they have trouble focusing on two or more dimensions of a problem at the same time. Instead, preoperational children engage in (47) _____ where they focus on a single aspect of the problem when more are relevant. In addition, preoperational children lack (48) _____ or the process of mentally reversing an action. Preoperational children also have trouble with (49) _____ or the processes of change from one state to another and so their thought is (50) _____. (Try writing preoperational children's responses to one of the conservation problems demonstrating each of these concepts.)

Piaget also believed that preoperational children were (51) _____ because they tend to view the world from their own perspective and have trouble recognizing other points of view. They have trouble relating subclasses of objects to the whole class of objects because they tend to center on the most perceptually salient feature of the task, and so they have trouble solving (52) _____ _____ problems. Sometimes preoperational children engage in (53) _____ _____ and conclude that because two events occurred together, they must be causally related. They may also show (54) _____, or a

85

tendency to attribute life-like qualities to inanimate objects. (In what ways was Piaget mistaken about preoperational children's abilities?)

School-age children (roughly 7 to 11 years) are in Piaget's (55) _____ _____ stage of cognitive development. They have mastered the (56) _____ _____ that were missing from preoperational thought. They are able to conserve, although they do not always solve all conservation at the same time, something Piaget referred to as (57) _____ _____. They are also able to order items along a quantifiable dimension, called (58) _____, and have mastered (59) _____, which is a cognitive operation that allows children to recognize the relationships among elements in a series. Finally, concrete operational children can solve (60) _____ _____ problems because they understand that subclasses are included in a whole class.

The language of preschool-age children is developing rapidly with their ability to use symbols. Their understanding of grammatical rules is often evident in the mistakes they make. For example, children often overapply rules they have learned to cases that are irregular, an error called (61) _____. Chomsky proposed that language be described in terms of (62) _____ _____, which consists of rules of syntax for transforming basic sentences into other forms. (Can you provide an example of a transformational rule?) School-age children refine their pronunciation skills, produce longer and more complex sentences and develop an ability to think about language, an understanding called (63) _____ _____.

There are several theoretical explanations of how children come to learn language at such an early age with no formal training. The (64) _____ theorists believe that children learn language the same way they learn everything else--through observation, imitation, and reinforcement. This theory seems to best explain how children acquire the (65) _____ of language, but not the (66) _____ of language. (What evidence supports this explanation of language acquisition?) The (67) _____ explanation proposes that humans have an inborn mechanism, called a (68) _____ _____ _____, that allows children to infer the rules governing the speech they hear and then apply these rules to their own speech. (What evidence supports this explanation of language acquisition?) This theory may explain syntactical developments better.

The (69) _____ perspective acknowledges that both the learning and nativist theories have some valuable aspects. Innate capacities and the language environment interact to influence language development. The social-communication theorists emphasize how the social interactions between infants and adults contribute to language and cognitive developments. Adults typically converse with infants using (70) _____, a simplified speech that is spoken slowly and in a high-pitched voice. (What other things do adults do to facilitate language development?)

According to Piaget, adolescents are entering the stage of (71) _____ _____. They are able to reason logically about (72) _____ and (73) _____ ideas. They also use systematic problem-solving strategies, rather than trial-and-error approaches often used by children in earlier stages. One type of reasoning is (74) _____-_____, where individuals reason from specific observations to a general conclusion. Another type of reasoning is (75) _____-_____, where individuals reason from general ideas to specific implications of these ideas. Mastery of formal operational thought takes place over several years and is often quite slow.

As a result of formal operational thought, adolescents often show (76) _____ _____, which is where adolescents have trouble differentiating their own thoughts and feelings from those of other people. This form of egocentrism develops as a result of adolescents' emerging (77) _____, their ability to think about thinking. Adolescent egocentrism takes two forms. One is the (78) _____ _____, which involves confusing your own thoughts with those of a hypothetical audience. (Can you provide an example of this phenomenon?) A second form of adolescent egocentrism is the (79) _____ _____, which is a tendency to think that your thoughts or feelings are unique and that others cannot possibly experience the same thoughts or feelings.

Formal operational thought is not always mastered consistently by adolescents or by adults. We tend to apply formal operational thought to areas with which we have some expertise and knowledge. Despite the fact that formal operational thought is not completely mastered by all adults, some researchers believe that Piaget did not go far enough with cognitive development and have posited growth beyond formal operations. Arlin has suggested that advanced thinkers enter a (80) _____-_____ stage where they use their knowledge to develop new questions or problems. Other researchers suggest that adults are more likely than adolescents to believe in (81) _____, which means that they believe that knowledge depends on the subjective perspective of the person with the knowledge. Adults may also have better (82) _____ thinking, which involves that ability to uncover and resolve contradictions between ideas. Finally, adults seem to be better able to think about systems of knowledge than adolescents. (Can you provide an example of thinking about systems?)

Cross-sectional studies with older adults suggest that they perform poorly on concrete and formal operational tasks. (How should these findings be interpreted?) With respect to language skills, some older adults may have communication problems associated with hearing problems, but language skills do not generally decline. In fact, knowledge of (83) _____ tends to increase throughout the life span.

Piaget's contributions must be viewed in the context of various challenges to the theory. (What are Piaget's major contributions?) One criticism of Piaget is that his estimates of the (84) _____ of development were not always correct. For example, the abilities of preschool-age children were probably underestimated, while the abilities of adolescents were probably overestimated. Piaget has also been criticized for blurring the distinction between competence and (85) _____. (Why is this distinction important?) Some researchers do not believe that development is best characterized by a series of coherent (86) _____ or qualitative changes in thinking. Piaget believed that cognition was the basis for many other developments, including language. Other researchers believe more attention needs to be given to how language affects thought. Finally, Piaget has been criticized for not really (87) _____ development, but only describing development. (How successful have training studies been and what implications do these training studies have for Piaget's theory?)

REVIEW OF KEY TERMS AND CONCEPTS

Below is a list of terms and concepts from this chapter. Match each one with its appropriate definition. You might also want to try writing definitions in your own words and then checking your definitions with those here in the Study Guide or in the text.

A, not B, error
accommodation
adaptation
adolescent egocentrism
animism
assimilation
babbling
centration
class inclusion
clinical method
cognition
concrete operations stage
conservation
cooing
decentration
deferred imitation
dialectical thinking
egocentrism
empirical-inductive reasoning
formal operations stage
functional grammar
holophrase
horizontal decalage
hypothetical-deductive reasoning
imaginary audience

metalinguistic awareness
morpheme
motherese
object permanence
organization
overextension
overregularization
personal fable
phoneme
phonology
pragmatics
preoperational stage
primary circular reaction
problem-finding stage
relativism
reversibility
scheme (schema)
secondary circular reaction
semantics
sensorimotor stage
seriation
symbolic capacity
syntax
telegraphic speech
tertiary circular reaction

intelligence
language
language acquisition device (LAD)
logical operation
metacognition

transductive reasoning
transformational grammar
transitivity
underextension

_____1.   Repetition of consonant-vowel combinations.

_____2.   A tendency to view the world from one's own
                      perspective and to have trouble recognizing other
                      points of view.

_____3.   The basic unit of sound in a language.

_____4.   A single word that, when combined with gestures or
                      intonation, conveys the meaning of an entire sentence.

_____5.   An inborn tendency to combine existing schemes into
                      new and more complex schemes.

_____6.   The ability to think about thinking.

_____7.   Young children's tendency to use fairly specific
                      words to refer to a general class of objects or
                      events.

_____8.   Understanding that objects continue to exist even
                      when those objects are no longer directly experienced.

_____9.   Confusing your own thoughts with the thoughts of a
                      hypothetical audience for your behavior.

_____10.   An inborn tendency to adjust to the demands of the
                      environment.

_____11.   Reasoning from one particular event to another and
                      concluding that because two events occur together,
                      they are causally related.

_____12.   An error often made by 8 to 12 month old infants who
                      successfully find an object hidden at one location and
                      then watch the object being hidden at a second
                      location and continue to search at the first hiding
                      location.

_____13.   Imitation of models who are no longer present.

_____14.   The process of interpreting new experiences in terms
                      of existing cognitive structures.

_____15. The activity of knowing and the processes through which knowledge is acquired and problems are solved.

_____16. Repetition of vowel-like sounds associated with positive affective states.

_____17. Young children's tendency to use a general word too narrowly.

_____18. An inborn mechanism for acquiring language that allows children to infer rules governing others' speech and then use these rules to produce their own speech.

_____19. A tendency to attribute life-like qualities to inanimate objects.

_____20. A form of simplified speech used by adults when speaking to young children.

_____21. Piaget's third stage of cognitive development when children can logically reason about physical objects and experiences.

_____22. The rules of syntax specifying how to transform basic sentences into other forms.

_____23. Two or three word sentences that contain only critical content words.

_____24. The process of mentally "undoing" an action.

_____25. Term used to describe children's inability to solve all problems that supposedly require the same mental operations.

_____26. Piaget's first stage of cognitive development where infant's understanding of the world is constructed through their senses and actions.

_____27. Thinking about language and its properties.

_____28. The process of modifying existing cognitive structures in order to understand or adapt to new experiences.

_____29. The analysis of early language in terms of the semantic relations between words.

_____30. An interview technique in which a child's response to each question determines the next question.

_____31. An action centered on the infant's that is repeated for pleasure.

_____32. The relationship between words or symbols and what they represent or mean.

_____33. A type of reasoning where specific implications are derived from general ideas or hypotheses, and are then systematically tested.

_____34. Piaget's fourth stage of cognitive development when children can reason logically about hypothetical and abstract ideas.

_____35. The basic unit of language which conveys meaning.

_____36. An organized pattern of thought or action used to interpret our experiences.

_____37. An action centered on objects in the infant's environment that is repeated for pleasure.

_____38. A type of reasoning where general conclusions are derived from specific observations.

_____39. Problem in differentiating one's own thoughts and feelings from those of other people.

_____40. The ability to use images, words, or gestures to represent objects and experiences.

_____41. Actions on objects are modified to discover new and interesting results.

_____42. A cognitive operation that allows children to mentally order items along a quantifiable dimension.

_____43. A tendency to think that you and your thoughts and feelings are unique.

_____44. The system of rules specifying how to combine words to form sentences.

_____45. An action performed in one's head on the objects of thought.

_____46. Piaget's second stage of cognitive development where children reason using symbols but do not reason logically.

_____47. A cognitive operation that allows children to recognize the relationship among elements in a series.

91

_____48. A system of symbols that can be combined according to agreed-on rules to create messages.

_____49. Understanding that certain properties of a substance or object remain the same despite superficial changes in appearance.

_____50. Rules specifying how language is to be used appropriately in different social contexts.

_____51. A possible stage beyond formal operations where individuals are able to uncover and resolve contradictions among ideas.

_____52. The system of speech sounds of a language.

_____53. A stage beyond formal operations, proposed by Arlin, in which individuals can use knowledge to form new questions or problems.

_____54. According to Piaget, this is a basic life function that helps an organism adapt to its environment.

_____55. The overapplication of grammatical rules to irregular nouns and verbs.

_____56. The tendency to focus on a single aspect of problem when more aspects are relevant.

_____57. An understanding that knowledge depends on the subjective perspective of the person with the knowledge.

_____58. The understanding that subclasses are included in a whole class.

_____59. The ability to focus on two or more dimensions of a problem at one time.

RESEARCH SUMMARY AND REVIEW

For each of the following studies, briefly summarize the main point(s) of the research and indicate why the research is important. Don't worry about specific details that are not central to the main points, or memorizing names of researchers. Questions you might ask yourself include: Does the research support or refute a theory or hypothesis presented in the text? How does it further our understanding of some concept? Does it provide an example of a point being made in the text? Use the text to check your understanding.

1. Bower's (1982) research on object permanence (p 206): _____

    _____

    _____

    _____

    _____

2. Gelman's (1972) research on conservation of number (p 212): _____

    _____

    _____

    _____ _____

    _____ _____

3. Krauss and Glucksburg's (1977) research on communication (p 215 &
    217): _____ _____

    _____ _____

    _ _____

    _ _____

    _____

4. Martorano's (1977) research on formal operational thought (p 222):

    _____

    _____

    _____

    _____

5. McGhee's (1979) research on humor and its relation to cognitive
    development (page 216): _____

    _____

    _____

    _____

    _____

93

For additional practice, pull out some other research discussed in this chapter or research discussed in class lectures and summarize the main points of the studies.

For each multiple choice question, read all alternatives and then select the best answer.

1. Which of the following illustrates Piaget's clinical method?
   a. asking children standardized questions and recording their answers
   b. giving children paper and pencil questionnaires to learn the ages when children can solve certain problems
   c. questioning children as a group to learn about general problem solving strategies
   d. asking children questions that are individually tailored to their previous responses

2. An example of accommodation is
   a. believing that all four-legged animals with fur are dogs
   b. realizing that a cat fits into a different category than a dog
   c. the confusion that a child experiences when new events challenge old schemas
   d. a child who sees a cat and refers to it as a dog, but is then corrected by the parent

3. Which of the following statements best characterizes Piaget's position on the nature-nurture issue?
   a. the environment is most important to the development of intellectual capacity
   b. innate mechanisms are primarily responsible for determining intelligence
   c. cognitive skills result from an interaction of innate characteristics and environmental experiences
   d. some cognitive skills result from innate characteristics while others are influenced only by environmental experiences

4. Assimilation is
   a. interpreting the world around us in terms of our current cognitive structures
   b. the modification of existing schemas to account for new experiences
   c. the innate tendency to meaningfully organize information
   d. combining existing schemes into more complex ones

5. The basic sound units in a language are called _____ and the basic units of meaning are called _____
   a. phonology; semantics
   b. semantics; phonology
   c. morphemes; phonemes
   d. phonemes; morphemes

6. A primary circular reaction involves repeating some action that is centered on
   a. the surrounding environment
   b. the infant's own body
   c. some other person's body
   d. one of the primitive reflexes

7. By age 8 to 12 months, an infant is able to
   a. find a hidden object that the infant watched being hidden
   b. use a trial and error method of experimenting with the world
   c. demonstrate a certain amount of insight
   d. imitate the behavior of an absent model

8. Which of the following is an example of the first "true" object permanence in sensorimotor substage 4?
   a. closely watching a doorway through which someone has passed and can no longer be seen
   b. correctly searching for a shoe under the bed even though the child had not seen the shoe hidden in this location
   c. searching for a toy where the child just watched it being hidden
   d. using goal directed behavior to systematically check all possible hiding locations for a toy

9. Calling all four-legged animals "doggie" is an example of
   a. overregularization
   b. underextension
   c. overextension
   d. telegraphic speech

10. Which of following is the best example of telegraphic speech?
   a. "Is the ball here?"
   b. "More milk."
   c. "Shoes under the table."
   d. "Dog!"

11. Piaget suggested that preschoolers have difficulty understanding conservation because they
   a. tend to concentrate on all the dimensions of the problem at one time
   b. tend to focus on only one aspect of a problem when more aspects are relevant
   c. persist in mentally reversing actions performed in the transformation
   d. have not yet achieved abstract reasoning

12. Which of these statements demonstrates transductive reasoning?
    a. "It's not afternoon because Daddy isn't home from work yet."
    b. "The sun hides behind the mountain because it knows that it is nighttime."
    c. "I want to go play outside, so Mommy does too."
    d. "That chair made me trip!"

13. Which of the following terms is used to describe the inconsistency that children show in solving problems that require the same cognitive operations?
    a. transductive reasoning
    b. vertical decalage
    c. horizontal decalage
    d. static thought

14. Seriation involves
    a. the realization that properties of objects do not change even though appearance might be altered
    b. understanding that subclasses are included in the whole class
    c. understanding the relationships among elements in a series
    d. mentally arranging elements along a quantifiable scale

15. Learning theorists argue that language is acquired through
    a. biologically programmed capacities
    b. imitation of others' language and reinforcement for recognizable speech
    c. cognitive understanding of speech sounds and their relationship to real objects and actions
    d. a device that allows children to sift through language and generate rules that govern the language

16. Chomsky's nativist theory of language acquisition seems to best explain how children acquire _____ while learning theory seems to best explain acquisition of _____.
    a. syntax; pragmatics
    b. semantics, phonology
    c. syntax; semantics
    d. semantics; syntax

17. Formal operational children are different than concrete operational children in that
    a. formal operational children can deal with possibilities
    b. formal operational children focus on realities
    c. concrete operational children systematically test all possible solutions to a problem
    d. concrete operational children are more likely to experience horizontal decalage

18. An example of empirical-inductive reasoning is
    a. drawing a third eyeball on a hand rather than on a face
    b. placing pictures which vary on several dimensions in proper sequence
    c. developing a hypothesis and then determining all the possible implications of this general hypothesis
    d. using observations to determine that a pendulum on a short string swings more quickly than one on a long string

19. Which of the following is an example of a personal fable?
    a. believing that life is a tragedy, thus every precaution needs to be taken to ensure safety for everyone
    b. feeling self-conscious in front of an audience
    c. believing that everyone is aware of your feelings
    d. believing that no one has ever felt romantic love more strongly

20. Piaget has been criticized by recent developmentalists who suggest that
    a. Piaget was somewhat pessimistic concerning the timing of cognitive abilities in adolescents
    b. Piaget was overly optimistic concerning the abilities of infants and young children
    c. development is a gradual process rather than a stagelike process
    d. development is stagelike but stages follow a different pattern than what Piaget suggested

21. Adults typically use formal operational thought
    a. only in their areas of expertise
    b. in all appropriate situations
    c. on new and more difficult tasks but not on old and familiar tasks
    d. consistently, once it is acquired

22. Dialectical thinking refers to
    a. the ability to accept opposing ideas
    b. rethinking or reorganizing knowledge to discover new questions or problems
    c. the ability to locate and resolve contradictions between opposing ideas
    d. understanding that knowledge depends on the interpretation of that knowledge by the knower

23. Research with older adults solving Piagetian tasks shows that
    a. nearly all are reasoning at the formal operational level
    b. older adults perform worse than younger adults on many concrete operational tasks
    c. older adults perform similarly to younger adults on all Piagetian tasks
    d. older adults are more egocentric than younger adults and tend to use transductive reasoning

1.   Apply Piaget's description of cognitive development to the issues of divorce and birth of a new sibling. What would a child's understanding of these two events be in each of Piaget's stages of cognitive development?

2.   Consider how deafness affects language development of children. Questions to think about include: Do you need to hear speech to develop speech? More generally, do you need to be exposed to a language (spoken or unspoken) in order to develop a language? What is the relationship between thought and language? Is language an important basis for thought (Is it a <u>necessary</u> basis for thought)?

Before you leave this chapter, go back and take another look at the learning objectives presented at the beginning of the chapter. Rephrase each objective into a question and check to see whether you have mastered them. A good way to check your understanding of a concept is to see if you can teach it to someone else. Take turns doing this with a small group of people. Whenever you are unsure or unclear about a response, go back to the text and find out what information you are missing in order to provide a clear and complete response.

ANSWERS

Summary and Guided Review (Fill-in the blank)

1.	cognition	22.	pragmatics
2.	clinical method	23.	sensorimotor
3.	flexibility	24.	behavioral
4.	standardized	25.	reflexive activity
5.	intelligence	26.	primary circular reaction
6.	schemes	27.	secondary circular reaction
7.	behavioral	28.	coordination
8.	symbolic	29.	secondary schemes
9.	logical operation	30.	tertiary circular reactions
10.	innate	31.	thought
11.	organization	32.	four
12.	adaptation	33.	deferred imitation
13.	assimilation	34.	object permanence
14.	accommodation	35.	A, not B
15.	disequilibrium	36.	invisible
16.	language	37.	cooing
17.	phonology	38.	babbling
18.	phonemes	39.	holophrases
19.	semantic	40.	overextend
20.	morphemes	41.	underextend
21.	syntax	42.	telegraphic speech

43. functional grammar
44. preoperational
45. conservation
46. decentration
47. centration
48. reversibility
49. transformations
50. static
51. egocentric
52. class inclusion
53. transductive reasoning
54. animism
55. concrete operations
56. logical operations
57. horizontal decalage
58. seriation
59. transitivity
60. class inclusion
61. overregularization
62. transformational grammar
63. metalinguistic awareness
64. learning
65. semantics

66. syntax
67. nativist
68. language acquisition device
69. interactionist
70. motherese
71. formal operations
72. hypothetical
73. abstract
74. empirical-inductive
75. hypothetical-deductive
76. adolescent egocentrism
77. metacognition
78. imaginary audience
79. personal fable
80. problem-finding
81. relativism
82. dialectical
83. semantics
84. timing
85. performance
86. stages
87. explaining

Key Terms

1. babbling
2. egocentrism
3. phoneme
4. holophrase
5. organization
6. metacognition
7. overextension
8. object permanence
9. imaginary audience
10. adaptation
11. transductive reasoning
12. A, not B, error
13. deferred imitation
14. assimilation
15. cognition
16. cooing
17. underextension
18. language acquisition device
19. animism
20. motherese
21. concrete operations stage
22. transformational grammar
23. telegraphic speech
24. reversibility

25. horizontal decalage
26. sensorimotor stage
27. metalinguistic awareness
28. accommodation
29. functional grammar
30. clinical method
31. primary circular reaction
32. semantics
33. hypothetical-deductive reasoning
34. formal operations stage
35. morpheme
36. scheme
37. secondary circular reaction
38. empirical-inductive reasoning
39. adolescent egocentrism
40. symbolic capacity
41. tertiary circular reaction
42. seriation
43. personal fable
44. syntax
45. logical operation
46. preoperational stage
47. transitivity
48. language

49. conservation
50. pragmatics
51. dialectical thinking
52. phonology
53. problem-finding stage
54. intelligence
55. overregularization
56. centration
57. relativism
58. class inclusion
59. decentration

Self Test

1.	D	13.	C
2.	B	14.	D
3.	A	15.	B
4.	A	16.	C
5.	D	17.	A
6.	B	18.	D
7.	A	19.	D
8.	C	20.	C
9.	C	21.	A
10.	B	22.	C
11.	B	23.	B
12.	A		

Chapter Eight
Learning and Information Processing

After reading and studying the material in this chapter, you should be able to do the following:

1. Explain habituation.

2. Explain classical conditioning and provide an example.

3. Explain operant conditioning and provide an example.

4. Distinguish between negative reinforcement and punishment.

5. Explain how the timing and frequency of reinforcement affect learning.

6. Explain the process of observational learning.

7. Distinguish between learning and performance and indicate why this distinction is important.

8. Describe the information-processing approach to cognition.

9. Discuss whether newborns can learn through habituation, classical conditioning, operant conditioning, and observational learning, and note limitations of newborns' learning capabilities.

10. Describe how infant memory is assessed and the findings regarding infant memory.

11. Describe the memory strategies used by children and adults.

12. Define metamemory and discuss how it changes with age.

13. Describe knowledge base and how it is related to learning and memory.

14. Discuss how problem solving capacities change during childhood.

15. Describe developments in information processing of adolescents.

16. Discuss changes in memory and cognition that occur in adulthood.

17. Discuss explanations for the declines that occur in learning and memory as people get older.

The following summary provides an overview of the main points contained in this chapter of the text. Fill-in the blanks with terms that appropriately complete the sentence. Although blank spaces are provided, you may want to write your answers on a separate piece of paper, which will make it easier to compare your answers to the correct answers provided at the end of this chapter.

Scattered throughout the summary are questions in parentheses. These are meant to encourage you to think actively as you are reading and connect this summary to the more detailed information provided in the text. You can answer these questions as you are filling in the blanks or you can fill-in all the blanks, then go back and reread the entire summary, addressing the questions in order to provide more depth of understanding.

Learning is defined as a relatively permanent change in behavior that results from one's (1) _____. This chapter presents four types of learning. One form of learning, called (2) _____, is evident when an individual stops responding to a stimulus that is repeatedly presented. A second form of learning is (3) _____ _____, where a stimulus that initially had no effect on an individual comes to elicit a response through its association with a (4) _____ that already produces the desired response. A stimulus that elicits the desired response without prior learning experiences is an (5) _____ stimulus. A stimulus that produces the desired response only after being associated with a stimulus that always elicits the response is a (6) _____ stimulus. An unlearned response to an unlearned stimulus is an (7) _____ response, while a learned response to a conditioned stimulus is a (8) _____ response. (Can you provide an example of classical conditioning that is not in the text?) Many (9) _____ responses are thought to be learned through classical conditioning. Responses learned this way can be unlearned through the same process, called (10) _____.

A third form of learning is (11) _____ _____, where behaviors or responses become more or less probable depending on their consequences. One possible consequence is (12) _____ _____, where something administered following a behavior strengthens that behavior. Behaviors could also be strengthened by removing something adverse following the behavior, a process called (13) _____ _____. Decreasing the strength of a behavior is accomplished through (14) _____, which can be positive or negative. (Can you describe ways to make use of punishment effective?) Sometimes, a behavior is followed by no consequences, which eventually leads to (15) _____ since the behavior is not being reinforced.

The systematic application of learning principles in order to change behavior is called (16) _____ _____. By reinforcing closer and closer approximations of a behavior that is

ultimately desired, it is possible to (17) _____ a complex
behavior. Reinforcing a behavior every time it occurs is providing
(18) _____ reinforcement and tends to result in extinction
of the behavior once the reinforcement has been discontinued.
Reinforcing only some instances of a behavior is providing
(19) _____ reinforcement, which tends to result in slower
extinction if the reinforcements are provided on an (20) _____
schedule.

   A fourth form of learning is (21) _____ learning, which
results from observing the behavior of other people. Learning a
behavior does not necessarily mean an individual will (22) _____
the behavior. The process of (23) _____ _____
means that if the learner observes the model getting reinforced for his
or her actions, the learner will be more likely to perform the behavior.
(Can you describe the cognitive processes that are involved in
observational learning?)

   The four forms of learning just described are part of the
(24) _____ approach to learning. Another approach to
learning is the (25) _____-_____ perspective,
which uses a computer analogy. A popular information-processing model
posits that information coming into the information-processing system
(i.e., the person) is briefly held in a (26) _____
_____. If the person pays attention to this information, it
will be moved into (27) _____-_____, or working,
memory. Information to be remembered for any length of time must
somehow be moved into (28) _____-_____ memory.

   In order to remember something, it must first be (29) _____
and then (30) _____, or held in long-term memory. When the
information is needed, it must be (31) _____ from long-term
memory. Retrieval of information by reproducing it without cues is
called (32) _____, which is more difficult than
(33) _____ of information, or indicating whether or not the
information has been previously experienced. Using the information-
processing system to achieve a goal or make a decision is
(34) _____ _____. Monitoring the information-
processing system are a number of (35) _____ _____.

   Research suggests that newborns show habituation, and can learn
through classical and operant conditioning, and possibly through
observational learning. However, they are limited in their capacities.
(Can you provide evidence of each type of learning in newborns and the
limitations on each?) Newborns also show evidence of (36) _____
memory. (How has this been demonstrated?)

   Although the basic learning processes are present during infancy,
learning and memory clearly improve during childhood. There are four
main hypotheses about why this improvement occurs. One possibility is
that basic (37) _____ change. For example, some neo-

Piagetian theorists propose that working memory space increases during childhood. However, research does not show that total capacity changes, although children do get more efficient at using the space they have as many processes become (38) _____ and require little effort.

Another possibility for the improvement in learning and memory is that (39) _____ _____ improve with age. Although young children can (40) _____ remember when they are highly motivated, their memory strategies are not always very effective. One strategy is to use (41) _____, or repeating the items to be remembered. Another strategy is (42) _____ or classifying items to be remembered into meaningful groups. A third strategy is to use (43) _____ or create meaningful links between the items to be remembered. Rehearsal typically develops first, followed by use of (44) _____ and finally by spontaneous use of (45) _____ in adolescence. Memory strategies like these are thought to develop through three stages. The first is (46) _____ _____ where children lack basic cognitive skills to benefit from using a strategy, even if the strategy is provided for the children. The second stage is (47) _____ _____ where children fail to produce a strategy, but if it is provided, they can use it and benefit from it. The third stage is (48) _____ strategy use where the strategy is spontaneously and effectively used to aid learning and memory.

A third explanation for the improvement in learning and memory is that knowledge about memory and other cognitive processes changes with age. Knowledge of memory and memory processes is called (49) _____ and does improve with age. (Can you provide evidence that shows growth in this skill?) However, these improvements in metamemory are not always found to be strongly associated with increases in memory. A fourth possibility is that increased knowledge of the world in general, or (50) _____ _____, leads to improvements in memory. There is research evidence that children who have an extensive knowledge base in a particular area can outperform adults who are novices in the same area.

Problem solving capacities also change during childhood and have been tested using a (51) _____ learning task. In a (52) _____ _____ type problem, after learning which stimulus value is "correct" in one set of trials, children must learn to respond to the opposite value in subsequent trials. In a (53) _____ _____ problem, children must switch to an entirely different stimulus dimension than the one that has previously been "correct." According to operant conditioning theory, the (54) _____ _____ should be easier. (Can you explain why this is the case?) Young children (preschool-age) do find the (55) _____ problems easier, but school-age children find the (56) _____ problems easier to learn. This change in the way children learn and solve problems at about the time they enter school is called the (57) _____ shift. One reason for this might be that children entering school use (58) _____

_____, or language as a tool of thought. Problem solving has also been studied by information-processing theorists. (Can you describe the logic behind the balance-beam task used by Siegler to assess problem-solving abilities?)

During adolescence, memory strategies improve, and adolescents make more (59) _____ use of strategies. They also use strategies more (60) _____ and spontaneously. Adolescents know more in general, so their (61) _____ _____ expands, and they also show improvements in their (62) _____, or understanding of their learning and memory processes.

During adulthood, developing (63) _____ in a field facilitates memory and problem solving within this field. Self-reports and research indicate that memory declines with age, but declines are slight and usually do not occur until one's 60's or 70's. Also, since much of the research in this area has used (64) _____-_____ designs, the apparent declines could be due to other factors. The memory store that shows the greatest decline is (65) _____-_____ memory. Memory for the distant past is termed (66) _____ long-term memory. This type of memory typically declines less than elderly adults' performance on immediate long-term memory tasks, suggesting that the elderly have trouble learning new material and then retrieving it from long-term memory. (What are some other limitations of older adults' memory?)

Possible explanations for the declines observed in older adults are basically the same as those considered for young children's performance. Unlike young children, older adults do not seem to have deficient (67) _____ _____. Metamemory problems also do not seem to contribute greatly to memory declines in older adults. Older adults do not always spontaneously use effective strategies, in other words, they show a (68) _____ _____. They also need to devote more time and mental effort to memory tasks than younger adults. It is also possible that the declines in memory observed for older adults compared to younger adults are due to (69) _____ differences. Older adults may not be as motivated to perform as younger adults and often respond cautiously in laboratory studies. Finally, when older adults are tested in the laboratory, the context of remembering is usually quite different from everyday contexts in which they normally learn and remember.

Older adults also seem to perform more poorly than young adults on problem solving tasks. On a twenty-questions task, asking (70) _____-_____ questions is most efficient. Older children and young adults use this strategy, but older adults do not unless the task is altered to make it more familiar to them, another example of a (71) _____ _____.

Below is a list of terms and concepts from this chapter. Match each one
with its appropriate definition. You might also want to try writing
definitions in your own words and then checking your definitions with
those here in the Study Guide or in the text.

behavior modification	operant conditioning
classical conditioning	organization (as a memory strategy)
conditioned response (CR)	partial reinforcement
conditioned stimulus (CS)	positive reinforcement
constraint-seeking questions	problem solving
continuous reinforcement	production deficiency
counterconditioning	punishment
elaboration	recall memory
encoding	recognition memory
extinction	rehearsal
5-to-7 shift	remote long-term memory
habituation	retrieval
infantile amnesia	reversal shift
information-processing approach	sensory register
knowledge base	shaping
learning	short-term memory
long-term memory	storage
metamemory	time out
negative reinforcement	unconditioned response (UCR)
nonreversal shift	unconditioned stimulus (UCS)
observational learning	verbal mediation

_____1. A form of learning in which behaviors or responses
become either more or less probable depending on their
consequences.

_____2. A memory strategy that involves repeating items to be
remembered.

_____3. A failure to produce a strategy, but if a strategy is
provided, individuals can use it and benefit from it.

_____4. A learning problem where the learner has to respond to
the opposite end of the stimulus dimension that has
been "correct" up to this point.

_____5. Reinforcing closer and closer approximations of the
behavior that is ultimately desired.

_____6. Getting information out of long-term memory when it is
needed.

_____7. A memory strategy that involves classifying items to
be remembered into meaningful groups.

_____8. A type of memory that requires individuals to indicate whether they have previously experienced a stimulus.

_____9. A learned response to a conditioned stimulus.

_____10. Any stimulus that increases the likelihood of a behavior in the future when administered following the behavior.

_____11. A memory store which temporarily stores a limited amount of information and allows active operation of this information.

_____12. A relatively permanent change in behavior that results from one's experiences.

_____13. A memory strategy that involves creating meaningful links between the items to be remembered.

_____14. Reinforcing a behavior every time it occurs.

_____15. A memory store that is relatively permanent and holds our knowledge of the world and our past experiences.

_____16. Knowledge of memory and memory processes.

_____17. A learning problem where the learner must switch to an entirely different stimulus dimension than the one that has been "correct" to this point.

_____18. A form of learning in which a stimulus that initially had no effect on an individual comes to elicit a response through its association with a stimulus that already produces the desired response.

_____19. Getting information into the information-processing system, and processing it.

_____20. The process of extinguishing a response learned through classical conditioning by applying classical conditioning principles.

_____21. A type of memory that requires individuals to reproduce a previously encountered stimulus without cues.

_____22. A stimulus that elicits the desired response without learning experiences.

_____23. The lack of memory for early years of life.

_____24. A process of eliminating a behavior by removing its reinforcing consequences.

_____25. The holding of information in long-term memory.

_____26. The use of the information-processing system to achieve a goal or make a decision.

_____27. An individual's knowledge of a content area.

_____28. A change in the way children learn and solve problems that occurs at about the time they enter school.

_____29. A stimulus that produces the desired response only after being associated with a stimulus that always elicits the response.

_____30. A form of learning that results from observing the behavior of other people.

_____31. The use of language as a tool for thought.

_____32. Any stimulus that follows a behavior and decreases the likelihood of the behavior reoccurring.

_____33. An approach to cognition that uses a computer analogy and emphasizes mental processes involved in attention, perception, memory, and decision making.

_____34. Memory for the distant past.

_____35. A problem solving strategy that asks questions that rule out several possible solutions rather than just one.

_____36. Reinforcing only some instances of a behavior.

_____37. A very brief, but literal image or record of stimuli.

_____38. Any stimulus that increases the likelihood of a behavior occurring in the future when removed following the behavior.

_____39. An unlearned response to an unconditioned stimulus.

_____40. A form of learning in which an individual stops responding to a stimulus that is repeatedly presented.

_____41. The systematic application of learning principles to change behavior in positive ways.

_____42. Removing the opportunity to have one's misbehavior positively reinforced.

RESEARCH SUMMARY AND REVIEW

For each of the following studies, briefly summarize the main point(s) of the research and indicate why the research is important. Don't worry about specific details that are not central to the main points, or memorizing names of researchers. Questions you might ask yourself include: Does the research support or refute a theory or hypothesis presented in the text? How does it further our understanding of some concept? Does it provide an example of a point being made in the text? Use the text to check your understanding.

1. Bandura's (1965) study on modeling aggression (pp 240-1): _____

_____

_____

_____

_____

2. Chi's (1978) research on memory of novices and experts (p 252):

_____

_____

_____

_____

3. Siegler's (1981) balance-scale study of children's problem solving (pp 254-255): _____

_____

_____

_____

_____

For additional practice, pull out some other research discussed in this chapter or research discussed in class lectures and summarize the main points of the studies.

For each multiple choice question, read all alternatives and then select the best answer.

1. In _____ conditioning, a learner must first emit a response, while in _____ conditioning, a stimulus elicits a response from the learner.
    a. classical; operant
    b. operant; classical
    c. operant; observational
    d. observational classical

2. You turn on the can opener to open the dog's food and dog comes running into the room. In this example, food is the _____; the sound of the can opener is the _____; and running into the room in response to the sound is the _____.
    a. unconditioned stimulus; conditioned stimulus; unconditioned response
    b. conditioned stimulus; unconditioned stimulus; conditioned response
    c. unconditioned stimulus; conditioned stimulus; conditioned response
    d. conditioned stimulus; conditioned response; unconditioned response

3. A stimulus can serve as reinforcement or as punishment depending on whether it
    a. is pleasurable or not (negative) for the subject receiving it
    b. increases or decreases the frequency of the behavior it follows
    c. occurs before or after the behavior in question
    d. is administered or taken away from the person

4. Which of the following is an example of negative reinforcement?
    a. Giving a child a dessert as a reward for eating his/her vegetables at dinner
    b. Paying a child for each "A" received on his or her report card
    c. When a parent stops nagging a child when the child finally cleans his or her room
    d. Cutting a child's television viewing by 30 minutes each time the child "talks back"

5. Which of the following is necessary in order to learn through observation (modeling)?
    a. Observing the model getting rewarded or punished for his/her actions
    b. Being provided with an opportunity to imitate the model's actions immediately after the observation
    c. Hearing the model describe the consequences of his/her actions
    d. Observing and remembering the model's actions

6. Partial reinforcement occurs when a new behavior is reinforced
    a. every time it occurs
    b. some of the times that it occurs
    c. by the removal of an unpleasant stimulus
    d. by the addition of a pleasant stimulus

7. In order to effectively use punishment as a deterrent to bad
    behavior a parent should
    a. delay punishment until both parents can address the behavior
        together with the child
    b. speak quietly so the child does not feel intimidated
    c. explain the inappropriateness of the behavior and the reasons
        for punishment
    d. punish the behavior when it is extreme but not necessarily
        punish when the behavior is mild or moderate

8. Encoding involves information that is
    a. moved from a sensory register to short-term memory to long-term
        memory
    b. maintained in long-term memory
    c. pulled out from long-term memory when needed
    d. simple to process

9. Which of the following is true regarding classical conditioning?
    a. Newborns can be easily classically conditioned.
    b. Classical conditioning is not possible until at least 8-12
        months of age.
    c. Newborns can be classically conditioned but not always reliably
        or easily.
    d. Infants can be classically conditioned if they understand what
        it is the experimenter is trying to condition.

10. Research on imitation suggests that
    a. young infants can show imitation but this may be a reflex-like
        action
    b. infants of all ages reliably show imitation
    c. young infants reliably imitate novel acts but older infants have
        lost this ability
    d. imitation is not evident at all until about 8-12 months of age

11. The lack of memory for one's early years of life is termed
    a. production deficiency
    b. mediation deficiency
    c. infantile memory loss
    d. infantile amnesia

12. An example of elaboration is
    a. repeating "red, chair, dog" several times
    b. consolidating "red" and "green" into a color group and "chair" and "table" into a furniture group
    c. noting that the red chair and the green piano remind you of Christmas when you sit on the chair and play the piano
    d. saying the words to be remembered out loud

13. The ability to benefit from a memory strategy but the failure to use it spontaneously is termed
    a. production deficiency
    b. mediation deficiency
    c. metamemory
    d. learning disability

14. In their area of expertise, expert children perform
    a. better than novice adults
    b. the same as novice adults
    c. worse than novice adults
    d. the same as children with good overall problem solving skills

15. An example of a nonreversal shift is
    a. learning that "round" is correct and later learning that "square" is correct
    b. learning that "round" is correct and later learning that "blue" is correct
    c. learning that the larger object is correct
    d. learning to use trial and error method of problem solving

16. One difference between the memory strategy use by preadolescents and use by adolescents is that adolescents
    a. randomly select a strategy
    b. use fewer strategies to remember important information
    c. remember more irrelevant information than younger children
    d. are better able to distinguish the more relevant points from the irrelevant points

17. Which of the following statements accurately describes memory performance of adults?
    a. Memory systematically declines throughout adulthood.
    b. Memory declines may occur after age 60 and are typically slight.
    c. Memory does not change from adolescence through middle adulthood, but after this, memory declines quite rapidly.
    d. Older adults experience no memory declines because they use more memory strategies than younger adults.

18. In comparison to younger adults, older adults
    a. process new information more quickly than younger adults
    b. exhibit production deficiencies but are capable of using organizational strategies
    c. recall information just as quickly as younger adults
    d. have difficulty using organizational and elaborative strategies

19. With which of the following tasks would older adults have the <u>least</u> problem?
    a. a memory task where the material is unfamiliar
    b. a task where they are asked to recall rather than recognize names
    c. a memory task where they can use well-practiced memory strategies
    d. a timed memory task

20. On problem-solving tasks such as discrimination learning, older adults perform
    a. similarly to young adults
    b. similarly to children
    c. better than young adults
    d. better than children but worse than young adults

APPLICATION

As children's eyewitness testimony in court proceedings has increased, we have seen more research on children's reliability as witnesses. Based on what you know about memory development from this chapter, what conclusions and suggestions can you make regarding use of children as witnesses?

Before you leave this chapter, go back and take another look at the learning objectives presented at the beginning of the chapter. Rephrase each objective into a question and check to see whether you have mastered them. A good way to check your understanding of a concept is to see if you can teach it to someone else. Take turns doing this with a small group of people. Whenever you are unsure or unclear about a response, go back to the text and find out what information you are missing in order to provide a clear and complete response.

ANSWERS

Summary and Guided Review (Fill-in the blank)

1. experience
2. habituation
3. classical conditioning
4. stimulus
5. unconditioned
6. conditioned
7. unconditioned
8. conditioned
9. emotional
10. counterconditioning
11. operant conditioning
12. positive reinforcement
13. negative reinforcement
14. punishment
15. extinction
16. behavior modification
17. shape
18. continuous
19. partial
20. unpredictable

21. observational
22. perform
23. vicarious reinforcement
24. behavioral
25. information-processing
26. sensory register
27. short-term
28. long-term
29. encoded
30. stored
31. retrieved
32. recall
33. recognition
34. problem solving
35. control processes
36. recognition
37. capacities
38. automatized
39. memory strategies
40. deliberately
41. rehearsal
42. organization
43. elaboration
44. organization
45. elaboration
46. mediation deficiency

47. production deficiency
48. mature
49. metamemory
50. knowledge base
51. discrimination
52. reversal shift
53. nonreversal shift
54. nonreversal shift
55. nonreversal
56. reversal
57. 5-to-7
58. verbal mediation
59. deliberate
60. selectively
61. knowledge base
62. metacognition
63. expertise
64. cross-sectional
65. long-term
66. remote
67. knowledge base
68. production deficiency
69. cohort
70. constraint-seeking
71. production deficiency

Key Terms

1. operant conditioning
2. rehearsal
3. production deficiency
4. reversal shift
5. shaping
6. retrieval
7. organization
8. recognition memory
9. conditioned response (CR)
10. positive reinforcement
11. short-term memory
12. learning
13. elaboration
14. continuous reinforcement
15. long-term memory
16. metamemory
17. nonreversal shift
18. classical conditioning
19. encoding
20. counterconditioning
21. recall memory

22. unconditioned stimulus (UCS)
23. infantile amnesia
24. extinction
25. storage
26. problem solving
27. knowledge base
28. 5-to-7 shift
29. conditioned stimulus
30. observational learning
31. verbal mediation
32. punishment
33. information-processing approach
34. remote long-term memory
35. constraint-seeking questions
36. partial reinforcement
37. sensory register
38. negative reinforcement
39. unconditioned response (UCR)
40. habituation
41. behavior modification
42. time out

Self Test

1.	B	11.	D
2.	C	12.	C
3.	B	13.	A
4.	C	14.	A
5.	D	15.	B
6.	B	16.	D
7.	C	17.	B
8.	A	18.	B
9.	C	19.	C
10.	A	20.	B

Chapter Nine
Mental Abilities

After reading and studying the material in this chapter, you should be able to do the following:

1. Describe the various perspectives on whether intelligence is a single ability or many abilities.

2. Distinguish between fluid and crystallized intelligence.

3. Describe Sternberg's triarchic theory of intelligence.

4. Describe the Stanford-Binet and Wechsler intelligence tests and indicate how they differ from one another.

5. Discuss intelligence testing today.

6. Describe how infant intelligence is measured and its relation to later intelligence.

7. Discuss whether IQ scores are stable during childhood and whether they predict school achievement.

8. Discuss how timing of puberty relates to mental abilities and indicate whether this hypothesis is supported by research.

9. Discuss whether IQ is related to occupational success.

10. Describe the ways that intellectual abilities change with age.

11. Discuss the factors that are associated with declining intellectual abilities in older adults.

12. Discuss factors that influence IQ scores, including home environment, birth order, family size, social class, and racial and ethnic differences.

13. Describe characteristics of gifted children.

14. Explain how mental retardation is defined, possible causes, and outcomes.

15. Discuss creativity, including how it is measured and its relation to intelligence.

16. Discuss the outcome of compensatory education.

The following summary provides an overview of the main points contained in this chapter of the text. Fill-in the blanks with terms that appropriately complete the sentence. Although blank spaces are provided, you may want to write your answers on a separate piece of paper, which will make it easier to compare your answers to the correct answers provided at the end of this chapter.

Scattered throughout the summary are questions in parentheses. These are meant to encourage you to think actively as you are reading and connect this summary to the more detailed information provided in the text. You can answer these questions as you are filling in the blanks or you can fill-in all the blanks, then go back and reread the entire summary, addressing the questions in order to provide more depth of understanding.

The (1) _____ approach views intelligence as a trait or set of traits that can be measured. A statistical procedure called (2) _____ _____ has been used by psychometricians to identify clusters of tests or test items that are strongly related to one another, but unrelated to other items. Spearman used factor analysis to study intelligence and concluded that a (3) _____ factor contributed to performance on many different tasks. Thurstone identified seven distinct (4) _____ mental abilities. Guilford proposed that intelligence consists of as many as 120 different mental abilities. His (5) _____-_____-_____ model focuses on the contents, operations, and products of intelligence. Cattell and Horn propose that intelligence consists of two major dimensions. The ability to solve novel problems is (6) _____ intelligence and the ability to use knowledge acquired through experiences is (7) _____ intelligence.

A more recent theory of intelligence is Sternberg's (8) _____ model, which emphasizes three aspects of intelligent behavior. According to this model, intelligent behavior depends on the (9) _____ in which it is displayed and so can be expected to vary from one culture or subculture to another. Intelligent behavior is also affected by the (10) _____ that one has with a situation or task. The intelligent response to a task the first time it is encountered may differ from what is considered intelligent after many encounters with the same task. The increased efficiency that comes with familiarity and practice with a task reflects (11) _____. The third aspect of Sternberg's triarchic model includes the information-processing (12) _____.

Binet and Simon designed the first intelligence test, calculating a child's IQ or (13) _____ _____ from a child's obtained (14) _____ _____ on the test and the child's chronological age. The revised version of this original test is the (15) _____-_____. The (16) _____ _____, or standards of typical performance, are based on a

large and representative sample of people. The (17) _____
Scales of intelligence separate IQ into a verbal and a
(18) _____ component. (Why might it be important to consider
these two components separately?) If a large number of IQ scores are
plotted on a graph, they form a (19) _____ _____,
which shows that more people score around the mean of 100 and fewer
people score at the extremes of the curve. One of the newer
intelligence tests is the Kaufman Assessment Battery for Children, which
included both minority and handicapped children in its norm sample to
remedy what some view as a weakness of the Stanford-Binet and Wechsler
tests. Another new test is Feuerstein's Learning Potential Assessment
Device, which focuses on children's (20) _____ to learn
rather than what they have already learned. (Can you explain how
administration of Feuerstein's test is different from the Stanford-Binet
or Wechsler?)

Infant intelligence is typically measured with the
(21) _____ Scales of Infant Development. This test includes
a motor scale and a mental scale, which are used to assign a
(22) _____ _____. A third component of the test
is an infant behavioral record. Scores on the Bayley do not accurately
predict later IQ, but they can be used to chart developmental progress
and diagnose (23) _____ problems and mental retardation.
(What reasons are offered in the text for this lack of predictive
ability?) Recent research by Fagan suggests that later IQ may be better
predicted by performance on some measures of infant (24) _____.
(Why might this be a better predictor?)

There is a fairly strong relationship between IQ scores obtained at
different times throughout childhood. However, although group scores
are fairly stable, scores of individual children can fluctuate quite
substantially. (What do these findings suggest?) The
(25) _____-_____ hypothesis suggests that
intellectual development of children from impoverished environments is
diminished and this effect builds over time so that children's
intelligence actually seems to decline. (Is there any research support
for this hypothesis?) IQ scores are often used to predict
(26) _____ _____ and they are fairly accurate in
doing this. Children in school with similar IQs may differ in their
characteristic ways of approaching problems, or their
(27) _____ _____. Children who are
(28) _____ respond to problems quickly, typically giving the
first answer that comes to mind. Children who are (29) _____
respond more slowly to problems after considering several possible
solutions. (What are some advantages and disadvantages of each style?)

The IQ scores of adolescents accurately predict adult IQ scores and
IQ scores of adolescents continue to predict school achievement.
Beginning in adolescence, females perform better than males on tests of
(30) _____ ability while males perform better than females on
tests of (31) _____ reasoning and spatial ability. Waber
proposed that these sex differences relate to the timing of

(32) _____. According to this theory, early maturation cuts short the process of (33) _____ and consequently would effect abilities that require greater specialization. Since females typically mature earlier than males, they develop better verbal abilities, but visual/spatial skills would be less developed. (Does research support this theory of sex differences?)

In adults, there is a relationship between IQ scores and (34) _____ status such that so-called higher status jobs are filled with people who, overall, have higher IQs than people in low-status jobs. However, once people obtain high status jobs, IQ scores are not related to actual job performance. IQ scores are somewhat predictive of job success in (35) _____ status occupations.

Early cross-sectional research on intelligence across the life span indicated that IQ scores steadily decreased from about age 20 on. However, (36) _____ research indicates that IQ does not decline across early and middle adulthood, and only modest declines in IQ occur in old age. One major factor contributing to these different findings is (37) _____ or generational effects. (Can you describe how this factor contributes to different conclusions?) Sequential studies of changes in intelligence show that some gains in intelligence are made throughout middle adulthood, and declines typically occur only late in life. (Do you remember what sequential designs are from chapter 1?) This research also indicates that (38) _____ intelligence declines earlier and more sharply than (39) _____ intelligence.

For individuals who do experience a decline in intellectual performance, poor (40) _____ is often the culprit. People also tend to experience a (41) _____ _____ months or a few years before they die. Another factor contributing to declining intellectual performance is lack of (42) _____ in some older adults' lives.

Differences in IQ scores across the life span are influenced by both hereditary and (43) _____ factors. An instrument for measuring the amount and type of intellectual stimulation in a child's home is the (44) _____ _____. Scores on this inventory predict children's IQ scores fairly well. In particular, (45) _____ involvement with the child, provision of appropriate (46) _____ materials, and opportunities for various types of (47) _____ were strongly related to the child's cognitive functioning. IQ scores are also affected by the child's (48) _____ _____ in the family and the size of the family. (Can you explain why these two factors might effect intellectual performance?) In addition, social class differences affect IQ scores, such that children who come from disadvantaged backgrounds score lower than children from middle-class homes.

A great deal of controversy has surrounded the finding that children of different racial and ethnic backgrounds score lower on IQ tests than white Anglo-American children. There are several possible reasons for this. One is that the tests are (49) _____ because they are more appropriate for children from white, middle-class backgrounds. In an attempt to eliminate or reduce this possibility, (50) _____ _____ IQ tests have been developed. Differences between racial and ethnic groups are still apparent on these tests. Another possibility is that minority children are not as highly (51) _____ in testing situations as white, middle-class children. (Can you explain why?) A third possibility is that there are (52) _____ differences between ethnic and racial groups that contribute to observed differences on IQ tests. There are, in fact, genetic differences (53) _____ groups, but these differences do not translate into differences (54) _____ groups. (Can you explain why within-group differences cannot be used to argue that there are between-group differences?) The finding that IQ scores of black children increase when these children are adopted into white, middle-class homes suggests that group differences result from (55) _____ factors.

Individuals who have high IQ scores or show special abilities are considered (56) _____. Terman's longitudinal of gifted children dispelled a number of myths about gifted individuals. In short, gifted individuals were not the social misfits or weaklings that many people believed them to be. As adults, children from Terman's study were generally healthy, happy, and productive. Terman's subjects, however, were not only gifted, they also came from advantaged family backgrounds. So it is unclear whether intelligence per se contributed to their favorable outcomes. Individuals who show below average intellectual functioning and impairments in (57) _____ behavior are considered (58) _____ _____. (What are the different levels of mental retardation?) Retardation that is due to some identifiable biological cause is termed (59) _____ retardation and usually accounts for the more severe and profound cases of retardation. Retardation that is due to a combination of low genetic potential and poor environment is (60) _____/_____ retardation and usually results in mild retardation. Individuals who are retarded but have some area where they display extraordinary talent are known as (61) _____ _____.

Individuals who can produce novel responses or works are considered to be (62) _____. Creativity involves (63) _____ thinking, or the ability to come up with a variety of ideas or solutions to a problem. IQ tests typically measure (64) _____ thinking, which involves coming up with the one "correct" answer to a problem. Creativity is often measured by the total number of different ideas that one can generate in response to a problem, or (65) _____ _____. Children who are creative tend to show more freedom, originality, humor, violence, and playfulness, and engage in more pretend play than children who are not creative. Scores on tests of creativity are somewhat related to later creative performance, but this relationship is weak. In adulthood, creative output typically increases throughout early adulthood and declines only in older adulthood. This pattern varies, though, depending on the field of work.

REVIEW OF KEY TERMS AND CONCEPTS

Below is a list of terms and concepts from this chapter. Match each one with its appropriate definition. You might also want to try writing definitions in your own words and then checking your definitions with those here in the Study Guide or in the text.

automatization
convergent thinking
creativity
crystallized intelligence
cultural/familial retardation
culture bias
cumulative-deficit hypothesis
developmental quotient (DQ)
divergent thinking
factor analysis
fluid intelligence
giftedness
HOME inventory
ideational fluency

idiot savant
impulsivity
intelligence quotient (IQ)
mental age (MA)
mental retardation
normal distribution
organic retardation
psychometric approach
reflectivity
structure-of-intellect model
terminal drop
test norms
triarchic theory of intelligence

_____1. A bell-shaped distribution with most scores falling close to the average score.

_____2. A cognitive style of responding slowly to problems after considering several possible solutions.

_____3. Intelligence that allows us to use our minds to solve novel problems.

_____4. Retardation that is due to some combination of low genetic potential and a poor environment

_____5. An index of an infant's performance on developmental tasks relative to other infants the same age.

_____6. The rapid decline in intellectual abilities that often occurs within a few years before dying.

_____7. A theoretical perspective that views intelligence as a trait or set of traits on which people differ and these differences can be measured.

_____8. The type of thinking that produces a single answer to question or problem.

_____9.   The ability to use knowledge acquired through specific learning and life experiences.

_____10. The ability to produce novel responses or works.

_____11. The hypothesis that impoverished environments inhibit intellectual growth, and these negative effects accumulate over time.

_____12. On an intelligence test, the level of age-graded problems that a child can solve.

_____13. A cognitive style of responding to problems quickly, giving the first answer that comes to mind.

_____14. Sternberg's information-processing theory of intelligence that emphasizes the context, experience, and information-processing components of intelligent behavior.

_____15. Standards of typical performance on a test as reflected by average scores and the range of scores around the average.

_____16. The type of thinking that produces a variety of solutions to a problem when there is no one right answer.

_____17. The total number of different ideas that one can generate when asked to think of all the possible solutions to a problem or question.

_____18. The increased efficiency of information-processing that comes with familiarity and practice.

_____19. A condition where individuals have high IQ scores or show special abilities in areas valued by society.

_____20. Retardation that is due to some identifiable biological cause associated with hereditary factors, diseases, or injuries.

_____21. A statistical procedure used to identify clusters of tests or test items that are related to one another but are unrelated to other items.

_____22. An index of a person's performance on an intelligence test relative to chronological age.

_____23. The notion that IQ tests favor children from certain cultural backgrounds, namely white middle-class backgrounds.

_____24. Guilford's model of intelligence that consists of as many as 120 different intellectual abilities.

_____25. A person who has an extraordinary talent but who is otherwise mentally retarded.

_____26. A condition where individuals perform significantly below average on intelligence tests and show deficits in adaptive behavior skills during the developmental period.

_____27. An instrument for measuring the amount and type of intellectual stimulation in a child's home environment.

RESEARCH SUMMARY AND REVIEW

For each of the following studies, briefly summarize the main point(s) of the research and indicate why the research is important. Don't worry about specific details that are not central to the main points, or memorizing names of researchers. Questions you might ask yourself include: Does the research support or refute a theory or hypothesis presented in the text? How does it further our understanding of some concept? Does it provide an example of a point being made in the text? Use the text to check your understanding.

1. Scarr and Weinberg's (1977; 1983) research on adopted children (pp 289-290): _____

_____

_____

_____

_____

2. Schaie and colleagues' (1983; 1986) longitudinal research on intellectual abilities (pp 282-283): _____

_____

_____

_____

_____

3.   Terman's (1954) classic study of gifted individuals (p 291): _____

_____

_____

_____

_____

For additional practice, pull out some other research discussed in this
chapter or research discussed in class lectures and summarize the main
points of the studies.

SELF TEST _____

For each multiple choice question, read all alternatives and then select
the best answer.

1.   Which of the following is an example of crystallized intelligence?
     a.   remembering unrelated word pairs (e.g., dog-couch)
     b.   solving verbal analogies
     c.   realizing the relationship between geometric figures
     d.   solving word comprehension problems (e.g, what does
          "participate" mean?)

2.   The _____ emphasizes the importance of context,
     experience and information-processing components in defining
     intelligent behavior.
     a.   triarchic theory of intelligence
     b.   psychometric approach to intelligence
     c.   factor analysis approach
     d.   structure-of-intellect model

3.   _____ refers to an efficiency of information processing
     that appears with practice.
     a.   Experience
     b.   Automatization
     c.   Impulsive cognitive style
     d.   Giftedness

4.   If someone achieves a score of 100 on the Stanford-Binet
     intelligence test, it means that
     a.   This person scored higher than approximately 68% of the
          population.
     b.   This person is somewhat below average in intelligence.
     c.   This person's MA and CA levels were the same.
     d.   This person could answer all the questions appropriate for 10-
          year-olds.

5. On the Wechsler Intelligence Scale for Children, a learning disability would be most clearly indicated by which of the following?
    a. Finding a large discrepancy between verbal IQ and performance IQ
    b. Finding that the verbal IQ and performance IQ scores were within several points of one another
    c. Finding that both the verbal IQ and performance IQ scores were very low
    d. Finding that the test was culturally biased because the child tested was not from a white, middle-class background

6. The Bayley Scale of Infant Development is a useful indicator of
    a. childhood intelligence
    b. whether or not the child is gifted
    c. a child's developmental progress through major milestones
    d. problem solving abilities that the child possesses

7. Feuerstein's Learning Potential Assessment Device measures
    a. what children have learned
    b. infant intelligence
    c. children's abilities to learn by observing an adult solve the task
    d. children's potential to learn new things with minimal guidance

8. Correlations of IQ measured during early and middle childhood with IQ measured during adolescence and young adulthood indicate that for individuals, IQ scores
    a. are quite stable
    b. can fluctuate quite a bit
    c. generally increase with age
    d. generally decrease with age

9. Correlations between scores on infant intelligence tests and scores on later intelligence tests show
    a. that infants who score high typically score high as children and adolescents
    b. that infant intelligence scores can predict later intelligence for those who score around the mean of 100
    c. little relationship between infant intelligence and later intelligence
    d. that infant intelligence scores can predict childhood intelligence but not adult intelligence

10. The cumulative-deficit hypothesis suggests that
    a. lack of intellectual stimulation produces an overall deficit in intelligence that is stable over time
    b. lack of intellectual stimulation depresses intellectual growth more and more over time
    c. lack of intellectual stimulation early in life is less damaging than lack of intellectual stimulation later in life
    d. parents with low IQ scores will have children with low IQ scores

11. The relationship between IQ and occupational status indicates that
    a. IQ scores are more likely to predict job preference than job performance
    b. people with high IQ scores do not work in low status occupations
    c. people with high IQ scores are more likely to work in high status occupations than people with low IQ scores
    d. IQ scores determine job performance for all levels of IQ scores and all occupations

12. A child using a reflective cognitive style would
    a. evaluate several possible hypotheses before answering
    b. always perform better than a child using an impulsive style
    c. respond quickly to a problem, using the first hypothesis that comes to mind
    d. use efficient memory strategies to store information

13. Which of the following best predicts IQ scores in early childhood?
    a. parental involvement with child
    b. scores on the Bayley Scale of Infant Development
    c. whether parent's discipline style includes punishment
    d. the number of siblings that a child has

14. Research on ethnic and racial differences in IQ scores shows that differences
    a. do not really exist
    b. result from genetic differences between racial groups
    c. can be reduced with the appropriate environmental intervention
    d. do exist but cannot be reduced or eliminated

15. Which of the following demonstrates how intellectual abilities change with age?
    a. Overall, intellectual abilities decline significantly with age.
    b. Crystallized intelligence declines with age.
    c. Fluid intelligence declines with age.
    d. No decline in intelligence occurs with age.

16. A variety of factors have been found to influence IQ, including which of the following?
    a. First borns tend to have slightly higher IQ scores than later borns.
    b. The increased stimulation of a large family increases the children's IQ.
    c. Parents who have high IQ scores will have children who have even higher IQ scores.
    d. Ethnicity has little impact on IQ scores.

17. Gifted children tend to
    a. be socially maladjusted
    b. be healthy and happy
    c. be ill-equipped emotionally to handle stress
    d. have considerable difficulty skipping grades

18. Ideational fluency refers to
    a. never answering a problem with a response that has been produced before
    b. the type of thinking that is typically measured on standardized intelligence tests
    c. developing responses that are valued by society
    d. the number of novel responses produced

19. Standardized intelligence tests typically measure
    a. divergent thinking
    b. convergent thinking
    c. creativity
    d. everyday problem-solving skills

20. With respect to creativity in adulthood,
    a. creative endeavors decrease throughout adulthood
    b. creative endeavors increase in young adulthood and then usually peak and remain steady in middle adulthood
    c. creative endeavors are at their peak during college years and early adulthood
    d. creative endeavors decline significantly for older adults in all fields

APPLICATION

This chapter of the text presented several different perspectives about intelligence. What is your own personal theory of intelligence? What traits, abilities, or skills make up intelligence? Do you define intelligence consistently across the life span? For example, are the abilities that make a school-age child intelligent the same abilities that make a forty-year-old intelligent? How does this issue relate to measurement of intelligence and use of intelligence test scores for prediction? Once you have thought about your personal definition of intelligence, consider how you would measure it. What kinds of tasks or problems would tap your idea of intelligence at different periods of the life span?

Before you leave this chapter, go back and take another look at the learning objectives presented at the beginning of the chapter. Rephrase each objective into a question and check to see whether you have mastered them. A good way to check your understanding of a concept is to see if you can teach it to someone else. Take turns doing this with a small group of people. Whenever you are unsure or unclear about a response, go back to the text and find out what information you are missing in order to provide a clear and complete response.

ANSWERS

Summary and Guided Review (Fill-in the blank)

1. psychometric
2. factor analysis
3. general
4. primary
5. structure-of-intellect
6. fluid
7. crystallized
8. triarchic
9. context
10. experience
11. automatization
12. components
13. intelligence quotient
14. mental age
15. Stanford-Binet
16. test norms
17. Wechsler
18. performance
19. normal distribution
20. potential
21. Bayley
22. developmental quotient
23. neurological
24. attention
25. cumulative-deficit
26. academic achievement
27. cognitive style
28. impulsive
29. reflective
30. verbal
31. mathematical
32. puberty
33. lateralization
34. occupational
35. moderate
36. longitudinal
37. cohort
38. fluid
39. crystallized
40. health
41. terminal drop
42. stimulation
43. environmental
44. HOME inventory
45. parental
46. play
47. stimulation
48. birth order
49. biased
50. culture fair
51. motivated
52. genetic
53. within
54. between
55. environmental
56. gifted
57. adaptive
58. mentally retarded
59. organic
60. cultural/familial
61. idiot savants
62. creative
63. divergent
64. convergent
65. ideational fluency

Key Terms

1. normal distribution
2. reflectivity
3. fluid intelligence
4. cultural/familial retardation
5. developmental quotient (DQ)
6. terminal drop
7. psychometric approach
8. convergent thinking
9. crystallized intelligence
10. creativity
11. cumulative-deficit hypothesis
12. mental age (MA)
13. impulsivity
14. triarchic theory of intelligence
15. test norms
16. divergent thinking
17. ideational fluency
18. automatization
19. giftedness
20. organic retardation
21. factor analysis

22.	intelligence quotient (IQ)	25.	idiot savant
23.	culture bias	26.	mental retardation
24.	structure-of-intellect model	27.	HOME inventory

Self Test

1.	D	11.	C
2.	A	12.	A
3.	B	13.	A
4.	C	14.	C
5.	A	15.	C
6.	C	16.	A
7.	D	17.	B
8.	B	18.	D
9.	C	19.	B
10.	B	20.	B

Chapter Ten
Self-Conceptions, Personality,
and Emotional Expression

After reading and studying the material in this chapter, you should be able to do the following:

1. Describe how psychoanalytic theory and social learning theory explain personality development.

2. Define self-concept and self-esteem and trace the emergence of self-concept during infancy, including the development of a categorical self.

3. Explain temperament and the categories of temperamental style identified in infants.

4. Explain how social comparisons figure in a child's developing sense of self.

5. Discuss developments in self-esteem of children.

6. Name and describe Erikson's first four stages of psychosocial development that occur during infancy and childhood.

7. Describe developments in self-concept and self-esteem that occur during adolescence.

8. Discuss Erikson's psychosocial conflict of adolescence.

9. Describe what is known about the four identity statuses.

10. Discuss how social influences affect identity formation.

11. Discuss whether there are enduring personality traits.

12. Discuss whether people change in systematic ways and reasons why people change or remain the same.

13. Describe the development of intimacy in adulthood.

14. Describe the psychosocial stages of middle adulthood and old age.

15. Discuss whether infants display and experience emotional states.

16. Discuss how children learn to use, control, and interpret emotions.

17. Describe ways that self-esteem can be improved throughout the lifespan.

The following summary provides an overview of the main points contained in this chapter of the text. Fill-in the blanks with terms that appropriately complete the sentence. Although blank spaces are provided, you may want to write your answers on a separate piece of paper, which will make it easier to compare your answers to the correct answers provided at the end of this chapter.

Scattered throughout the summary are questions in parentheses. These are meant to encourage you to think actively as you are reading and connect this summary to the more detailed information provided in the text. You can answer these questions as you are filling in the blanks or you can fill-in all the blanks, then go back and reread the entire summary, addressing the questions in order to provide more depth of understanding.

An organized set of attributes, motives, values, and behaviors unique to an individual is considered that person's (1) _____. Personalities are often described in terms of (2) _____ that are thought to be relatively consistent across situations and times. (3) _____ believed that personality was formed in infancy and early childhood and changed very little after this. Erikson believed that personality continued to grow and change across the life span. Social learning theories propose that personality is strongly influenced by (4) _____ factors and can change when these factors change.

(5) _____ refers to one's perceptions of one's self and (6) _____ is one's overall feelings about the characteristics that make up the self. One of the first signs that infants recognize themselves as distinct individuals is when infants recognize themselves in a mirror. Infants begin to form a (7) _____ self and classify themselves along dimensions such as age and gender. The ability to recognize self depends in part on (8) _____ development and also on social experiences. Our understanding of self is often thought to reflect how others people respond to us, a concept known as the (9) _____-_____ self. (Can you describe how other people might affect our self-concepts?)

The tendency to respond in predictable ways to events is referred to as (10) _____. Researchers have classified most infants into one of three categories of temperament. About 40% of the infants studied were classified as (11) _____, meaning that they had regular habits, were typically happy and content, and were adaptable to new experiences. About 10% of the infants were considered (12) _____ because they were active, irritable, did not have regular habits, and responded negatively to new experiences. About 15% of the infants were (13) _____ and were inactive, somewhat moody, and had somewhat regular habits. One aspect of temperament--the tendency to be inhibited or uninhibited--seems to be related to later personality. (Can you describe the relationship between this dimension of temperament and later personality?)

Preschool children's self-concepts tend to be (14) _____ and physical. School-age children are able to use internal traits to describe themselves and begin to compare their abilities to those of companions. This leads to (15) _____ _____ where children use comparisons to evaluate themselves. Self-esteem is also developing during childhood. Research indicates that children have well-defined self-perceptions and these perceptions are (16) _____ with how others view them. Children are also able to distinguish between their competencies in different areas. (What factors contribute to the development of high or low self-esteem?)

A number of important personality dimensions do not stabilize until childhood. Traits that persist seem to be those that are valued by (17) _____, while those that disappear or change may conflict with cultural norms.

According to Erikson's psychosocial stages of development, infants confront the conflict of (18) _____ versus (19) _____. Toddlers must achieve a sense of (20) _____ or risk feelings of shame and doubt. Preschool children and kindergartners struggle with the conflict of (21) _____ versus (22) _____ while school-age children must master (23) _____ or possibly develop feelings of inferiority.

The self-concepts of adolescents become more (24) _____ and they are more self-aware than younger children. Adolescents' descriptions of themselves are also more (25) _____ or coherent than those of younger children. Although adolescents may have somewhat lower self-esteem, their self-esteem when they leave adolescence is about the same as when they entered adolescence. Erikson believed that adolescents are faced with the important psychosocial task of (26) _____ versus (27) _____ _____. Adolescents who have faced a crisis about who they are and what they believe in, and who have made a commitment, have achieved (28) _____ _____ status. Adolescents who have faced a crisis (or are currently facing one) but have not yet made a commitment fall into the (29) _____ status. Adolescents who have not experienced a crisis and have not made commitment are in the (30) _____ status, while adolescents who have not experienced a crisis but have made a commitment fall into the (31) _____ status. Achieving identity is related to (32) _____ experiences. (Can you describe what some of these influences are and how they are related to identity achievement?)

Self-esteem does not vary across adulthood, although adults of different ages are likely to feel good (or bad) about themselves for different reasons. In addressing whether personality is stable across

adulthood, two questions arise. One question is whether an individual's
(33) _____ within a group on some personality trait remains
the same. A second question is whether there is stability in the
(34) _____ level of some personality trait within a group.
Longitudinal research has focused on two major dimensions of
personality. One is (35) _____, or the degree to which one
is active and sociable. The second is (36) _____, or the
degree to which one is emotionally unstable, anxious, depressed, and
easily upset. With respect to the first question above, individual
rankings on these two dimensions of personality are fairly stable across
time. (Can you provide a concrete example of what this means for a
specific individual?) With respect to the second question, cross-
sectional research suggests that older adults have different
personalities than younger adults. However, these results may reflect
(37) _____ or generational effects, suggesting that the
(38) _____ context in which people develop affects their
personality.

Personality does seem to grow from adolescence to middle adulthood,
but there is little systematic change in personality from middle
adulthood to later adulthood. The personalities of some people may
remain stable, while those of other people change across the life span.
Personalities may remain stable because of the influence of
(39) _____ factors or because childhood experiences continue
to impact on personality throughout the life span. It is also possible
that personalities remain stable because environments remain stable.
Changes in the environment might explain why some personalities change,
and maturation and aging might also contribute to change. Some types of
people seem more likely to change than others. (Can you explain what
"types" are more changeable than others?)

According to Erikson, young adults face the psychosocial task of
(40) _____ versus (41) _____. Research supports
Erikson's claim that individuals' must achieve a sense of
(42) _____ before being able to develop true intimacy.
Middle-age adults are concerned with the psychosocial crisis of
(43) _____ versus (44) _____ as they work to
produce something lasting and important for future generations.
Vaillant, another psychoanalytic theorist, believes that there is an
additional stage between Erikson's young and middle-age adult crises
called (45) _____ _____. (Can you describe what
this means?) Finally, older adults face the psychosocial conflict of
(46) _____ versus (47) _____. Elderly adults may
engage in a process of (48) _____ _____ where they
reflect on unresolved issues in order to come to terms with their lives.

Humans are emotional beings from very early in life. Infants show
a wide range of emotional expressions during the first year of life. It
is not clear whether infants' emotional displays mean the same as those
same displays made by adults. Elementary school children learn the
(49) _____ _____ for when and what emotions to
display under various circumstances. The popular notion that elderly

people do not show strong emotional responses or that emotions are somehow not as important to older adults, has not been supported by recent research.

For those children and adults who have low self-esteem, there are a variety of techniques for improving self-esteem. Classrooms are often designed so that children receive feedback about themselves that affects their general sense of self-worth. One suggestion is that children with low self-esteem could benefit from (50) _____ classrooms where different abilities are recognized. Some older adults may have lower self-esteem because of the negative messages about aging that our society often sends. Prejudice against elderly people is called (51) _____ . Those elderly who can ignore negative stereotypes of aging may feel better about themselves than elderly who believe the negative stereotypes about old age.

REVIEW OF KEY TERMS AND CONCEPTS

Below is a list of terms and concepts from this chapter. Match each one with its appropriate definition. You might also want to try writing definitions in your own words and then checking your definitions with those here in the Study Guide or in the text.

ageism
autonomy versus shame and doubt
categorical self
diffusion status
display rules
foreclosure status
generativity versus stagnation
identity
identity achievement status
identity versus role confusion
industry versus inferiority
initiative versus guilt

integrity versus despair
intimacy versus isolation
life review
looking-glass self
moratorium status
personality
self-concept
self-esteem
social comparison
temperament
trust versus mistrust

_____ 1. Noting how one compares to others and using that information to judge one's self.

_____ 2. An identity status where a person has not experienced a crisis and has not achieved a commitment.

_____ 3. A clear sense of who you are, where you are heading, and where you fit into society.

_____ 4. Psychosocial conflict in which a young child tries to accept more grown-up responsibilities that she/he may not be able to handle.

_____5. An identity status where a person has experienced a crisis and has made a commitment to certain goals.

_____6. The psychosocial conflict during elementary school in which children need to acquire important academic and social skills.

_____7. Classification of one's self along dimensions such as age and sex.

_____8. The tendency to respond in predictable ways to events.

_____9. An identity status where a person has not experienced a crisis but has made a commitment.

_____10. One's understanding of oneself, including one's unique attributes or traits.

_____11. The process of reflecting on unresolved conflicts of the past in order to come to terms with one's self and derive new meaning from the past.

_____12. The psychosocial conflict of young adulthood that involves developing strong friendships and intimate relationships.

_____13. The first psychosocial conflict in which infants must develop a basic sense of trust.

_____14. A person's feelings about the characteristics that make up his or her self.

_____15. Psychosocial conflict of adolescence in which children must develop a sense of who they are socially, sexually, and professionally.

_____16. The notion that our understanding of self is a reflection of how other people view us and respond to us.

_____17. The psychosocial conflict of older adulthood that involves assessing one's life and finding it meaningful.

_____18. An identity status where a person is currently experiencing a crisis or actively addressing identity issues and has not yet made a commitment.

_____19. The organized combination of attributes, motives, values, and behaviors that is unique to each individual.

_____20. The psychosocial conflict of middle adulthood that
                involves being productive in one's work and with one's
                family.

_____21. Cultural rules specifying what emotions should or
                should not be expressed and under what circumstances.

_____22. The psychosocial conflict in which toddlers must learn
                some independence.

_____23. Term used to describe prejudice against elderly
                people.

RESEARCH SUMMARY AND REVIEW

For each of the following studies, briefly summarize the <u>main point(s)</u>
of the research and indicate why the research is important. Don't worry
about specific details that are not central to the main points, or
memorizing names of researchers. Questions you might ask yourself
include: Does the research support or refute a theory or hypothesis
presented in the text? How does it further our understanding of some
concept? Does it provide an example of a point being made in the text?
Use the text to check your understanding.

1. Lewis and Brooks-Gunn's (1979) research on recognition of self (p
    307): _____

    _____

    _____

    _____

2. Thomas and Chess and colleagues' (1970, 1977, 1984, 1986) research
    on temperament (p 308, 310): _____

    _____

    _____

    _____

3. Harter's (1982) research on development of self-esteem (p 311):

    _____

    _____

4. Costa and colleagues' (1983; 1984) longitudinal research of
    personality (p 320-321): _____

    _____

    _____

    _____

    _____

5. Saarni's (1984) study on learning to control display of emotions (p
    329): _____

    _____

    _____

    _____

    _____

For additional practice, pull out some other research discussed in this
chapter or research discussed in class lectures and summarize the main
points of the studies.

SELF TEST

For each multiple choice question, read all alternatives and then select
the best answer.

1. According to Erik Erikson, personality
    a. develops in the first five or six years after birth and changes
        little after this
    b. develops and changes throughout the life span
    c. development is complete in adolescence once a sense of identity
        has been achieved
    d. is formed in childhood and only changes later in life under
        extreme environmental conditions

2. Self-esteem refers to a person's
    a. cognitive understanding of self
    b. perception of his or her abilities and traits
    c. overall evaluation of his or her worth as a person
    d. knowledge of who they are

3. Someone who adheres to social learning theory would believe that
   a. personality develops through a series of systematic stages that are similar for all people
   b. personality is shaped by the environment during childhood, but once it is formed, changes very little in response to environmental changes
   c. some aspects of personality are determined only by genetic factors while other are determined only by environmental factors
   d. personality traits are only consistent across the life span if the person's environment remains the same

4. Infants with a spot of rouge on their noses who recognize themselves in a mirror will
   a. reach for the nose of their mirror image
   b. reach for their own nose
   c. look behind the mirror
   d. begin to cry indicating that they are confused

5. An infant who is classified as "slow-to-warm-up"
   a. follows a somewhat regular schedule, is inactive, and somewhat moody
   b. follows a somewhat regular schedule, is active, and tolerates frustrations fairly well
   c. follows a regular schedule, appears content, and is adaptable to new experiences
   d. does not follow a regular schedule, is inactive, and reacts very negatively to new experiences

6. Research on inhibited and uninhibited children finds that
   a. whether one is uninhibited or inhibited as a toddler determines whether one will be sociable or not as an adult
   b. inhibited toddlers are more likely to turn out to be shy children than uninhibited toddlers
   c. inhibited toddlers were securely attached as infants
   d. uninhibited children typically have parents who use a permissive style of parenting

7. A child who can compare her abilities to those of her companions is likely to be in Piaget's _____ stage of cognitive development.
   a. sensorimotor
   b. preoperational
   c. concrete operational
   d. formal operational

8. According to Erikson, toddlers (2 years) should be developing a sense of
   a. trust
   b. independence
   c. initiative
   d. industry

9. When Harter's self-perception scale was administered to children in third through ninth grades, it was found that
    a. only the oldest children had well-defined self-concepts
    b. children typically did not distinguish between their competencies in different areas
    c. children showed a "halo effect" by evaluating themselves high in all areas
    d. children's ratings of themselves were consistent with how other rated them

10. Preschool-age children (4-5 years) struggle with the psychosocial conflict of
    a. autonomy versus shame and doubt
    b. initiative versus guilt
    c. industry versus guilt
    d. identity versus role confusion

11. According to Erikson, a third grader who has problems with reading and math may develop a sense of
    a. doubt
    b. guilt
    c. inferiority
    d. role confusion

12. Adolescents who have experienced a crisis involving identity but have not resolved the crisis or made a commitment are classified in Marcia's _____ status.
    a. diffusion
    b. moratorium
    c. foreclosure
    d. identity achievement

13. An adolescent who says "My parents taught me that abortion is wrong and so I just would not consider having an abortion or voting for someone who supports abortion." This statement reflects which identity status?
    a. diffusion
    b. moratorium
    c. foreclosure
    d. identity achievement

14. Longitudinal research on personality traits of extraversion and neuroticism suggests that
    a. these traits are relatively consistent over time in adults
    b. these traits change considerably over time in adults
    c. these two traits are positively correlated with one another
    d. these traits can not be reliably measured in adults

15. Findings from cross-sectional research that different age groups of adults differ in personality may reflect
    a. the fact that personality is affected by the historical context in which it develops
    b. changes in the way personality has been measured over the years
    c. the fact that personality begins to disintegrate as we age
    d. the fact that people grow more similar as they get older

16. Elderly adults face Erikson's psychosocial conflict of
    a. integrity versus stagnation
    b. generativity versus stagnation
    c. intimacy versus despair
    d. integrity versus despair

17. Compared to adults who do not achieve a firm sense of identity, those adults who do achieve a sense of identity are
    a. equally likely to form genuine intimacy with another person
    b. more likely to form genuine intimacy with another person
    c. are less likely to form intimate relationships because they feel very good about themselves as individuals
    d. more likely to form many pseudointimate relationships but no intimate relationships

18. Emotional expressions in infants
    a. begin to emerge at the end of the first year
    b. depend on the infant's cognitive awareness of the situation
    c. are initially programmed by biology, but are then shaped by sociocultural factors
    d. reflect the same inner emotional states as they do in adults

19. Display rules for emotion refer to
    a. the rules for how to display specific emotions through facial expressions
    b. the use of another person's emotional response to evaluate an ambiguous situation
    c. the relationships between internal emotional state and external emotional response
    d. cultural definitions of what emotions should be displayed under what circumstances

20. Research suggests that children who grow up in homes where there is little overt emotional expression
    a. have serious emotional problems as adults
    b. compensate by being highly expressive with their friends
    c. are particularly good at interpreting emotional displays by others
    d. were very verbal about their emotions even though they did not physically express their emotions

Consider your own identity development. Can you identify a crisis (or crises) that has made you confront or question who you are and what you believe? Have you made a commitment to certain personal, occupational, religious, and political choices? Has the commitment been made after seriously exploring various options? In what ways have you demonstrated a commitment? Which of Marcia's identity statuses seems to best characterize your identity formation at this point?

Before you leave this chapter, go back and take another look at the learning objectives presented at the beginning of the chapter. Rephrase each objective into a question and check to see whether you have mastered them. A good way to check your understanding of a concept is to see if you can teach it to someone else. Take turns doing this with a small group of people. Whenever you are unsure or unclear about a response, go back to the text and find out what information you are missing in order to provide a clear and complete response.

ANSWERS

Summary and Guided Review (Fill-in the blank)

1. personality
2. traits
3. Freud
4. environmental
5. self-concept
6. self-esteem
7. categorical
8. cognitive
9. looking-glass
10. temperament
11. easy
12. difficult
13. slow-to-warm-up
14. concrete
15. social comparison
16. consistent
17. society
18. trust
19. mistrust
20. autonomy
21. initiative
22. guilt
23. industry
24. abstract
25. integrated
26. identity
27. role confusion
28. identity achievement
29. moratorium
30. diffusion
31. foreclosure
32. social
33. ranking
34. average
35. extraversion
36. neuroticism
37. cohort
38. historical
39. hereditary
40. intimacy
41. isolation
42. identity
43. generativity
44. stagnation
45. career consolidation
46. integrity
47. despair
48. life review
49. display rules
50. multidimensional
51. ageism

Key Terms

1. social comparison
2. diffusion status
3. identity
4. initiative versus guilt
5. identity achievement status
6. industry versus inferiority
7. categorical self
8. temperament
9. foreclosure status
10. self-concept
11. life review
12. intimacy versus isolation
13. trust versus mistrust
14. self-esteem
15. identity versus role confusion
16. looking-glass self
17. integrity versus despair
18. moratorium status
19. personality
20. generativity versus stagnation
21. display rules
22. autonomy versus shame and doubt
23. ageism

Self Test

1.	B	11.	C
2.	C	12.	B
3.	D	13.	C
4.	B	14.	A
5.	A	15.	A
6.	B	16.	D
7.	C	17.	B
8.	B	18.	C
9.	D	19.	D
10.	B	20.	C

Chapter Eleven
Gender Roles and Sexuality

After reading and studying the material in this chapter, you should be able to do the following:

1. Explain the terms gender roles, gender-role norms, gender-role stereotypes, gender typing, and gender identity.

2. Differentiate between the expressive role and instrumental role.

3. Describe four actual psychological differences between the sexes.

4. Describe gender-role development in preschool-age children, including acquisition of gender identity, gender stereotypes, and gender-typed behavior.

5. Discuss Money and Ehrhardt's biosocial theory of gender-role development, including how biological and social factors interact to influence gender-roles.

6. Describe Freud's psychoanalytic theory of gender-role development and indicate whether the theory is supported by evidence.

7. Discuss the social learning theory of gender-role development, including what support exists for this theory.

8. Discuss the cognitive-developmental theory of gender-role development, including the role of acquiring gender identity, gender stability, and gender consistency.

9. Describe Martin and Halverson's schematic-processing model of gender-role development.

10. Discuss how all the theories of gender-role development can be integrated to provide the most accurate picture of development.

11. Describe what children know about sex and reproduction and how sexual behavior changes during childhood.

12. Describe adolescents' understanding of gender roles and their sexuality, including sexual attitudes.

13. Discuss the differences in how males and females resolve identity and intimacy issues.

14. Define androgyny and parental imperative, and discuss how the parental imperative affects masculinity, femininity, and androgyny.

15. Describe changes in sexual activity during adulthood.

SUMMARY AND GUIDED REVIEW

The following summary provides an overview of the main points
contained in this chapter of the text. Fill-in the blanks with terms
that appropriately complete the sentence. Although blank spaces are
provided, you may want to write your answers on a separate piece of
paper, which will make it easier to compare your answers to the correct
answers provided at the end of this chapter.

Scattered throughout the summary are questions in parentheses.
These are meant to encourage you to think actively as you are reading
and connect this summary to the more detailed information provided in
the text. You can answer these questions as you are filling in the
blanks or you can fill-in all the blanks, then go back and reread the
entire summary, addressing the questions in order to provide more depth
of understanding.

Males and females differ in a number of ways. They differ
biologically because they have different (1) _____, which
trigger release of different levels of (2) _____. Males and
females also differ because societies expect them to adopt different
patterns of behavior or (3) _____ _____ specifying
how they should act. (4) _____-_____ _____ are
expectations that society holds for what males and females should be
like and these create (5) _____-_____ _____, or
generalizations about what males and females are like. Children learn
their biological sex and acquire the behaviors and values that society
considers appropriate for members of that sex through a process of
(6) _____ _____. Girls in our society have
traditionally been encouraged to adopt an (7) _____
role that involves being nurturant, kind, cooperative, and sensitive to
other's needs. Boys have been encouraged to adopt an
(8) _____ role that involves being dominant, independent,
assertive, and competitive.

Research with males and females consistently shows four
psychological differences. Females have greater (9) _____
_____ ability than males. Beginning in adolescence, males
outperform females on tests of (10) _____/_____
ability and (11) _____ reasoning. As early as two years of
age, males tend to be more (12) _____ than females. (What
are some stereotypes of males and females that are unfounded?) Findings
of psychological sex differences are based on (13) _____ for
males and females and do not apply to all individuals.

Our society begins to treat males and females differently at
(14) _____. By age 2 1/2 to 3, children show that they have
acquired (15) _____ _____ because they know
whether they are male or female. Even before this time, children are

beginning to act in ways that society finds gender appropriate.

According to Freud, infants are in the (16) _____ of psychosexual development. The genitals of infants are sensitive to stimulation and both male and female infants have been observed to engage in masturbation-like activities, although these are not (17) _____ in the sense that they are for adults.

At about the same time that young children acquire gender identity, they begin to learn (18) _____ _____ or society's ideas about what males and females are like. Children around 6 or 7 years believe that these stereotypes are absolute while older children are more flexible in their thinking about gender-role stereotypes. (Why is there this developmental difference in thinking about gender-role stereotypes?) Children begin to acquire (19) _____-_____ behaviors. They prefer toys that society deems gender-appropriate and they develop a preference for same-sex playmates. (20) _____ are under more pressure than (21) _____ to behave in gender-appropriate ways. (Can you explain why this is true?)

There are several theories that try to explain the development of gender roles. Money and Ehrhardt proposed a (22) _____ theory that focuses on the interaction of (23) _____ and (24) _____ influences. According to this theory, several critical events contribute to gender-role development. One is receiving an X or Y chromosome, which triggers a second event, the release of (25) _____, which stimulates the development of a male internal reproductive system. A third event occurs at 3 to 4 months after conception when testosterone triggers development of male external genitals or, in its absence, development of female external genitalia. Testosterone also affects development of the (26) _____ and (27) _____ system. Hormones released during (28) _____ will stimulate the growth of the reproductive system and secondary sex characteristics. These biological events trigger a number of (29) _____ events that will further differentiate males and females.

Biological theories such as this help explain why (30) _____ are more vulnerable to X-linked recessive disorders. Children who are chromosomally XX but who were exposed to male hormones prenatally are called (31) _____ _____. (How are these girls behaviorally different from other girls?) The level of male hormones may also relate to (32) _____ in animals and humans. Social factors also have an impact on gender development. Evidence suggests that there may be a (33) _____ or sensitive period between 18 months and 3 years of age when gender identity is established. (Can you explain the evidence that suggests this?)

According to Freud's psychoanalytic theory, both biology and environment contribute to gender-role development. Preschool-age children are in the (34) _____ stage of psychosexual

145

development. They experience love for their parent of the other sex and as a result of this, jealousy and conflict. The conflict is resolved through (35) _____ with the same-sex parent. (What is the psychoanalytic rationale for why boys seem to learn gender stereotypes and gender-typed behaviors faster than girls?)

Social learning theorists believe that gender-role development occurs through (36) _____ _____ where children are reinforced for sex-appropriate behaviors and punished for behaviors considered appropriate for members of the other sex. According to this view, sex-role development also occurs through (37) _____ _____ where children adopt attitudes and behaviors of same-sex models. (Which parent is more likely to reward children for same-gender behavior?)

Cognitive-developmental theory argues that gender-role development depends on level of cognitive development. Children must first acquire (38) _____ _____ or the recognition of being male of female. They must also understand that gender identity is (39) _____ across time and (40) _____ across situations. (What level of cognitive development is needed for understanding of gender stability and gender consistency?) According to this view, once children understand that biological sex is unchanging, they begin to develop behaviors and attitudes of same-sex models. (What is one problem with this view of gender-role development?) An information processing model (Martin and Halverson) suggests that children acquire (41) _____ _____, which are organized expectations and beliefs about males and females and these beliefs influence the things that children pay attention to and remember. (How can all these perspectives be integrated to provide the most comprehensive explanation of gender-role development?)

Children's understanding of reproduction has been related to their level of (42) _____ development. They often interpret information about sex and reproduction in terms of what they already know (assimilation). Children between 9 and 11 years begin to understand that sexual (43) _____ plays a role in reproduction but still may not comprehend that it is the union of a sperm and an egg that creates a life.

Contrary to what Freud believed, sexual interest and experimentation (44) _____ during childhood. Freud argued that school-aged children were in a (45) _____ _____ in which sexuality was repressed. Children's sexual behaviors are influenced by parental and societal (46) _____. In (47) _____ societies, children are typically not allowed to express any sexuality. In (48) _____ societies, there are rules prohibiting sexual behaviors by children but children often violate the rules without punishment. In (49) _____ societies, children are free to express their sexuality and in fact, may be encouraged to explore their sexuality. (Where does the U.S. fit in this classification?)

Adolescents tend to adhere more strictly to (50) _____
_____ than do younger children. (Why is this the case?)
Sexual morality of adolescents has changed during this century and
includes: 1) Sex with (51) _____ is acceptable. 2) The
(52) _____ _____ is declining but has not
disappeared. 3) There is increased confusion about (53) _____
_____ since individuals must now decide for themselves what
is right or wrong, rather than adhering to general rules. Sexual
behaviors have also changed during the last century. Adolescents engage
in sexual behaviors at earlier ages and more adolescents are having
sexual intercourse. Since many sexually active adolescents fail to use
(54) _____ _____, one out of ten teenage girls
gives birth before the age of 18.

According to Erikson's theory, adolescents are working on
establishing an (55) _____ and young adults are working on
establishing (56) _____. Males and females seem to differ in
how they address these issues. Males have traditionally focused more on
(57) _____ goals while females have focused on
(58) _____ aspects of identity. Males are also more likely
than females to achieve (59) _____ before (60) _____.
With respect to resolving intimacy and identity issues, females have
several options. (Can you describe what these options are?)

In adulthood, male and female roles are often similar until
marriage and parenthood begin to differentiate the roles. Sandra Bem
argues that masculinity and femininity are two separate psychological
dimensions. Someone who is (61) _____ has masculine-
stereotyped traits as well as feminine-stereotyped traits. Gutmann
refers to demands placed on a person by parenthood as the
(62) _____ _____. The demands often mean that
men emphasize their masculine qualities and women emphasize their
feminine qualities. Gutmann proposes that when no longer constrained by
the parental imperative, psychologically masculine men adopt more
(63) _____ qualities and psychologically feminine women
adopt more (64) _____ qualities. Gutmann's hypothesis is
partially supported. Parenthood does tend to make people more
traditionally sex-typed, but they tend to become (65) _____
in the postparental phases of life, rather than replacing sex-typed
traits with other-sex traits.

Androgynous people tend to be more flexible in their
(66) _____ than traditionally sex-typed persons. The
(67) _____ traits that a person has rather than androgyny in
general, are associated with high self-esteem and good adjustment. And
while androgynous parents seem to raise children who are androgynous,
some evidence suggests that these children are less competent and less
socially responsive and assertive than children of traditionally sex-
typed parents.

Young adults incorporate their (68) _____ into their

identities. Sexual preference of most adults is (69) _____.
In married couples, sexual activity declines over the course of their
marriage and problems with the marriage can lead to (70) _____
sexual activity. Even though frequency of sexual activity declines as
people get older, people continue to be sexual beings. In part, this
decline results from (71) _____ changes in men and women as
they get older. Sexual capacity can also be affected by diseases and
use of prescribed drugs, which both increase as a person gets older.
Societal (72) _____ and lack of a (73) _____ also
contribute to the decline of sexual activity of older adults.

Changing gender-role attitudes and behaviors is possible but not
easy. Young children are more receptive to changes than older children
but do not always retain changes brought about by short term training.

REVIEW OF KEY TERMS AND CONCEPTS

Below is a list of terms and concepts from this chapter. Match each one
with its appropriate definition. You might also want to try writing
definitions in your own words and then checking your definitions with
those here in the Study Guide or in the text.

androgenized females   gender-role stereotypes
androgyny   gender schemas
double standard   gender stability
expressive role   gender typing
gender consistency   identification
gender identity   instrumental role
gender-role norms   parental imperative
gender roles

_____1. The understanding that gender identity is stable over
                   time.

_____2. Behavior patterns and traits that define how to act as
                   female or male in a particular society.

_____3. Belief that sexual behaviors that are acceptable for
                   males are not acceptable for females.

_____4. Organized sets of beliefs and expectations about males
                   and females that influence the type of information
                   that is attended to and remembered.

_____5. Generalizations about what males and females are like.

_____6. The understanding that gender is constant despite
                   changes in appearance or activities.

_____7. Process by which children learn their biological sex
               and acquire the motives, values, and behaviors
               considered appropriate for members of that sex.

_____8. A gender-role norm that encourages boys to be
               dominant, independent, assertive, and competitive.

_____9. Societal standards about what males and females should
               be like.

_____10. Requirements or demands imposed on a person by
               parenthood.

_____11. An awareness of one's self as male or female.

_____12. The possession of both masculine-stereotyped traits
               and feminine-stereotyped traits.

_____13. A gender-role norm that encourages girls to be kind,
               nurturant, cooperative and sensitive to the needs of
               others.

_____14. Females who were exposed prenatally to male hormones
               and have external genitals that appear masculine.

_____15. The process of internalizing the attitudes and
               behaviors of the same-sex parent.

RESEARCH SUMMARY AND REVIEW

For each of the following studies, briefly summarize the <u>main point(s)</u>
of the research and indicate why the research is important. Don't worry
about specific details that are not central to the main points, or
memorizing names of researchers. Questions you might ask yourself
include: Does the research support or refute a theory or hypothesis
presented in the text? How does it further our understanding of some
concept? Does it provide an example of a point being made in the text?
Use the text to check your understanding.

1. Kuhn, Nash, and Brucken's (1978) research on gender stereotypes
    (page 341): _____

_____

_____

_____

_____

2. Damon's (1977) research on gender-role expectations (page 342):

_____

_____

_____

_____

3. Guttentag and Bray's (1976) research on changing gender-role
    behaviors (page 365): _____

_____

_____

_____

_____

For additional practice, pull out some other research discussed in this
chapter or research discussed in class lectures and summarize the main
points of the studies.

SELF TEST
_____

For each multiple choice question, read all alternatives and then select
the best answer.

1. The process by which children learn their biological sex and acquire
    the motives, values, and behaviors considered appropriate for the
    members of that sex is called
    a. gender typing
    b. gender-role norms
    c. gender differences
    d. gender consistency

2. Females in our society have historically been encouraged to assume
    a(n)
    a. gender role
    b. instrumental role
    c. expressive role
    d. androgynous role

3. Which one the following is <u>true</u> regarding psychological differences between males and females?
   a. Males and females do not actually differ on any psychological traits or abilities.
   b. Wherever there is a difference between males and females, males outperform females.
   c. There are no differences between males and females throughout childhood, but beginning in adolescence, males outperform females in most areas.
   d. Females typically outperform males on verbal tasks and males typically outperform females on tests of mathematical reasoning.

4. Most children can correctly label themselves as males or females by age _____ and begin to understand that one's sex does not change around age _____.
   a. 5 years; 11 years
   b. 3 years; 6 years
   c. 18 months; 3 years
   d. 2 years; 3 years

5. Money and Ehrhardt's biosocial theory of gender-role development suggests that
   a. there are real biological differences between boys and girls and these differences influence how people react to the children
   b. biological differences between males and females cause them to behave differently and to have different levels of expertise in areas such as math and verbal skills
   c. biological differences males and females may exist, but these differences have no impact on psychological differences between males and females
   d. biological factors affect males' behavior but not females' behavior

6. A woman who receives male hormones while she is pregnant may deliver a child who is
   a. genetically XY and has external genitals that appear feminine
   b. genetically XX and has external genitals that appear masculine
   c. genetically XX and becomes very masculine appearing following puberty
   d. mentally retarded

7. According to Freud's psychoanalytic explanation, boys resolve their Oedipus complexes and girls resolve their Electra complexes
   a. when they move into the phallic stage of development
   b. out of love for their parents
   c. by identifying with the parent of the other sex
   d. by identifying with the same-sex parent

8. Social learning theorists explain sex-typing as the result of
    a. the child's understanding of gender identity and gender
        constancy
    b. the child's desire to be like his or her parents
    c. the parents' differentially reinforcing behaviors and the
        child's observation of same-sex models
    d. chromosomal and hormonal differences between males and females

9. According to cognitive-developmental theorists, gender-role
    development
    a. begins with children's understanding that they are girls or boys
    b. begins with children imitating same-sex models
    c. begins when parents differentially reinforce boys and girls
    d. depends on observational learning

10. When children realize that their gender is stable over time, they
    have achieved _____, and when they realize that their gender is
    stable over situations, they have achieved _____.
    a. gender stability; gender identity
    b. gender identity; gender consistency
    c. gender consistency; gender stability
    d. gender stability; gender consistency

11. Gender schemas
    a. determine a child's behavior in ambiguous situations
    b. influence the kinds of information that children attend to
    c. refer to the child's understanding that their gender is stable
        over time
    d. reflect the fact that children have difficulty understanding
        their appropriate gender roles

12. Which of the following accurately characterizes developmental
    changes in thinking about gender roles?
    a. Preschoolers are the most rigid in their thinking about gender
        roles.
    b. The period of young adulthood is when people hold the most
        rigid beliefs about gender roles.
    c. Children in early elementary school and adolescence hold the
        most rigid beliefs about gender roles.
    d. Children in middle childhood hold the most rigid beliefs about
        gender roles.

13. Which of the following is _true_ regarding changes in sexual
    attitudes?
    a. Regardless of how they may act, most adolescents believe that
        premarital sex is wrong.
    b. Most adolescents are quite knowledgeable about sex and clearly
        understand today's sexual norms.
    c. The "double standard" for male and female sexual behavior no
        longer exists.
    d. Most adolescents believe that sex with affection is OK.

14. In Sandra Bem's model, an androgynous individual is a person who is
    a. high in both masculine and feminine traits
    b. high in masculine traits and low in feminine traits
    c. low in masculine traits and high in feminine traits
    d. low in both masculine and feminine traits

15. With respect to androgyny, research indicates that
    a. androgynous people are less flexible in their behavior than sex-typed people
    b. children of androgynous parents are more socially responsible and assertive than children of sex-typed people
    c. the possession of masculine traits leads to higher self-esteem and good adjustment
    d. the possession of feminine traits by men leads to better adjustment

APPLICATION

Consider the ramifications if governmental and political positions were held primarily by women rather than primarily by men, as they are now. How would our society change? What things would be different and what things would remain the same?

Before you leave this chapter, go back and take another look at the learning objectives presented at the beginning of the chapter. Rephrase each objective into a question and check to see whether you have mastered them. A good way to check your understanding of a concept is to see if you can teach it to someone else. Take turns doing this with a small group of people. Whenever you are unsure or unclear about a response, go back to the text and find out what information you are missing in order to provide a clear and complete response.

ANSWERS

Summary and Guided Review (Fill-in the blank)

1.	chromosomes	13.	averages
2.	hormones	14.	birth
3.	gender roles	15.	gender identity
4.	gender-role norms	16.	oral
5.	gender-role stereotypes	17.	sexual
6.	gender typing	18.	gender stereotypes
7.	expressive	19.	gender-typed
8.	instrumental	20.	boys
9.	verbal	21.	girls
10.	visual/spatial	22.	biosocial
11.	mathematical	23.	biological
12.	aggressive	24.	social

25. testosterone
26. brain
27. nervous
28. puberty
29. social
30. males
31. androgenized females
32. aggression
33. critical
34. phallic
35. identification
36. differential reinforcement
37. observational learning
38. gender identity
39. stable
40. consistent
41. gender schemas
42. cognitive
43. intercourse
44. increase
45. latency period
46. attitudes
47. restrictive
48. semirestrictive
49. permissive

50. gender roles
51. affection
52. double standard
53. sexual norms
54. birth control
55. identity
56. intimacy
57. vocational
58. interpersonal
59. identity
60. intimacy
61. androgynous
62. parental imperative
63. feminine
64. masculine
65. androgynous
66. behavior
67. masculine
68. sexuality
69. heterosexual
70. extramarital
71. physiological
72. attitudes
73. partner

Key Terms

1. gender stability
2. gender roles
3. double standard
4. gender schemas
5. gender-role stereotypes
6. gender consistency
7. gender typing
8. instrumental role

9. gender-role norms
10. parental imperative
11. gender identity
12. androgyny
13. expressive role
14. androgenized females
15. identification

Self Test

1.	A	9.	A
2.	C	10.	D
3.	D	11.	B
4.	B	12.	C
5.	A	13.	D
6.	B	14.	A
7.	D	15.	C
8.	C		

Chapter Twelve
Choices: Motives and Morals

LEARNING OBJECTIVES

After reading and studying the material in this chapter, you should be able to do the following:

1. Distinguish between physiological and psychological motives, and give an example of each.

2. Define morality and the three basic components of morality.

3. Compare and contrast Piaget's two stages of moral reasoning.

4. Describe Kohlberg's levels and stages of moral reasoning.

5. Discuss how social learning theorists explain moral behavior.

6. Discuss the strengths and weaknesses of each of the theories.

7. Describe factors that influence motivation of infants.

8. Discuss whether infants are amoral.

9. Discuss achievement motivation during childhood, including factors that influence achievement motivation such as attributions.

10. Explain the development of moral reasoning during childhood.

11. Describe how children learn to resist temptation and what factors influence resistance.

12. Discuss parenting characteristics that contribute to the development of morality.

13. Describe changes in achievement motivation and morality that occur during adolescence.

14. Describe motivations of adults.

15. Discuss factors that promote moral growth.

16. Evaluate Kohlberg's theory or moral reasoning, addressing whether research supports the theory, and the claims that the theory might be biased or incomplete.

17. Discuss how religion relates to, and affects, morality.

18. Discuss ways to stimulate moral development.

   The following summary provides an overview of the main points contained in this chapter of the text. Fill-in the blanks with terms that appropriately complete the sentence. Although blank spaces are provided, you may want to write your answers on a separate piece of paper, which will make it easier to compare your answers to the correct answers provided at the end of this chapter.

   Scattered throughout the summary are questions in parentheses. These are meant to encourage you to think actively as you are reading and connect this summary to the more detailed information provided in the text. You can answer these questions as you are filling in the blanks or you can fill-in all the blanks, then go back and reread the entire summary, addressing the questions in order to provide more depth of understanding.

   A (1) _____ is a condition or state that directs a person's behavior toward a goal. (2) _____ motives include things like hunger, thirst, and sex, and (3) _____ motives include the needs for mastery, achievement, and affiliation.

   A set of principles that allow a person to distinguish right from wrong is termed (4) _____. Morality includes an emotional, or (5) _____, component, a behavioral component, and a (6) _____ component that focuses on how a person reasons and makes decisions about moral dilemmas.

   Freud's psychoanalytic theory focused on moral (7) _____. A child who has done something wrong typically feels some negative emotion such as guilt or shame. Freud believed that morality was not present until the (8) _____ developed during the phallic stage of psychosexual development. At this time, children (9) _____ the moral standards of the same-sex parent.

   Cognitive developmental theorists such as Piaget and Kohlberg focused on moral (10) _____. Piaget proposed that preschool children are in a (11) _____ period where they show little concern or awareness of rules. Elementary school children are usually in the stage of (12) _____ morality where they believe that rules are moral (13) _____ and consequences are more important than intentions. They also believe in (14) _____ _____, which is the idea that rule violations will always be punished. Older children and adolescents move into the stage of (15) _____ morality where they view rules as agreements between individuals and believe that intentions are more important than consequences.

   Following in Piaget's footsteps, Kohlberg developed a theory of moral reasoning that consists of three levels, each with two stages. The (16) _____ level consists of stage 1, the

156

(17) _____-and-obedience orientation, where the emphasis is on the (18) _____ of an act, and stage 2, (19) _____ _____, where an act is judged by whether it satisfies personal needs or results in personal gain. The (20) _____ level consists of stage 3, the "good boy" or "good girl" morality, where actions are right if they please others or are approved by others, and stage 4, the authority and social-order-maintaining morality with its focus on conforming to laws and rules. The last level of moral reasoning is (21) _____ morality, which includes stages 5 and 6. Stage five is the morality of contract, individual rights, and democratically accepted law, and stage six is the morality of individual principles of conscience. (Can you provide responses that portray these six different stages?)

Social learning theorists focus more on moral (22) _____. A major difference between social learning theory and the other theories of moral development is that social learning theories view morality as (23) _____-_____ behavior rather than a general trait.

Infants are thought to have (24) _____ motivation, or the desire to successfully interact with one's environment. Through interactions with the environment, infants form perceptions about their (25) _____ and perceptions about their ability to control the environment. Effectance, or (26) _____, motivation is influenced by the presence of appropriate stimulation, an environment that is (27) _____, and a secure relationship with a caregiver. (Can you describe how these factors influence mastery motivation?) Another motive that is present during infancy is the (28) _____ motive, which is the desire to interact with other people.

Infants in our society are often viewed as lacking any sense of morality, or as being (29) _____. Although infants are not held morally responsible for their actions, they are learning lessons about what is right and wrong. Infants display some rudimentary signs of (30) _____ or understanding another person's feelings. They are not yet capable of sharing or helping another person or otherwise displaying (31) _____.

The need for (32) _____ is a motive to compete and succeed whenever one's behavior is being evaluated against a standard. Children tend to strive for achievement because they have an (33) _____ orientation and want to earn external incentives, or because they have an (34) _____ orientation and have their own personal needs for competence. Children who are high in need achievement tend to earn better grades than children who are low. In addition, the value of success and the expectations of success impact on performance.

Locus of (35) _____ is the extent to which people view themselves personally responsible for what happens to them. Individuals

157

with an (36) _____ locus of control assume that they are personally responsible for what happens to them, while individuals with an (37) _____ locus of control attribute outcomes to external causes. Children with internal locus of control tend to earn higher grades than children with external locus of control. Another factor that affects attributions is (38) _____, or the degree to which a cause is changeable. For example, effort would be an unstable cause because this can change depending the amount of effort one expends on a task. (Can you provide examples of responses that reflect stable and unstable, internal and external causes?) High achievers tend to attribute their successes to (39) _____ and stable factors and their failures to (40) _____ factors or lack or effort. Low achievers often attribute their failures to internal and stable causes, which may cause them to develop (41) _____ _____ or the belief that one cannot control the consequences of certain situations and so fail to act in these situations. (Is it possible to reduce or eliminate this attribution style?)

Children typically reason at the (42) _____ level when tested with Kohlberg's moral dilemmas. Research on Piaget's theory of moral reasoning indicates that he underestimated young children. When Piaget's moral reasoning tasks are simplified, even young children can consider (43) _____ when making moral judgments. Turiel claims that children in Piaget's heteronomous stage encounter two kinds of rules. (44) _____ rules focus on basic rights and privileges of individuals and (45) _____-_____ rules focus on what social consensus deems right or wrong. Even young children understand the difference between these two types of rules and understand that violating (46) _____ rules is the more serious transgression. Research with children on resistance to temptation indicates that moral behavior is not consistent across (47) _____. (How have researchers studied resistance to temptation?)

Moral development has been related to parental discipline styles. Disciplining by withholding attention, love, or approval is termed (48) _____ _____. (49) _____ _____ is the use of physical power to gain compliance to rules. (50) _____ involves explaining to a child why a behavior is wrong and pointing out how it affects other people. The use of (51) _____ is associated with higher levels of moral maturity than use of the other two discipline styles. (Can you explain why this is true?)

During adolescence, students seem to operate more on the basis of (52) _____ rewards such as grades rather than internal satisfaction. Their expectations for success also decline, possibly because adolescents have the (53) _____ capabilities to realize when they are or are not succeeding at a task. Most adolescents reason at the (54) _____ level of Kohlberg's model; few advance to reason at the (55) _____ level.

Achievement motivation of adult men shows no consistent pattern across the adult years but overall, seems fairly consistent for young, middle-age, and older men. Achievement motivation of women declines, at least as it pertains to (56) _____-_____ motivation. In general, the need to affiliate with others remains stable across the adult years for men but declines with age for women. Changes in motives during adulthood are influenced more by life situations or (57) _____ _____ than by age. Some adults move into Kohlberg's (58) _____ level of moral reasoning and moral reasoning does not deteriorate in old age.

Cognitive developmental theorists claim that cognitive growth and relevant social experiences contribute to moral development. Research suggests that general cognitive abilities and (59) _____-_____ abilities are necessary but not sufficient for moral development. (Can you specify how different levels of cognitive reasoning are related to different levels of moral reasoning?) Kohlberg believed that one important social experience was interacting with others, particularly peers, in order to be exposed to different levels of moral reasoning, which could create cognitive (60) _____. This was thought to be necessary in order to advance to higher levels of reasoning. (What are some other important social experiences that affect moral development?)

Kohlberg has been criticized for several reasons. One important criticism is that his theory is biased against women. In some studies, women reason at stage (61) _____ while men reason at stage (62) _____. Carol Gilligan argues that women reason using a morality of (63) _____ and men reason using a morality of (64) _____. (Can you explain what these perspectives mean?) Gilligan claims that neither focus is "right;" they are simply different ways to reason and reflect differences in how boys and girls are traditionally raised in our society. (What are the other criticisms of Kohlberg's theory?)

Many adults (and children) are involved in religion. There is a relationship between being highly religious and sense of well-being. The term (65) _____ is used to describe the ways in which we find meaning in our lives and includes religious beliefs. Fowler proposed six stages of faith that are similar to Kohlberg's six stages of moral reasoning. The stages of faith are related to one's level of cognitive development and are influenced by social experiences. Some adults achieve the stage of (66) _____-_____ faith where they develop their own unique philosophies after serious reflection.

There are several ways to stimulate moral development. One way is participation in group discussions where one is exposed to different levels of moral thought. Ideally, these discussions should expose one to reasoning that is just slightly more mature than one's own level. In addition to merely being exposed to higher levels of moral reasoning, one needs to actively interpret and analyze the comments made by others

in the group. Kohlberg suggested developing the (67) _____
_____ in a school setting to foster moral development. This
involves having teachers and students jointly decide on rules and
disciplinary actions.

REVIEW OF KEY TERMS AND CONCEPTS

Below is a list of terms and concepts from this chapter. Match each one
with its appropriate definition. You might also want to try writing
definitions in your own words and then checking your definitions with
those here in the Study Guide or in the text.

affiliative motive
altruism
amoral
attribution theory
autonomous morality
conventional morality
effectance motivation
empathy
faith
heteronomous morality
immanent justice
individuative-reflective faith
induction
internalization
Just Community

learned helplessness
locus of control
love withdrawal
moral affect
moral reasoning
moral rules
morality
motive
need for achievement
postconventional morality
power assertion
preconventional morality
premoral period
social-conventional rules

_____1. The belief that rule violations will invariably be
                        punished.

_____2. Standards of what behaviors are right or wrong based
                        on rights and privileges of individuals.

_____3. Kohlberg's fifth and sixth stages in which judgments
                        are based on broad principles of justice that have
                        validity separate from the views of any particular
                        person or group.

_____4. The cognitive process of deciding whether an act is
                        right or wrong.

_____5. A type of discipline style based on physical power of
                        the adult over the child.

_____6. According to Piaget, the preschool years when children
                        show little awareness of rules and are not considered
                        able to reason about moral issues.

_____7. Kohlberg's first two stages of moral reasoning where the personal consequences of a person's actions are used as the basis for judgments.

_____8. The belief that one cannot control the consequences of certain situations and as a result, failure to act in these situations.

_____9. A condition or state that directs a person's behavior toward a goal.

_____10. Behaviors such as helping or sharing that are motivated by desire to help other people rather than by self-interest.

_____11. The motive to successfully interact with one's environment.

_____12. A type of discipline style based on explanations that focus on how the misbehavior affects other people.

_____13. A set of principles that allow a person to distinguish right from wrong and act on this distinction.

_____14. A motive to compete and strive for success whenever one's behavior can be evaluated against a standard.

_____15. Kohlberg's third and fourth stages in which actions are judged by whether they conform to the rules set forth by others.

_____16. Understanding and experiencing another person's feelings.

_____17. The ways in which we make or find meaning in our lives, including religious beliefs.

_____18. The emotional component of morality, consisting of feelings about right and wrong actions.

_____19. The lack of any sense of morality.

_____20. A type of discipline style based on threatened or actual loss of love or attention.

_____21. A dimension of personality concerning the degree to which people view themselves personally responsible for what happens to them.

_____22. A sense of meaning, developed after serious reflection, that is one's own unique philosophy.

_____23. The process of acquiring the standards of other people.

_____24. Piaget's second stage of moral reasoning when children view rules as agreements between people and intentions are more important than consequences of actions.

_____25. The theory that our explanations of behavior influence our future expectancies of success and our motivation to succeed.

_____26. The motive to interact with other people.

_____27. A moral environment in which students and teachers jointly decide on rules and disciplinary actions.

_____28. Piaget's first stage of moral reasoning when children believe that rules are moral absolutes and consequences of actions are more important than intentions.

_____29. Standards of what behaviors are right or wrong based on social consensus.

RESEARCH SUMMARY AND REVIEW

For each of the following studies, briefly summarize the main point(s) of the research and indicate why the research is important. Don't worry about specific details that are not central to the main points, or memorizing names of researchers. Questions you might ask yourself include: Does the research support or refute a theory or hypothesis presented in the text? How does it further our understanding of some concept? Does it provide an example of a point being made in the text? Use the text to check your understanding.

1. Hartshorne and May's (1928-30) classic study on morality (p 385):

_____

_____

_____

_____

2. Nelson's (1980) study on moral reasoning (pp 383-384): _____

_____

_____

3. Veroff, Reuman, and Feld's (1984) study of adult motivations (pp 390-391): _____

_____

_____

_____

For additional practice, pull out some other research discussed in this chapter or research discussed in class lectures and summarize the main points of the studies.

SELF TEST

For each multiple choice question, read all alternatives and then select the best answer.

1. Cognitive-developmental theorists have been most concerned with how children
    a. feel about their moral actions
    b. act when faced with a moral dilemma
    c. reason when faced with a moral dilemma
    d. learn the difference between right and wrong

2. According to Freud's psychoanalytic theory
    a. children reach moral maturity around age 6 or 7 when they resolve their Oedipal (or Electra) conflicts
    b. girls are more morally mature than boys since they have less to fear during the phallic stage of development
    c. children reach moral maturity in adolescence when they enter the genital stage of development
    d. the reasons behind an act are more important than how one feels about a moral action

3. Piaget argued that young elementary school children
    a. are largely unaware of moral rules and so do not always act appropriately
    b. base decisions on both consequences of an action and intentions of the actor
    c. believe that rules can be changed at any time
    d. believe that the consequences of an action are more important than intentions of the actor

4. A child in Piaget's _____ stage of morality would believe that punishments should be tailored to fit the crime.
   a. autonomous
   b. heteronomous
   c. moral absolutes
   d. preconventional

5. If a child who is asked whether stealing some candy is a acceptable answers that it is OK, then this child
   a. is at Kohlberg's preconventional level of moral reasoning
   b. is at Kohlberg's conventional level of moral reasoning
   c. is at Kohlberg's postconventional level of moral reasoning
   d. could be reasoning at any of Kohlberg's levels

6. A child says that it is wrong to cheat because he or she might get caught would be in Kohlberg's _____ stage.
   a. punishment-and-obedience orientation (stage 1)
   b. instrumental hedonism (stage 2)
   c. "good boy" or "good girl" morality (stage 3)
   d. authority and social-order-maintaining morality (stage 4)

7. Someone who refuses to bend a rule to accommodate an exception to the rule because, this person says, "a rule is a rule," is likely in Kohlberg's _____ stage.
   a. instrumental hedonism (stage 2)
   b. "good boy" or "good girl" morality (stage 3)
   c. authority and social-order-maintaining morality (stage 4)
   d. morality of contract, individual rights, and democratically accepted law (stage 5)

8. A teenager who begins smoking because all his friends are doing it, is probably in Kohlberg's _____ stage.
   a. instrumental hedonism (stage 2)
   b. "good boy" or "good girl" morality (stage 3)
   c. authority and social-order-maintaining morality (stage 4)
   d. morality of contract, individual rights, and democratically accepted law (stage 5)

9. Social learning theorists argue that morality is
   a. a generalized trait inherent to the person and subject to little change
   b. a situation-specific trait that is subject to change
   c. an emotional reaction and cannot be directly observed
   d. established in early childhood and changes little after this

10. Understanding and experiencing another person's feelings is termed
    a. altruism
    b. empathy
    c. moral maturity
    d. affiliation

11. A child with an internal locus of control might say which of the following?
    a. I did well on that test because I knew the material.
    b. I did well on that test because it was easy.
    c. I did well on that test because the teacher likes me.
    d. I did well on that test because Dad promised me money for getting an "A."

12. Children who score high in need for achievement
    a. have parents who use an authoritarian style of parenting
    b. have parents who praise success with external rewards and punish failures
    c. get the same grades as other children but feel happier about them
    d. tend to get better grades than children who score low on need for achievement

13. Research on attributions indicates that
    a. high achievers tend to attribute their successes to internal and stable causes
    b. high achievers tend to attribute their failures to internal and stable causes
    c. low achievers tend to attribute everything to external causes
    d. high achievers tend to give up once they fail a task

14. Standards of what behaviors are right or wrong based on rights and privileges of individuals are termed
    a. postconventional rules
    b. social-conventional rules
    c. moral rules
    d. heteronomous rules

15. Recent studies of Piaget's theory of moral reasoning suggest that
    a. there is no relationship between level of cognitive development and moral reasoning
    b. Piaget underestimated children's moral reasoning capabilities
    c. Piaget overestimated children's moral reasoning capabilities
    d. Piaget focused too much attention on children's actions in a moral situation

16. Studies of children's moral behavior show that
    a. behavior is remarkably consistent across situations
    b. behavior is relatively inconsistent across situations
    c. how one acts in a moral situation is very similar to one's reasoning about hypothetical dilemmas
    d. behavior is consistent with one's values

17. Parents who use an inductive style of discipline
    a. indoctrinate their child with their own values and beliefs
    b. withhold attention until their child complies with rules
    c. use their power to get their child to comply with rules
    d. explain to their child why the behavior is wrong and emphasize
       how it affects other people

18. Moral maturity can be fostered by
    a. using an inductive style of discipline
    b. using love-withdrawal as the major disciplinary method
    c. using power assertion as the major disciplinary method
    d. harsh discipline that leaves the child in no doubt about whether
       a behavior is acceptable or not

19. Achievement motivation in men
    a. decreases across adulthood
    b. increases across adulthood
    c. remains the same as it had been throughout childhood and
       adolescence
    d. shows no specific pattern but depends in part on whether the
       person's efforts have met with success or failure in the past

20. Carol Gilligan claims that men and women score at different levels
    on Kohlberg's moral dilemmas because
    a. males operate on the basis of a morality of justice and women do
       not
    b. Freud was right--females are less morally mature
    c. males are more concerned about the needs of others
    d. males reason about real life dilemmas while women reason about
       hypothetical moral issues

21. People who engage in serious reflection about life and develop their
    own unique philosophy are in Fowler's _____ stage of faith.
    a. mythic-literal
    b. synthetic-conventional
    c. individuative-reflective
    d. conjunctive

APPLICATION
_____

Consider how use of punishment affects development of moral reasoning
and behavior. What kind of message does punitive discipline send to
children? What type of moral reasoning and behavior is it likely to
foster and why?
_____

Before you leave this chapter, go back and take another look at the
learning objectives presented at the beginning of the chapter. Rephrase
each objective into a question and check to see whether you have
mastered them. A good way to check your understanding of a concept is
to see if you can teach it to someone else. Take turns doing this with

a small group of people. Whenever you are unsure or unclear about a
response, go back to the text and find out what information you are
missing in order to provide a clear and complete response.

<u>ANSWERS</u>

Summary and Guided Review (Fill-in the blank)

1.	motive	35.	control
2.	physiological	36.	internal
3.	psychological	37.	external
4.	morality	38.	stability
5.	affective	39.	internal
6.	cognitive	40.	external
7.	affects (emotions)	41.	learned helplessness
8.	superego	42.	preconventional
9.	internalize	43.	intentions
10.	reasoning	44.	moral
11.	premoral	45.	social-conventional
12.	heteronomous	46.	moral
13.	absolutes	47.	situations
14.	immanent justice	48.	love withdrawal
15.	autonomous	49.	power assertion
16.	preconventional	50.	induction
17.	punishment	51.	induction
18.	consequences	52.	external
19.	instrumental hedonism	53.	cognitive
20.	conventional	54.	conventional
21.	postconventional	55.	postconventional
22.	behaviors	56.	career-related
23.	situation-specific	57.	social contexts
24.	effectance	58.	postconventional
25.	competence	59.	perspective-taking
26.	mastery	60.	disequilibrium
27.	responsive	61.	three
28.	affiliative	62.	four
29.	amoral	63.	care
30.	empathy	64.	justice
31.	altruism	65.	faith
32.	achievement	66.	individuative-reflective
33.	extrinsic	67.	Just Community
34.	intrinsic		

Key Terms

1.	immanent justice	6.	premoral period
2.	moral rules	7.	preconventional morality
3.	postconventional morality	8.	learned helplessness
4.	moral reasoning	9.	motive
5.	power assertion	10.	altruism

11. effectance motivation
12. induction
13. morality
14. need for achievement
15. conventional morality
16. empathy
17. faith
18. moral affect
19. amoral
20. love withdrawal

21. locus of control
22. individuative-reflective faith
23. internalization
24. autonomous morality
25. attribution theory
26. affiliative motive
27. Just Community
28. heteronomous morality
29. social-conventional rules

Self Test

1.	C	12.	D
2.	A	13.	A
3.	D	14.	C
4.	A	15.	B
5.	D	16.	B
6.	A	17.	D
7.	C	18.	A
8.	B	19.	D
9.	B	20.	A
10.	B	21.	C
11.	A		

Chapter Thirteen
Participation in the Social World

After reading and studying the material in this chapter, you should be able to do the following:

1. Describe the development of a caregiver's attachment to an infant, including features of infants that facilitate attachment.

2. Describe the development of an infant's attachment to a caregiver, including fears that can result from attachment.

3. Describe the four major theories of attachment.

4. Evaluate the four major theories of attachment using available research.

5. Discuss how quality of attachment is assessed and how it is related to later development.

6. Describe the peer relationships of infants and early emergence of sociability.

7. Describe children's impressions of others and the development of perspective-taking skills.

8. Describe the developmental course of children's friendships and factors that contribute to peer acceptance and popularity.

9. Describe changes in social cognition that occur during adolescence.

10. Explain how peer group structures change from same-sex groups to dating relationships during adolescence.

11. Compare and contrast adolescent friendships with friendships of childhood.

12. Discuss conformity pressure during adolescence.

13. Discuss changes that occur in social cognition and social networks during the adult years.

14. Describe the filter model of mate selection.

15. Describe how the different attachment relationships between infant and caregivers can be related to different styles of loving.

16. Describe how adult friendships and relationships differ from earlier friendships.

17. Describe ways to help persons who are socially isolated and lonely.

SUMMARY AND GUIDED REVIEW

The following summary provides an overview of the main points contained in this chapter of the text. Fill-in the blanks with terms that appropriately complete the sentence. Although blank spaces are provided, you may want to write your answers on a separate piece of paper, which will make it easier to compare your answers to the correct answers provided at the end of this chapter.

Scattered throughout the summary are questions in parentheses. These are meant to encourage you to think actively as you are reading and connect this summary to the more detailed information provided in the text. You can answer these questions as you are filling in the blanks or you can fill-in all the blanks, then go back and reread the entire summary, addressing the questions in order to provide more depth of understanding.

Social relationships are important because they provide us with learning experiences and (1) _____ _____, or emotional and practical help that provides strength and helps protect us from stress. Some developmentalists believe that the relationship between parent and infant is the most important and may set the stage for all other social relationships. Relationships with members of one's social group, or (2) _____, are also important and are quite different from relationships with parents. One theorist placed special emphasis on the significance of (3) _____, or close friendships with peers of the same sex that emerge at around 9-12 years of age.

The nature of social relationships changes across the life span. The first relationship to develop is an (4) _____, which is a strong affection that binds one person to another. Infants express attachment by trying to maintain (5) _____ to the figure of their attachment and by showing a preference for this person. Just as infants become attached to caregivers, caregivers become attached to their infant. Infants have a number of features that seem to facilitate the development of attachment. (What are some of these features?) Sometimes a close relationship does not develop between infants and caregivers. This may result because some babies are more difficult to love, some adults have trouble responding to infants, and others have trouble reading their infants' signals and so do not have a (6) _____ relationship with them.

Infants progress through several phases as they develop a relationship with their caregivers. In the first phase, called (7) _____ _____ responsiveness, infants are responsive to social stimuli but show no preferences for one person over

170

another. In the second phase, (8) _____ _____
responsiveness, infants begin to show preferences for familiar
companions. In the third phase, (9) _____ _____
_____, infants will actively pursue the object of their
attachment. One sign that an attachment has formed is
(10) _____ _____, which occurs when infants are
separated from the object of their attachment. Infants may also show
(11) _____ _____, or a wary response to the
approach of an unfamiliar person. (What factors can affect this
response?) Once infants have formed an attachment, they often use that
attachment figure as a (12) _____ _____ for
exploration. They typically also use caregivers to (13) _____
_____, or to check the caregiver's response to an unfamiliar
situation.

There are four major theories of attachment. Freud believed that
since infants are in the (14) _____ stage of psychosexual
development, they become attached to any person who provides oral
pleasure. Erikson, another psychoanalytic theorist, believed a mother's
general responsiveness to her child fostered the development of
(15) _____, which was critical to attachment. Learning
theorists believe that infants become attached to caregivers because
they become a source of (16) _____ for the infants.
Cognitive-developmental theorists believe that formation of attachments
depends on the infant's cognitive capabilities. Infants must be able to
(17) _____ between social and nonsocial stimuli and must have
a sense of (18) _____ _____, or the understanding
that caregivers continue to exist even when they are absent. Ethologists
believe that all species are biologically predisposed to form
attachments because it is adaptive to do so. Some species engage in
(19) _____, an innate form of learning where the young will
follow and become attached to the first moving object they encounter
during a (20) _____ _____ early in life.

Research with monkeys suggests that feeding is _not_ critical for the
development of attachment. Harlow used the term (21) _____
_____ to describe the pleasurable sensations provided by
clinging to something soft and warm. Research indicates that the
availability of contact comfort contributes more to attachment than
feeding and so (22) _____ theory of attachment is not a good
explanation of how attachment develops. (23) _____ theory
has some support since infants do become attached to caregivers who are
generally responsive to their needs, and since caregivers who are
generally responsive are likely to be reinforcing to an infant, this is
also consistent with some versions of (24) _____ theory.
There is also some support for cognitive-developmental and ethological
theories of attachment. (Can you describe evidence that would support
each of these theories?)

Research with infants who have been raised in deprived environments
shows that social isolation early in life has an adverse effect on
development after the age of six months and the negative effects persist

into childhood and adolescence. Normal development seems to require
sustained interactions with responsive caregivers. Infants who are
deprived of social stimulation can recover when placed in affectionate
and responsive homes, but the length of deprivation and the new
caregivers' backgrounds influence the speed and completeness of the
recovery.

The (25) _____ _____ test is a procedure for
measuring the quality of an infant's attachment by observing the
infant's reaction to a series of mildly stressful events. Infants who
are (26) _____ attached show distress when separated from
their caregiver, joy when reunited, and use of caregiver as a secure
base. Infants characterized by (27) _____ attachment show
distress when separated from their caregiver, but are ambivalent about
being reunited, and do not really use the caregiver as a secure base.
Infants characterized by (28) _____ attachment show little
distress at separation from caregiver, avoid the caregiver when
reunited, and do not use the caregiver as a secure base. (What are the
outcomes for children who fall into these three categories of attachment
as infants?)

Infants are interested in other infants and begin to interact
socially with them around six months of age through smiles,
vocalizations, and gestures. Some researchers have suggested that
infants progress through three stages of sociability. In the first
stage, (29) _____-_____, two infants are engaged
together as they play with the same toy, but their focus is on the toy,
not on each other. In the second stage, (30) _____
_____, infants are more responsive to the behavior of their
play partner and in the third stage, (31) _____
_____, interactions between infants are more clearly social.
By the end of their second year, infants are able to distinguish between
infants as well as adults and act more sociable in the presence of
familiar infants.

Children are developing better (32) _____ _____
skills as evidenced by their abilities to think about the thoughts,
feelings, motives, and behaviors of themselves and others. Growth in
this area is distinct from, but related to, development of
(33) _____ of the physical world. Young children typically
describe others using (34) _____ terms. At around age 7 or
8, children begin to use (35) _____ terms to describe others,
and by age 11 or 12, children begin to compare and contrast others on
psychological dimensions. Children are also developing
(36) _____-_____ skills, or the ability to assume
another person's perspective. Selman has concluded that role-taking
skills develop in (37) _____. Preschool children tend to be
(38) _____ and have trouble assuming another person's
perspective. In the (39) _____-_____ stage,
children understand that others may hold different perspectives but
believe this occurs only because these others have received different
information. In the (40) _____-_____ stage,

children understand that others might receive the same information and still have a different perspective, but are not able to consider both their own perspective and another perspective at the same time. In the (41) _____ role taking stage, children can simultaneously consider two different perspectives but until they reach the stage of social and conventional system role taking, they do not try to understand other perspectives by comparing them to the social system in which they operate.

Children's interactions with their parents change as their social cognition skills increase. Children can engage in a (42) _____- _____ partnership where they are able to take the goals and plans of another person into consideration and act on the basis of this information. Children increasingly spend more time with their (43) _____ and in these interactions, children spend more and more time with same-sex peers. For preschool-age children, friendships are based largely on (44) _____ activity. School-age children are more likely to have (45) _____ friendships where each partner acts with respect and kindness towards the other. Friends are also more likely to be (46) _____ similar to one another. Peer acceptance is often studied through (47) _____ techniques where likes and dislikes among the members of a group are examined. Social cognition and role-taking skills have been found to be related to popularity. (Can you describe how these skills might relate to popularity among peers?)

Adolescents spend even more time with peers than children, and their social cognition skills are more developed allowing adolescents to think more abstractly about others. Adolescents move from same-sex peer groups to dating relationships. In late childhood, children are often members of same-sex (48) _____ and interact little with the other sex. Collections of several cliques constitute a (49) _____, which serves mainly as a vehicle for structured social activities. After interacting with other-sex peers in a group setting, adolescents often begin to form couples and crowds begin to dissolve. In our society, first dates typically occur around the age of (50) _____ and are usually informal arrangements. Friendships during adolescence focus on mutual (51) _____ and (52) _____-_____ between the partners. Adolescents tend to choose friends who are similar in (53) _____ traits. (How do males and females differ in their friendships during adolescence?)

Researchers have used (54) _____, or the tendency to change or develop opinions to go along with another person, to study parent and peer influence on adolescents. Conformity to adults tends to decrease with age. Conformity to peers to engage in (55) _____ acts remains steady across age, while conformity to peers to engage in antisocial acts increases with age, levels off, and then decreases by the end of high school. Despite the influence of peers during adolescence, parents and peers are not typically in conflict since adolescents consult peers and parents on different issues, not the same issues.

Friendships continue to be important during adulthood and adults show fairly refined social cognition skills. These skills depend more on (56) _____ _____ than on one's age in adulthood. Elderly adults who continue to use their social cognition skills show no decline in these abilities. The social network of most adults consists of spouse, children, other family members, and many nonfamily members. The main focus of adults' social networks varies depending on age and whether they are married, work, and have children. For many, however, the most important member of the social network is a spouse or romantic partner. Udry has suggested a (57) _____ model of mate selection where adults gradually sift through all potential partners and narrow down the selections until one partner remains. The first filter is (58) _____, suggesting that we are likely to select partners from those people who are near us geographically. The second filter is (59) _____ and the third is (60) _____ _____. The fourth filter is similarity or (61) _____ on values, attitudes, and interests. The (62) _____ filter suggests that partners often complement each other's strengths and weaknesses. Finally, partners must pass the last filter, which is readiness for marriage or commitment.

There may be some similarities between infants who are attached to a parent and adults who are in love with a romantic partner. Adults have been characterized by the same three categories used to describe infants' attachments. (Can you describe how these categories have been applied to adults?)

Friendships continue to be important to adults. Men and women continue to show different styles of interacting with friends. (What are these differences?) Adults especially value friendships that have lasted many years, even if the friends live geographically distant from one another. Adults typically perceive friendships as most satisfying when they are (63) _____ or balanced. Just as attachment is critical for normal infant and child development, friendships are important for normal adult development. However, it is the (64) _____ of friendships that is important, not the quantity of friendships. It seems important that adults have a (65) _____or person to whom they are particularly close and to whom they express their feelings and thoughts.

Some children and adults are socially isolated or lonely. These individuals often lack social cognition skills that can be improved through a variety of techniques to help develop better social relationships. (What are some of the methods that can help socially isolated individuals?)

Below is a list of terms and concepts from this chapter. Match each one with its appropriate definition. You might also want to try writing definitions in your own words and then checking your definitions with those here in the Study Guide or in the text.

attachment
chumship
clique
confidant
conformity
contact comfort
crowd
equity
filter model of mate selection
goal-corrected partnership
imprinting
insecure/avoidant attachment

insecure/resistant attachment
peer
secure attachment
secure base
separation anxiety
social cognition
social referencing
social support
sociometric techniques
Strange Situation test
stranger anxiety

_____1. An innate form of learning in which the young of a species will follow and become attached to a moving object (usually the mother) during a critical period early in life.

_____2. A caregiver-infant relationship characterized by distress at separation, ambivalence at being reunited, and little use of caregiver as a secure base.

_____3. Wariness or fear expressed by infants when separated from a caregiver to whom they are attached.

_____4. A small friendship group in adolescence.

_____5. The sense that there is a balance of contributions and benefits in relationships between spouses, friends, and other intimates.

_____6. A close friendship with peers of the same age that emerges at about age 9 to 12.

_____7. A collection of about four heterosexual cliques.

_____8. Harlow's term for the pleasure of clinging to something soft and warm.

_____9. A caregiver-infant relationship characterized by little distress at separation, avoidance of caregiver when reunited, and little exploration.

_____10. Members of one's social group, often people who are of similar age and behavioral functioning.

_____11. A spouse, relative, or friend to whom an individual feels an especially close attachment and with whom thoughts and feelings can be shared.

_____12. A series of mildly stressful events designed to measure the quality of an infant's attachment to a caregiver.

_____13. Wariness or fear expressed by infants when approached by an unfamiliar person.

_____14. The ability to think about the thoughts, feelings, motives and behaviors of one's self and others.

_____15. Emotional and practical help that provides strength to individuals and helps protect them from stress.

_____16. The tendency to change or develop opinions to go along with those of another person or group.

_____17. A phase of attachment in which children can take the goals and plans of a parent into consideration and adjust behavior accordingly.

_____18. The process of sifting through all potential partners to find one chosen partner.

_____19. An attachment figure who serves as a safe place from which an infant can explore the environment.

_____20. A strong affectionate tie that binds a person to an intimate companion.

_____21. A caregiver-infant relationship characterized by distress at separation, joy at being reunited, and use of caregiver as a secure base.

_____22. Using a familiar person's reaction to guide one's own behavior in an ambiguous situation.

_____23. Methods of studying social groups by determining likes and dislikes among the members of the group.

For each of the following studies, briefly summarize the <u>main point(s)</u> of the research and indicate why the research is important. Don't worry about specific details that are not central to the main points, or memorizing names of researchers. Questions you might ask yourself include: Does the research support or refute a theory or hypothesis presented in the text? How does it further our understanding of some concept? Does it provide an example of a point being made in the text? Use the text to check your understanding.

1. Harlow and Zimmerman's (1959) study of monkeys raised with surrogate mothers (page 412): _____

_____

_____

_____

2. Hazan and Shaver's (1987) study of adult attachment types (p 431-2):

_____

_____

_____

3. Selman and colleagues' (1976; 1980; 1989) research on role-taking abilities (p 419): _____

_____

_____

_____

4. Skolnick's (1986) longitudinal research of attachment (page 416):

_____

_____

_____

_____

For additional practice, pull out some other research discussed in this chapter or research discussed in class lectures and summarize the main points of the studies.

_____

For each multiple choice question, read all alternatives and then select the best answer.

1. Infants show attachment through which of the following behaviors?
    a. showing a preference for one person over another
    b. trying to maintain proximity to a person
    c. showing distress when a person leaves
    d. all of the above

2. At about 4 weeks of age, smiles are likely to be
    a. totally reflexive
    b. in response to a female voice
    c. in response to recognizing a familiar face
    d. directed toward the object of the infant's attachment

3. In the discriminating social responsiveness phase of developing attachment, infants
    a. respond to many different social stimuli such as voices and faces
    b. respond differently depending on the social situation
    c. show preferences for familiar companions
    d. show clear attachment by following the object of their attachment and protesting when this person leaves

4. Stranger anxiety would be greatest in which of the following situations?
    a. Seated on mother's lap at the doctor's office while mom warmly greets the doctor.
    b. Seated on mother's lap at home while mom warmly greets the next door neighbor.
    c. Seated on mother's lap at home while mom neutrally greets a salesperson.
    d. Seated across from mother at the doctor's office while mom neutrally greets the doctor.

5. According to Freud, infants become attached to their mothers because
    a. mothers become associated with pleasurable sensations
    b. mothers are generally responsive to their needs
    c. they are innately predisposed to form attachments
    d. mothers provide oral pleasure

6. Cognitive-developmental theorists believe that before attachment to caregivers can occur, infants must
   a. learn to associate caregiver with reinforcement
   b. be able to discriminate between social and nonsocial stimuli and understand that stimuli continue to exist even when not present
   c. be able to recognize caregiver and learn to follow the caregiver during a critical period early in life.
   d. have caregivers who consistently respond to their needs

7. The finding that infant monkeys in Harlow's research preferred the cloth surrogate over the wire surrogate regardless of which one had provided food
   a. supports Erikson's claim that general responsiveness is important to development of attachment
   b. shows that there is an innate predisposition to form attachments
   c. shows that Freud's emphasis on feeding behavior cannot fully explain development of attachment
   d. supports learning theory explanations of attachment since infants become attached to the mother who reinforced them with food

8. Social referencing refers to an infant's ability to
   a. recognize familiar companion
   b. compare self to others
   c. use other people's reactions to guide their own behavior
   d. imitate other people's behavior

9. Which of the following describes infants who are classified as having an insecure/resistant attachment?
   a. Infants use their mother as a secure base, they are upset when she leaves them, and welcome her when she returns.
   b. Infants are upset when their mother leaves them and are ambivalent when she returns.
   c. Infants are not really distressed when their mother leaves them and do not welcome her back when she returns.
   d. Infants are not really distressed when their mother leaves them and express joy when reunited with mother.

10. With respect to the relationship between security of attachment during infancy and social competence during adulthood, research suggests that
    a. quality of infant attachment does not predict adult social competence as well as peer relations during adolescence do
    b. quality of infant attachment has no relation to social competence during adulthood
    c. quality of infant attachment to parents is the most important predictor of adult social competence
    d. individuals who were securely attached as infants always have positive social relationships

11. Which of the following is <u>true</u> regarding the development of person perception?
    a. All ages typically describe others using concrete and physical terms.
    b. Older adults describe others using concrete terms while younger adults use psychological terms.
    c. All ages are capable of using psychological terms to describe others, but not all ages choose to use these terms.
    d. Children younger than 7 or 8 years typically describe others in concrete and physical terms.

12. Children in Selman's mutual role taking stage
    a. are unaware of other perspectives unless these perspectives are the same as their own
    b. understand that others may hold different perspectives but believe this is because they have received different information
    c. are able to compare other perspectives to the general social system in which these perspectives exist
    d. can simultaneously consider multiple perspectives

13. Effects of early social deprivation in human infants
    a. cannot be overcome
    b. can be overcome if the infants are placed with affectionate and responsive caregivers
    c. can be overcome if the infants are exposed to multiple caregivers
    d. are usually not significant

14. With respect to conformity to pressure during adolescence
    a. there is no difference between conformity to pressure from adults and pressure from peers
    b. conformity to peer pressure for antisocial acts increases while conformity to peer pressure for prosocial acts decreases
    c. adolescents are more likely to conform to peer pressure for prosocial acts than antisocial acts
    d. adolescents are more likely to conform to parental pressure than peer pressure

15. Which of the follow accurately represents the order of filters used for mate selection according to Udry's model?
    a. propinquity, attractiveness, social background, consensus, complementarity, readiness
    b. propinquity, complementarity, attractiveness, consensus, social background, readiness
    c. social background, propinquity, complementarity, attractiveness, consensus, readiness
    d. attractiveness, readiness, social background, propinquity, complementarity, consensus

Integrate the following concepts: Temperament style, quality of attachment, cognitive ability, role taking skills, and popularity and friendships. Explain how all these concepts are intertwined. How do they connect to one another? You do not need to relate each factor to <u>all</u> the other factors, but explain how one factor influences a second, which in turn influences a third, and so on.

Before you leave this chapter, go back and take another look at the learning objectives presented at the beginning of the chapter. Rephrase each objective into a question and check to see whether you have mastered them. A good way to check your understanding of a concept is to see if you can teach it to someone else. Take turns doing this with a small group of people. Whenever you are unsure or unclear about a response, go back to the text and find out what information you are missing in order to provide a clear and complete response.

ANSWERS

Summary and Guided Review (Fill-in the blank)

1.	social support	28.	avoidant
2.	peers	29.	object-centered
3.	chumships	30.	simple interactive
4.	attachment	31.	complementary interactive
5.	proximity	32.	social cognition
6.	synchronized	33.	cognition
7.	undiscriminating social	34.	concrete
8.	discriminating social	35.	psychological
9.	active proximity seeking	36.	role-taking
10.	separation anxiety	37.	stages
11.	stranger anxiety	38.	egocentric
12.	secure base	39.	social-informational
13.	social reference	40.	self-reflective
14.	oral	41.	mutual
15.	trust	42.	goal-directed
16.	reinforcement	43.	friends (or peers)
17.	discriminate	44.	common
18.	person permanence	45.	reciprocal
19.	imprinting	46.	psychologically
20.	critical period	47.	sociometric
21.	contact comfort	48.	cliques
22.	Freud's	49.	crowd
23.	Erikson's	50.	fourteen (14)
24.	learning	51.	intimacy
25.	Strange Situation	52.	self-disclosure
26.	securely	53.	psychological
27.	resistant	54.	conformity

55. prosocial
56. social experiences
57. filter
58. propinquity
59. attractiveness
60. social background

61. consensus
62. complementarity
63. equitable
64. quality
65. confidant

Key Terms

1. imprinting
2. insecure/resistant attachment
3. separation anxiety
4. clique
5. equity
6. chumship
7. crowd
8. contact comfort
9. insecure/avoidant attachment
10. peer
11. confidant
12. Strange Situation test

13. stranger anxiety
14. social cognition
15. social support
16. conformity
17. goal-corrected partnership
18. filter model of
    mate selection
19. secure base
20. attachment
21. secure attachment
22. social referencing
23. sociometric techniques

Self Test

1. D
2. B
3. C
4. D
5. D
6. B
7. C
8. C

9. B
10. A
11. D
12. D
13. B
14. B
15. A

Chapter Fourteen
The Family

After reading and studying the material in this chapter, you should be able to do the following:

1. Distinguish between the nuclear family and the extended family.

2. Describe changes that have occurred in the family during the 20th century.

3. Discuss how the father/infant relationship is similar to and different from the mother/infant relationship.

4. Describe indirect effects that parents can have on their children.

5. Describe the two dimensions of parenting and the effects of these dimensions on development.

6. Describe Baumrind's three patterns of parental control and the effects of these patterns on development.

7. Discuss the effects that a new baby can have on other children in the family.

8. Discuss the family relationship between adolescents and their parents.

9. Discuss how children affect husbands, wives, and their relationship.

10. Describe changes in the family that occur when the children mature and leave home.

11. Describe grandparenting roles.

12. Describe how various family relationships change during adulthood.

13. Describe adult life for individuals who do not marry and couples who do not have children.

14. Discuss effects of divorce on family relationships.

15. Discuss effects of remarriage on parents and children.

16. Discuss spouse abuse and child abuse, including reasons and possible solutions.

The following summary provides an overview of the main points contained in this chapter of the text. Fill-in the blanks with terms that appropriately complete the sentence. Although blank spaces are provided, you may want to write your answers on a separate piece of paper, which will make it easier to compare your answers to the correct answers provided at the end of this chapter.

Scattered throughout the summary are questions in parentheses. These are meant to encourage you to think actively as you are reading and connect this summary to the more detailed information provided in the text. You can answer these questions as you are filling in the blanks or you can fill-in all the blanks, then go back and reread the entire summary, addressing the questions in order to provide more depth of understanding.

The family is viewed as a (1) _____, meaning that it is a whole unit consisting of interrelated parts. The (2) _____ family consists of a mother, father, and at least one child. In an (3) _____ family, a family unit lives with other relatives. Family membership changes over time and the relationships within families also develop and change over time. The (4) _____ _____ is one way to characterize the sequence of changes in family membership and relationships that occur over time.

The changing family exists within a changing world and several social changes of the 20th century have significantly affected the family. Our society has a greater number of single adults and more adults are delaying marriage and childbearing than in the past. More women are participating in the labor force and our society has seen a rise in the divorce rate. There are more single-parent families and more (5) _____ families as divorced adults remarry. Finally, for a variety of reasons, adults today spend more years without children than in past generations.

Mothers are traditionally the primary caregivers for infants and mothers and infants typically develop an attachment to one another. The mother-infant relationship is (6) _____, meaning that mothers can affect the development of their infants and infants can affect the behavior of their mothers. Fathers are equally capable of parenting, however they differ from mothers in both the quantity and quality of the parenting that they actually provide. Mothers spend more time with children than fathers do, and mothers' interactions with their children tend to be related to providing care while fathers' interactions are more likely to be (7) _____ oriented. Fathers are likely to treat boys and girls more differently than do mothers and contribute to the gender-role development of both sons and daughters. Boys and girls both benefit intellectually from having fathers who are actively involved in their development. In addition to these effects, parents have many (8) _____ effects on their children through their ability to influence their spouses. (Can you

184

provide several examples of this type of effect?)

Good parenting is defined by the specific culture or subculture in which families live. One dimension of parenting, called (9) _____/_____, describes how affectionate parents are toward their child. A second dimension of parenting, (10) _____/_____, describes the degree of autonomy that parents allow their children. (Can you describe the four basic patterns of parenting that result from crossing these two dimensions?) Baumrind described three patterns of parental control that more specifically address how restrictive or permissive parents are with their children. An (11) _____ parenting style is one where children are allowed a fair amount of freedom, but rules are clearly stated, explained, and enforced. An (12) _____ parenting style is a highly restrictive style where parents impose many rules without explaining their importance, and often use physical means to gain compliance to the rules. A (13) _____ parenting style is a lax style of parenting where few rules are imposed on children and children are encouraged to express their feelings and impulses. (Which of these styles of parenting seems to have the "best" outcome in our society?) In general, warmth combined with (14) _____ parental control seems to be associated with healthy child development. The least successful parenting styles are those that involve hostility or rejection.

A second child in the family often creates (15) _____ _____, or feelings of competition, jealousy, and resentment between siblings. (How do first-borns react to the birth of a sibling?) While sibling relationships can involve negative conflicts, siblings also have many positive effects on one another. For example, siblings provide (16) _____ _____ for one another. Older siblings often provide (17) _____ services for younger siblings and serve as (18) _____ for new behaviors.

Some people believe that adolescents and their parents experience conflict because there is a (19) _____ _____, or discrepancy between the values and attitudes of different generations. While there are some differences between generations, particularly in terms of socialization experiences, parents and children are similar in many ways. Most teenagers view their relationship with their parents as (20) _____.

A major task of adolescence is to achieve (21) _____, which has two major components. One is (22) _____ autonomy, or the ability to rely on one's self rather than one's parents for emotional strength. The other component is (23) _____ autonomy, the ability to take care of one's self and function independently. As adolescents strive for autonomy, conflicts with parents become more frequent. (How can parents help adolescents successfully achieve autonomy?)

Most adults in our society marry and typically marry for love.

Marriage is a major adjustment for both partners. Many couples have children within a few years of getting married and this is another major life transition with both positive and negative changes. Marital satisfaction tends to (24) _____ from before to after the birth of a child and this change is more pronounced for women than men. (What factors contribute to individual differences in adjustment to parenthood?) Having a second child is another stressful event for the family and marital satisfaction typically remains somewhat depressed with the addition of more children to the family. Despite these declines, marital satisfaction is generally high overall.

As children reach maturity and leave their parent's home, the family system changes once again. The term (25) _____ _____ is used to describe the family structure after all children have left the home. Marital satisfaction tends to (26) _____ following the departure of children. (Why do parents react this way to their children leaving home?)

Many adults become grandparents in middle-age and do not fit the stereotyped image of white-haired elderly grandparents. Researchers have identified three major styles of grandparenting. (27) _____ grandparents are largely symbolic figures who do not interact a great deal with grandchildren. (28) _____ grandparents frequently see their grandchildren and enjoy sharing activities with them. (29) _____ grandparents assume a parentlike role and provide some degree of child care for their grandchildren. As grandchildren get older, the role of grandparents changes in predictable ways. Enjoyment and involvement seem to be highest when both grandchildren and grandparents are relatively young.

As noted above, marital satisfaction appears to decline when children enter the family and increases when children leave the family. Women tend to be more affected by changes in the family structure than men. Many factors other than stage of family life cycle determine marital satisfaction. (What are some of these factors?)

Sibling relationships also change across the life span. Adult siblings typically keep in touch with each other, but the relationship is less intense than when siblings were young and adult siblings rarely discuss intimate problems with each other. Nevertheless, siblings often report feeling close to one another. The sibling relationship can change in response to specific events, such as geographical moves, divorces, loss of a spouse, or illness.

Parents and children develop new relationships as the children become adults and leave home. The relationships are often more intimate, with recognition that each is an individual and has roles other than parent or child. Middle-aged adults continue to feel close to their parents. Many families are part of a (30) _____ _____ family where they live in separate households but have close and frequent interaction with other relatives. The relationships among different generations tend to be (31) _____, which

means that each contributes something to the relationship and gets
something back in return. Middle-aged adults often end up giving more
than they receive because they often experience demands from both the
older and younger generation, a condition called the
(32) _____   _____   _____.

Adult lifestyles in our culture have become quite diverse. Many
adults delay marriage, remain single, or become single through divorce
or death of a spouse. Living with a romantic partner without being
married, or (33) _____, is more common than it used to be.
Some couples use living together as a test of compatibility before
marrying. However, couples who live together before marrying actually
seem to be more dissatisfied with the marriage and more likely to
(34) _____ than couples who marry without first living
together. Adults who never marry have a somewhat lower overall sense of
happiness than married adults, but the difference in satisfaction is not
as large as it used to be. (35) _____ single adults tend to
be less satisfied than never married and currently married adults.

More couples are choosing not to have children than in the past.
Childless couples tend to have somewhat higher marital satisfaction than
couples with children during the child-rearing years. Following the
child-rearing years, couples with and without children are similar in
their levels of marital satisfaction.

Some adults form homosexual relationships. Gay and lesbian couples
are more similar to heterosexual couples than they are different. The
major difference is the (36) _____ that others express toward
the homosexual relationship.

Nearly half of recent marriages will end in divorce, making divorce
a typical part of the family life cycle. Divorce is a series of
experiences, not a single event that has finite beginning and end
points. It is unclear what processes cause divorce, but there are
several factors that seem to place some couples at a greater risk for
divorce than other couples. (What are some factors that increase the
likelihood of divorce?)

Families experiencing a divorce typically go through a
(37) _____ period during which there is much disruption. The
stress of a divorce places individuals at greater risk for depression,
physical problems, and even death. Adults experiencing divorce have
problems parenting. Custodial mothers tend to become less warm and more
(38) _____ in their discipline. While custodial mothers
often use a more restrictive style of parenting, noncustodial fathers
tend to be (39) _____. Most of the problems between parents
and children dissipate in the two years following a divorce, but the
divorce continues to affect both children and adults.

Most divorced parents remarry within five years after a divorce,
often creating (40) _____ families. While boys seem to
suffer more than girls when parents divorce, they apparently benefit

more than girls when their custodial mothers remarry. (What are some possible reasons for this finding?)

Unfortunately, some families experience violence in the forms of child abuse, spouse abuse, and elder abuse. Many child abusers were abused or neglected themselves as children. Infant (41) _____ are often interpreted differently by abusive and nonabusive mothers. Some children may have characteristics that make them more likely targets of abuse than other children. In addition to parent and child characteristics, the surrounding social climate and lack of social (42) _____ may contribute to the likelihood of abuse in the family. By identifying families that are high-risk candidates for family violence, it may be possible to provide the support necessary to prevent abuse from occurring. An organization called (43) _____ _____ may help those caregivers who are already abusive.

REVIEW OF KEY TERMS AND CONCEPTS

Below is a list of terms and concepts from this chapter. Match each one with its appropriate definition. You might also want to try writing definitions in your own words and then checking your definitions with those here in the Study Guide or in the text.

authoritarian parenting
authoritative parenting
autonomy
cohabitation
empty nest
extended family
family life cycle
generation gap
indirect effects

"middle generation squeeze"
modified extended family
nuclear family
permissive parenting
permissiveness/restrictiveness dimension
reconstituted family
sibling rivalry
warmth/hostility dimension

_____ 1. A family unit that consists of parent, stepparent, and at least one child.

_____ 2. A flexible parenting style in which parents set clear rules and provide explanations for rules but allow children some freedom and input.

_____ 3. The discrepancy between the values and attitudes of the different generations.

_____ 4. A family unit consisting of a mother, father, and at least one child.

_____ 5. An arrangement in which nuclear families live in separate households but have close ties and frequent interaction with other relatives.

_____6. Feelings of competition, jealousy, and resentment that can develop between brothers and sisters.

_____7. Single adults living with a romantic partner without being married.

_____8. A dimension of parenting that describes the degree of autonomy that parents allow their children.

_____9. A household in which a family unit lives with other relatives.

_____10. A critical task of adolescence involving development of independence in various realms.

_____11. The sequence of changes in family composition, roles, and relationships that occur from the time people marry to the time they die.

_____12. A restrictive parenting style in which parents impose many rules and use power tactics to ensure obedience to these rules.

_____13. Family situation following the departure of the children.

_____14. A dimension of parenting that describes how affectionate parents are toward their child.

_____15. Middle-aged adults who experience demands from both younger and older generations.

_____16. A parenting style in which adults make relatively few demands, encourage children to express their feelings, and rarely exert control over their behavior.

_____17. Effects that parents have on their children through their influence on their spouse's behavior.

RESEARCH SUMMARY AND REVIEW

For each of the following studies, briefly summarize the main point(s) of the research and indicate why the research is important. Don't worry about specific details that are not central to the main points, or memorizing names of researchers. Questions you might ask yourself include: Does the research support or refute a theory or hypothesis presented in the text? How does it further our understanding of some concept? Does it provide an example of a point being made in the text? Use the text to check your understanding.

1. Baumrind's (1967 and 1977) studies of the relationship between parenting styles and children's characteristics (page 445):

_____

_____

_____

_____

2. Hetherington and associates' (1981; 1982) findings regarding the effects of divorce (page 463): _____

_____

_____

_____

_____

For additional practice, pull out some other research discussed in this chapter or research discussed in class lectures and summarize the main points of the studies.

SELF TEST _____

For each multiple choice question, read all alternatives and then select the best answer.

1. A family unit consisting of a mother, father, and at least one child is termed a _____ family.
   a. reconstituted
   b. extended
   c. nuclear
   d. generational

2. The family life cycle
   a. refers to the sequence of changes in family membership and roles between marriage and death
   b. refers to family units that consist of a parent, a stepparent and at least one child
   c. refers to the changes that have occurred in the family system during the 20th century
   d. undergoes dramatic changes every 10 years

3. Compared to mother, fathers in general
   a. spend as much time with their children
   b. spend less time with their children
   c. treat boys and girls more similarly
   d. serve as disciplinarian in the family

4. Which type of parenting style places few demands on children and allows them to express their desires freely?
    a. permissive
    b. authoritative
    c. authoritarian
    d. love withdrawal

5. In which style of parenting do parents value obedience for its own sake and impose many rules that are typically not fully explained to children?
    a. permissive
    b. authoritative
    c. authoritarian
    d. love withdrawal

6. Children of parents who use a(n) _____ style of parenting are typically more self-reliant and achievement oriented than children raised with other styles of parenting
    a. permissive
    b. authoritative
    c. authoritarian
    d. love withdrawal

7. Which combination of parenting dimensions is associated with healthiest child development?
    a. hostility combined with reasonable levels of parental control
    b. warmth combined with little parental control
    c. warmth combined with total parental control
    d. warmth combined with moderate parental control

8. Feelings of rivalry or jealousy following the birth of a new sibling
    a. are strongest if parents maintain the same regular schedule they had for the first-born before the arrival of the new baby
    b. can be minimized if the first-born had already established a good relationship with parents
    c. can be minimized if the parents lavish the first child with attention
    d. are always worse if the first-born is a boy

9. With respect to adolescent-parent relationships, research indicates:
    a. there is a huge gap between generations in their values and attitudes
    b. adolescents generally report being unhappy with the relationship
    c. boys are much more dissatisfied with the relationship than girls
    d. adolescents are strongly influenced by their parents on important issues

10. The relationship between adult siblings
    a. disintegrates once the siblings leave school
    b. remains close although less intense than during childhood
    c. involves a great deal of sharing and discussing feelings
    d. continues to be as intense as during childhood

11. Which of the following is <u>true</u> regarding marital satisfaction?
    a. Marital satisfaction is highest following the birth of a child.
    b. Because of the adjustments that must be made, marital satisfaction is lowest right after marriage
    c. Marital satisfaction declines following the birth of a child
    d. Marital satisfaction declines across middle and older adulthood

12. Cohabiting couples who later marry
    a. are more dissatisfied with their marriages than couples who had not lived together before marrying
    b. are more satisfied with their marriages than couples who had not lived together before marrying
    c. are less likely to divorce than couples who had not lived together before marrying
    d. are basically no different from couples who had not lived together before marrying

13. Adults who never marry
    a. typically have some psychological problem
    b. are lonely and maladjusted
    c. are much happier and better adjusted than married adults
    d. are somewhat less happy than married adults

14. Evidence indicates that following a divorce
    a. both boys and girls settle quickly into a new lifestyle with few adjustment problems
    b. boys take longer to adjust than girls and exhibit more behavior problems
    c. girls take longer to adjust than boys and exhibit more depression
    d. neither boys or girls adjust to the new lifestyle within several years of the divorce

15. Reconstituted families where children in a mother-headed family acquire a stepfather
    a. seem to benefit boys more than girls
    b. seem to benefit girls more than boys
    c. seem to benefit boys and girls equally
    d. do not benefit any of the children, just the adults

16. Child abuse is <u>less</u> likely in families where
    a. the parents had been abused themselves and so they know the negative impact that abuse can have
    b. there are multiple sources of stress
    c. there is a strong support network available to parents
    d. parents have difficulty "reading" their child's signals

Write about what it is like to be a son, a daughter, a mother, a father, and a grandparent in today's family. Put yourself in each of these roles and view the family system from these perspectives. How would each of these individuals respond to, and be affected by, things such as the birth of a new baby, divorce, remarriage, and abuse?

Before you leave this chapter, go back and take another look at the learning objectives presented at the beginning of the chapter. Rephrase each objective into a question and check to see whether you have mastered them. A good way to check your understanding of a concept is to see if you can teach it to someone else. Take turns doing this with a small group of people. Whenever you are unsure or unclear about a response, go back to the text and find out what information you are missing in order to provide a clear and complete response.

ANSWERS

Summary and Guided Review (Fill-in the blank)

1. system
2. nuclear
3. extended
4. family life cycle
5. reconstituted
6. reciprocal
7. play
8. indirect
9. warmth/hostility
10. permissiveness/restrictiveness
11. authoritative
12. authoritarian
13. permissive
14. moderate
15. sibling rivalry
16. emotional support
17. caretaking
18. teachers
19. generation gap
20. positive
21. autonomy
22. emotional
23. behavioral
24. decline
25. empty nest
26. increase
27. remote
28. companionate
29. involved
30. modified extended
31. equitable
32. middle generation squeeze
33. cohabitation
34. divorce
35. divorced
36. prejudice
37. crisis
38. inconsistent
39. overpermissive
40. reconstituted
41. signals
42. support
43. Parents Anonymous

Key Terms

1. reconstituted family
2. authoritative parenting
3. generation gap
4. nuclear family
5. modified extended family
6. sibling rivalry
7. cohabitation
8. permissiveness/restrictiveness dimension
9. extended family
10. autonomy
11. family life cycle
12. authoritarian parenting
13. empty nest
14. warmth/hostility dimension
15. "middle generation squeeze"
16. permissive parenting
17. indirect effects

Self Test

1. C
2. A
3. B
4. A
5. C
6. B
7. D
8. B
9. D
10. B
11. C
12. A
13. D
14. B
15. A
16. C

Chapter Fifteen
Lifestyles: Play, School, and Work

After reading and studying the material in this chapter, you should be able to do the following:

1. Explain the terms play, work and leisure.

2. Describe the emergence and development of symbolic play during the first two years.

3. Discuss the positive and negative effects of alternative care on infant development.

4. Describe how play changes during early and middle childhood.

5. Discuss how play contributes to physical, intellectual, social, and emotional development.

6. Describe the effects of preschool on children's development.

7. Describe factors that contribute to effective schools and factors that have little impact on a school's effectiveness.

8. Explain the Pygmalion effect and its impact on student performance.

9. Explain mainstreaming, the effects of desegregation, and cooperative learning methods.

10. Discuss the positive and negative effects of television.

11. Describe the different activities in which adolescents are typically engaged and their implications.

12. Discuss how adolescents explore and make decisions about their future vocations.

13. Describe Levinson's theory of adult development and evaluate its usefulness.

14. Discuss how women's roles in the workplace have evolved and how these roles are integrated with women's roles in the home or family.

15. Describe how work and leisure affect adult development.

16. Compare and contrast activity theory and disengagement theory, and discuss the validity of these two theories.

17. Discuss how play can be used to enhance lifestyles across the life span.

SUMMARY AND GUIDED REVIEW

The following summary provides an overview of the main points contained in this chapter of the text. Fill-in the blanks with terms that appropriately complete the sentence. Although blank spaces are provided, you may want to write your answers on a separate piece of paper, which will make it easier to compare your answers to the correct answers provided at the end of this chapter.

Scattered throughout the summary are questions in parentheses. These are meant to encourage you to think actively as you are reading and connect this summary to the more detailed information provided in the text. You can answer these questions as you are filling in the blanks or you can fill-in all the blanks, then go back and reread the entire summary, addressing the questions in order to provide more depth of understanding.

(1) _____ is defined as an activity that is enjoyable and intrinsically motivated. (2) _____ is activity directed toward the goal of producing something useful. Work includes paid employment as well as unpaid activity in and around the home. Time that is free of obligations is (3) _____ time. People of all ages engage in play and work, but the balance between the two activities changes over the life span.

Infants first play with their own bodies and then begin to act on objects in their environment. Pretend, or (4) _____, play where one thing is used to represent another thing, emerges in rudimentary form around the end of the first year. According to Piaget, young children acquire (5) _____ _____, which allows them to use one thing to represent another. More refined symbolic play develops between the ages of 1 and 2. Through (6) _____, infants begin to act the role of someone other than themselves in their play. Through (7) _____, infants are able to engage in symbolic play with objects that are not "real." There is also increased (8) _____ of play so that infants can now string together a series of actions in a logical sequence.

More infants are attending day-care homes or centers than in the past. In general, infants who attend high quality day-care centers are no different from infants who are reared at home. It is important that the care at home or in a center be of high (9) _____. One-to-one interaction with familiar and competent caregivers is particularly important wherever the infant is raised. Infants who are at risk for developmental delay because they come from disadvantaged homes benefit from attending high quality day-care. (Can you explain why this is true?) Effects of day-care may also be influenced by

196

whether the infant is (10) _____ or not to a primary caregiver before entering the day-care. In addition, parental attitudes about day-care influence the success of the care. (How do parental attitudes influence effects of day-care?)

Children between the ages of 2 and 5 play quite a bit. Their play becomes more (11) _____. Parten devised a scale for classifying children's play. Children who are engaged in no particular activity are in the category of (12) _____ play. Children who play alone are engaged in (13) _____ play. (14) _____ play involves watching others as they play and (15) _____ play is when two children play next to each other but not with each other. In (16) _____ play, children interact with one another but only in (17) _____ play are children really united toward a common goal. Children increasingly engage in more associative and cooperative play, which are the most social of these play categories. Play of preschool-aged children also becomes more imaginative. Many children have (18) _____ _____ that they have invented.

Elementary school children engage in less symbolic play and more organized games with (19) _____. According to Piaget, children must be in the (20) _____-_____ stage to play games with rules.

Play is important for a number of reasons. It contributes to (21) _____ development since infants and children can move around and manipulate objects when they play. Play provides an opportunity to use language, which contributes to (22) _____ development. Play also contributes to (23) _____ development since children get an opportunity to role play, cooperate with others, and resolve conflicts. Emotional development is enhanced because children can express feelings that they might otherwise keep to themselves.

Around the age of 6, children begin spending a significant portion of their time at school. Many children attend a preschool prior to entering kindergarten and first grade. The average child is no better or worse for having gone to preschool. Children who come from disadvantaged homes often benefit (24) _____ from having this experience. In addition, children who attend preschool tend to be advanced in terms of (25) _____ development. Some elementary and secondary schools are more effective than others. Michael Rutter defines effective schools as those that promote (26) _____ _____, social skills (including polite and attentive behavior), positive attitudes toward learning, good attendance, voluntary continuation of schooling, and acquisition of skills that will enable students to find and hold jobs. Factors that do not contribute to effective schooling include the amount of monetary support that a school receives, the average size of classes (within a range of 20 to 40 students), and grouping according to ability, a technique called (27) _____ _____. Factors that

<u>do</u> contribute to the effectiveness of a school include a strong emphasis on (28) _____, well-managed classrooms (both in terms of classroom activities and discipline problems), and teachers who can work with other teachers. In addition, student characteristics interact with school factors to affect student outcome. (How does ability level interact with program characteristics?)

Schools have a difficult task since they must meet the needs of all students, not just the average, or the better, student. Unfortunately, many schools are best equipped to handle "normal," middle-class students. Minority students and students from low-income homes often have trouble in school. One problem is related to (29) _____ _____, or the Pygmalion effect. This means that students do better in school when they are expected to do well than when they are expected to do poorly. (How do teacher behaviors differ when interacting with students for whom they hold different expectations?)

Following the 1954 <u>Brown v. Board of Education</u> case, schools were ordered to (30) _____ so that black and white students were educated in the same schools. Unfortunately, school integration has not had large effects on children's racial attitudes. Prejudice among black and white students toward each other decreased somewhat, but not as much as hoped. Children with disabilities have also been integrated into the regular classroom through the process of (31) _____. The results of this have been mixed--Sometimes the outcome is positive and other times, the effects are nonexistent. Use of (32) _____ _____ methods have been successful. With these types of techniques, students of different races or ability levels are assigned to teams and are rewarded for team, not individual, performance.

It is no secret that today's children watch a lot of television. In families with a television set, families typically spend less time together engaged in other activities. Children who watch a lot of (33) _____ on television act more aggressively and children who are (34) _____ like to watch violent television programs. Television seems to (35) _____ children to violence because it makes them more tolerant and less emotionally upset by real life violence. Television programs also reinforce social (36) _____ such as traditional male and female roles. Television can also have a positive impact on children if they watch the "right" shows. Television can promote (37) _____, or helping and sharing, behaviors. It can also positively influence cognitive development and academic achievement. For example, children who regularly watch <u>Sesame Street</u> perform better on cognitive tests than children who do not watch much of this program.

Children today are also growing up with computers in some form. Some schools use (38) _____-_____ instruction, which has proven effective. Children have also been taught to program the computer, which can improve their performance on some Piagetian tasks, metacognition, and perhaps creativity.

198

Children are also beginning to think about career options. Children realize that they are going to be adults and that adults typically have a career. Children in preschool and elementary school typically focus on career options that are considered
(39) _____ _____.

Adolescents spend more of their waking hours engaged in
(40) _____ activities than in any other pursuit. Academic outcome for adolescents depends on their ability as well as the school quality, or climate in which they are expected to learn. According to one theory of vocational choice, adolescents move from the
(41) _____ stage to the (42) _____ stage where they begin to take their interests, capacities, and values into consideration. Following adolescence, individuals are likely to narrow down their vocational choice by also considering actual opportunities. (What other factors affect vocational choice?)

Work in and out of the home is critical to an adult's identity and development. Levinson proposed a theory of adult development that revolves around a person's (43) _____ _____, or overall pattern of a person's priorities and relationships with other people and with society. According to this theory, young adults are launching careers and exploring various career options. Middle-aged adults face a (44) _____ _____ and question their entire life structure. (What is the support for Levinson's theory and where is the theory weak?)

Older adults typically retire sometime in their 60's. One researcher has proposed that adjustment to retirement progresses through four phases. In the first, the (45) _____ phase, adults begin to plan for their upcoming retirement. In the
(46) _____ phase, they embrace retirement and enjoy the freedom it provides. In the (47) _____ phase, the novelty of retirement wears off, which may lead to the (48) _____ phase, where adults restructure their lifestyle. In general, retirement does not have negative effects on adult development, although it may reduce the person's income.

More and more women are working and are entering traditionally male-dominated careers. However, most women are still working in traditionally female-dominated jobs, which pay less than male-dominated jobs. Women may experience sex (49) _____ and
(50) _____ _____ because of the demands of both work and family. Related to this, women may also experience
(51) _____ _____ because of too much to do in too little time.

Work is important to adult development, just as play is important to child development. The (52) _____ _____ of a job, or extent to which the job provides opportunities for using one's mind and making independent decisions, is related to intellectual flexibility. Adults spend less time engaged in leisure activities than

children and adolescents because of work and family responsibilities.
Also, adults may be influenced by the (53) _____
_____ _____, a philosophy that makes people
suspect that leisure time contributes to moral weakness while work leads
to moral strength.

The text presents two general theories about successful aging. One
is the (54) _____ theory that suggests that adults will be
satisfied with their lives if they can continue to maintain their
preexisting activity levels. The other theory of aging holds that
successful aging requires (55) _____ of the aging individual
from society and vice versa. (Does one of these theories more
accurately portray successful aging?)

REVIEW OF KEY TERMS AND CONCEPTS

Below is a list of terms and concepts from this chapter. Match each one
with its appropriate definition. You might also want to try writing
definitions in your own words and then checking your definitions with
those here in the Study Guide or in the text.

ability tracking   play
activity theory   prosocial behavior
computer-assisted instruction   Protestant Work Ethic
cooperative learning methods   Pygmalion effect
disengagement theory   role conflict
imaginary companions   role overload
leisure   substantive complexity
life structure   symbolic capacity
mainstreaming   symbolic play
mentor   work
midlife crisis

_____1. An educational technique where students are grouped
                       according to ability and taught with others of similar
                       ability.

_____2. Teaching technique where students of different races
                       or ability levels are assigned to teams and are
                       rewarded for team, not individual, performance.

_____3. An overall pattern of life that reflects a person's
                       priorities and relationships with other people and the
                       larger society.

_____4. Time that is one's own to do with what one wants.

_____5. The feeling of having too much to do, or too many
                       roles to fulfill, in the time available.

_____6. Term used to describe the finding that students perform better when they are expected to do well than when they are expected to do poorly.

_____7. The theory that successful aging involves a mutual withdrawal of the aging person and society.

_____8. Pretend play where one thing is used to represent another.

_____9. The extent to which a job provides opportunities for using one's mind and making independent judgments.

_____10. Behavior such as sharing or helping that benefits another person.

_____11. The ability to use one thing to represent another.

_____12. The theory that aging adults will find their lives satisfying to the extent that they are able to maintain their existing levels of activity.

_____13. A goal-directed activity that is aimed toward producing something useful or providing subsistence.

_____14. Instructional methods that utilize the computer.

_____15. Playmates who exist only in the imagination of a particular child.

_____16. The feeling of being pulled in different directions by competing demands of different roles.

_____17. Someone who serves as a guide or advisor and provides support for another person's development.

_____18. An activity that is enjoyable, intrinsically motivated, and has an unrealistic quality.

_____19. A philosophy about work and leisure that makes people suspect that leisure time contributes to declining moral values while work leads to moral strength.

_____20. Questioning one's own life structure, including family and career, and raising issues about the direction of one's life.

_____21. Process of integrating students with disabilities into regular classrooms.

For each of the following studies, briefly summarize the <u>main point(s)</u>
of the research and indicate why the research is important. Don't worry
about specific details that are not central to the main points, or
memorizing names of researchers. Questions you might ask yourself
include: Does the research support or refute a theory or hypothesis
presented in the text? How does it further our understanding of some
concept? Does it provide an example of a point being made in the text?
Use the text to check your understanding.

1. Csikszentmihalyi and Larson's (1984) study of adolescents'
    activities (487-488): _____

    _____

    _____

    _____

    _____

2. Steinberg (1984) and colleagues' research of the effects of work on
    adolescents (p 490): _____

    _____

    _____

    _____

    _____

3. Rosenthal and Jacobson's (1968) classic study of teachers'
    expectancies (p 482): _____

    _____

    _____

    _____

    _____

For additional practice, pull out some other research discussed in this
chapter or research discussed in class lectures and summarize the main
points of the studies.

For each multiple choice question, read all alternatives and then select the best answer.

1. In order to be considered play, an activity must
    a. be intrinsically motivated
    b. be sanctioned by society
    c. consist of well defined rules
    d. be shared with a friend

2. The capacity for symbolic play emerges
    a. at birth
    b. around 6-7 months of age
    c. around 1 year
    d. around 3 years

3. Children whose pretend play includes several actions that are linked in logical sequence show _____ in their symbolic play.
    a. decentration
    b. decontextualization
    c. integration
    d. sequentiality

4. Infants in quality day-care homes or centers
    a. are not as attached to their mothers as home-reared infants
    b. are not significantly different from home-reared infants in terms of cognitive and social development
    c. initially experience no problems but are not as intellectually advanced as home-reared infants
    d. develop more behavior problems than home-reared infants

5. Children who do not actually participate in play with others but watch others play are engaged in _____ play.
    a. solitary
    b. unoccupied
    c. parallel
    d. onlooker

6. Symbolic play
    a. can be used to assess children's level of intellectual functioning
    b. can provide children the opportunity to work through problems
    c. shows the same pattern in all children
    d. increases when children enter elementary school

7. One factor that contributes significantly to school effectiveness is
    a. a comfortable setting where the emphasis is on academics
    b. average class size
    c. level of monetary support that the school receives
    d. strict guidelines and adherence to rules

8. Research on teaching methods suggests that
   a. it is possible to identify and develop one method that will be appropriate for all students
   b. low-ability students usually benefit from having a teacher who is demanding and tries to push them to work harder and harder
   c. high-ability students often benefit from having a teacher who is demanding and an educational program that is fast paced
   d. ability of students is not related to success of teaching style

9. The teacher-expectancy effect refers to the finding that
   a. low-ability students always perform worse than high-ability students
   b. students perform better when they are expected to do well than when they are expected to do poorly
   c. students perform better when they are expected to do poorly because they want to prove themselves to those people
   d. teachers' expectancies are usually well matched with students' expectancies

10. Compared to children who do not watch much television, children who watch a lot of commercial television
    a. have more traditional stereotypes about male and female roles in our society
    b. develop more flexible views about male and female roles in our society
    c. become more passive and less aggressive
    d. are less popular with their peers

11. Compared to children who watch very little of educational programs like Sesame Street, children who watch a lot of Sesame Street programs on television
    a. are more lethargic and apathetic about school activities
    b. are rated as less socially mature since these children spent less time interacting with their peers
    c. are rated as more prepared for school
    d. are more aggressive

12. Vocational choices
    a. are stable across an individual's life span
    b. become increasingly realistic across adolescence
    c. are usually not related to one's ability
    d. are influenced very little by environmental opportunities

13. Levinson's theory of adult development focuses on
    a. the interaction of one's self with other people and society
    b. the role of stress in adult development
    c. how adult males differ from females in values and career choices
    d. how career choices are made

14. According to Levinson's theory of adult development, men
    a. typically settle into their final career choice in early adulthood
    b. follow career paths that are similar to women's paths
    c. question their career and family choices very little
    d. experience a midlife crisis and question their life structure

15. Role conflict refers to
    a. the belief that hard work pays off and relaxation promotes moral decay
    b. the feeling that one has too much to do and too little time to accomplish it
    c. the competing demands of various roles such as family and work
    d. the feelings that women experience when they are in careers traditionally held by men

16. The theory that successful aging requires a gradual withdrawal from society is
    a. Levinson's theory
    b. disengagement theory
    c. withdrawal theory
    d. activity adjustment theory

APPLICATION

Design an "ideal" day-care situation using information you have learned about the cognitive, physical, social, and emotional developments of infants and preschoolers. Also remember to take into account other factors described in this chapter that influence the impact of day care. Be sure you design appropriate activities for your day-care center, capitalizing on infants' and children's lifestyles (e.g., changes in play). Will your day-care center include television or computers? How will these be used to maximize their benefits and minimize any problems?

Before you leave this chapter, go back and take another look at the learning objectives presented at the beginning of the chapter. Rephrase each objective into a question and check to see whether you have mastered them. A good way to check your understanding of a concept is to see if you can teach it to someone else. Take turns doing this with a small group of people. Whenever you are unsure or unclear about a response, go back to the text and find out what information you are missing in order to provide a clear and complete response.

Summary and Guided Review (Fill-in the blank)

1. play
2. work
3. leisure
4. symbolic
5. symbolic capacity
6. decentration
7. decontextualization
8. integration
9. quality
10. attached
11. social
12. unoccupied
13. solitary
14. onlooker
15. parallel
16. associative
17. cooperative
18. imaginary companions
19. rules
20. concrete-operational
21. physical
22. intellectual
23. social
24. cognitively
25. social
26. academic achievement
27. ability tracking
28. academics
29. teacher expectancies
30. desegregate
31. mainstreaming
32. cooperative learning
33. violence
34. aggressive
35. desensitizes
36. stereotypes
37. prosocial
38. computer-assisted
39. gender appropriate
40. leisure
41. fantasy
42. tentative
43. life structure
44. midlife crisis
45. preretirement
46. honeymoon
47. disenchantment
48. reorientation
49. discrimination
50. role conflict
51. role overload
52. substantive complexity
53. Protestant Work Ethic
54. activity
55. disengagement

Key Terms

1. ability tracking
2. cooperative learning methods
3. life structure
4. leisure
5. role overload
6. Pygmalion effect
7. disengagement theory
8. symbolic play
9. substantive complexity
10. prosocial behavior
11. symbolic capacity
12. activity theory
13. work
14. computer-assisted instruction
15. imaginary companions
16. role conflict
17. mentor
18. play
19. Protestant Work Ethic
20. midlife crisis
21. mainstreaming

<u>Self Test</u>

1.	A	9.	B
2.	C	10.	A
3.	C	11.	C
4.	B	12.	B
5.	D	13.	A
6.	B	14.	D
7.	A	15.	C
8.	C	16.	B

Chapter Sixteen
Psychological Disorders Throughout
the Life Span

<u>*LEARNING OBJECTIVES*</u>

After reading and studying the material in this chapter, you should be able to do the following:

1. Describe the criteria used for diagnosing psychological disorders.

2. Define developmental psychopathology and provide examples of the questions or issues studied by developmental psychopathologists.

3. Discuss infantile autism, including characteristics, causes, treatment, and prognosis.

4. Discuss depression-like conditions occurring during infancy and how these conditions are similar to or different from depression in adults.

5. Distinguish between undercontrolled and overcontrolled disorders.

6. Discuss hyperactivity, including symptoms, possible causes, treatment, and long-term prognosis.

7. Describe depression during childhood and indicate how it is similar to or different from depression during adulthood.

8. Discuss childhood problems in relation to the nature-nurture issue and the continuity-discontinuity issue.

9. Discuss whether psychological problems are more prevalent during adolescence than other periods of the life span.

10. Describe characteristics and causes of eating disorders.

11. Discuss reasons for juvenile delinquency and adolescent alcohol and drug use, noting factors that increase the likelihood of a problem in one of these areas.

12. Discuss the course and causes of depression and suicidal behavior during adolescence.

13. Discuss stress during adulthood, including causes, age differences, coping capacities, and age and gender differences in failing to cope.

14. Discuss depression during adulthood, including age and gender differences, causes, and how different coping strategies and attribution styles are related to depression.

15. Describe the various types of dementia, distinguishing between irreversible and reversible types.

16. Discuss treatments for psychological disorders across the life span.

SUMMARY AND GUIDED REVIEW

The following summary provides an overview of the main points contained in this chapter of the text. Fill-in the blanks with terms that appropriately complete the sentence. Although blank spaces are provided, you may want to write your answers on a separate piece of paper, which will make it easier to compare your answers to the correct answers provided at the end of this chapter.

Scattered throughout the summary are questions in parentheses. These are meant to encourage you to think actively as you are reading and connect this summary to the more detailed information provided in the text. You can answer these questions as you are filling in the blanks or you can fill-in all the blanks, then go back and reread the entire summary, addressing the questions in order to provide more depth of understanding.

There are three general ways to define abnormal behavior. The first is in terms of (1) _____ _____, or whether a person's behavior falls outside the normal range of behavior. The second classification uses (2) _____, or the extent to which a behavior interferes with personal and social adaptation. The third classification is whether or not a behavior causes (3) _____ _____. When applying any one of these classifications, there are other factors to consider in defining abnormal behavior. The expectations about how to act in a particular context, or the (4) _____ _____, must be considered, along with societal expectations about what behaviors are appropriate at various ages, or (5) _____ _____. More specific diagnostic criteria have been described by the American Psychiatric Association in DSM-III-R (Diagnostic and Statistical Manual of Mental Disorders. This manual specifies symptoms and behaviors associated with all psychological disorders. For example, DSM-III-R defines (6) _____ _____ as at least one episode of feeling profoundly depressed, sad, and hopeless, and/or losing interest in and the ability to derive pleasure from almost all activities. This definition excludes depression that is "normal," such as depression following the loss of a loved one. The study of the origins and course of abnormal behavior across the life span is called (7) _____ _____ and these psychologists are interested in the same issues that concern developmental psychologists.

A disorder beginning in infancy that is characterized by deviant social development, deviant language and communication skills, and repetitive, stereotyped behavior is (8) _____ _____.

The language of autistic children may include (9) _____, where a child repeats or echoes sounds or words produced by someone else. At least half of the children who have autism are also (10) _____ _____. Autism appears to have both genetic and environmental causes, although no specific causes have yet been pinpointed. Long-term prognosis for autistic children is generally (11) _____ and treatment focuses on (12) _____ training.

A depression-like state seen in infants who have lost an attachment figure is called (13) _____ depression. (What are the overt signs associated with this condition?) Another related condition is (14) _____ _____ _____, where infants who are raised in a stressful situation fail to grow normally and become underweight for their age. If removed from the stressful situation, infants recover their weight very quickly. Emotional trauma can reduce the production of (15) _____ _____ by the pituitary gland in individuals of all ages. (What effects do depressed parents have on their infants?)

Children who have (16) _____ disorders externalize their problems in ways that disturb other people and conflict with societal expectations. Children who have (17) _____ disorders internalize their problems. In general, (18) _____ are more likely to show undercontrolled disorders and (19) _____ are more likely to show overcontrolled disorders.

Children who are inattentive, impulsive, and show hyperactivity have (20) _____-_____ _____ disorder. Although all young children show these behaviors, children who are diagnosed with the disorder show them to a marked degree. Behaviors associated with hyperactivity vary with age. (Can you describe behaviors that might signal hyperactivity in infants and children of different ages?) Many hyperactive children are treated with Ritalin, a (21) _____ drug that reduces (for reasons not fully understood) hyperactive behaviors, and with (22) _____-_____ treatments. (What is the long-term prognosis for hyperactive children?)

It is now recognized that children can become depressed. Initially, some researchers believed that children showed (23) _____ _____ by expressing depression with symptoms not generally associated with depression in adults. However, it is apparent that children can be diagnosed with the same criteria that are used with adults. This does not mean that children and adults display depression with exactly the same behaviors. Preschool children are more likely to display the (24) _____ and (25) _____ symptoms than the (26) _____ symptoms that adults and older children will display. Many clinically depressed children continue to experience some episodes of depression later in childhood, adolescence, or adulthood.

Many people believe that the (27) _____ has a powerful effect on development, including development of abnormal behavior. There is a relationship between type of environment and whether a child has a disorder. However, this does not mean that the environment caused the disorder. It is possible that the disorder is (28) _____ based, or, because of the (29) _____ influences within families, the child's disorder may have helped create a disordered environment. Early childhood problems are more likely to (30) _____ than persist into adulthood. However, not all disorders disappear--Many adults who have disorders had problems as children.

Adolescence has been characterized as a period of (31) _____ _____ _____. While this might not be an accurate portrayal of this period, adolescents do seem to be more vulnerable to some forms of psychological disorders. Eating disorders are more often associated with adolescence than with other periods and are much more common among girls than boys. Refusal to maintain weight that is at least 85% of one's expected weight is termed (32) _____ _____. Binging and purging is associated with (33) _____ _____. Our society clearly influences eating disorders with its emphasis on thinness. In addition, some girls appear to have a genetic predisposition to develop an eating disorder, possibly because genes influence (34) _____. On top of this, girls who develop eating disorders typically experience disturbed (35) _____ _____.

Another problem associated with adolescence is (36) _____ _____, or lawbreaking by a minor. (37) _____ _____ are actions that are unlawful only if performed by a minor. Delinquency peaks around age 15 or 16, and is more common among boys than girls. (Why do adolescents engage in delinquent behavior?) Many adolescents have used, or currently use, drugs and alcohol. Three general factors have been found to distinguish problem drinkers from other adolescents. One factor is personal qualities, including value placed on (38) _____ _____ and independence. (How does the emphasis on these differ for problem drinkers and other adolescents?) Secondly, problem drinkers perceive their (39) _____ _____ differently. (How do their perceptions differ?) Third, problem drinkers are more likely to have other problem behaviors.

Adolescents who are depressed display many of the same cognitive symptoms that depressed adults display. They may, however, also show behaviors that would not normally be associated with depression in adults. The rate of (40) _____ has increased, making this the third leading cause of death among adolescents. Suicidal thoughts are common during adolescence. Adolescents are more likely than adults to attempt suicide, but are less likely to succeed at killing themselves.

Most adults must cope with some degree of (41) _____ in

211

their lives. Stress depends on one's perception of a situation. What is stressful for one person, may not be stressful for another person. In addition, people need to cope with (42) _____ _____, or everyday annoyances. Young adults seem to experience the greatest number of life changes and associated stress, while middle-aged and older adults gradually experience fewer and fewer stressful events. Ability to (43) _____ with stress does not change significantly across the life span.

A survey of prevalence of affective disorders and alcohol abuse showed that these were more common among young adults than middle-aged or older adults. In addition, women were more likely to report affective disorders, while men were more likely to report alcohol abuse. One of five adults will experience an affective disorder, such as depression, at some point in their lives. Contrary to a popular belief, elderly adults are not more depressed than younger adults. This may be because depression is often undiagnosed in the elderly. (Why might this be the case?) The (44) _____/_____ model suggests that psychopathology results from the interaction of a predisposition to a disorder and the experience of stressful events. Applying this to depression, a person might become depressed if they had a vulnerability for depression and if they experienced stress.   Explaining depression also requires consideration of an individual's (45) _____ _____, which includes personality and coping strategies. People who cope effectively typically have healthy (46) _____ styles, or ways of explaining events in their lives. Individuals who perceive no relationship between their actions and the consequences of a situation may develop the unhealthy attribution style of (47) _____ _____. Individuals who are vulnerable to depression tend to attribute (48) _____ life events to themselves. People who are self-confidant and easy-going often use (49) _____-_____ coping strategies, while people who are vulnerable to depression tend to use (50) _____ coping strategies. (Can you explain each of these coping strategies?) In addition to personal resources and stressful life events, a person's social environment must be considered to understand why some individuals develop depression.

Many people fear becoming senile as they get older. Senility, or (51) _____, is not a normal part of aging. It refers to progressive deterioration of intellectual functioning and personality. One form of dementia is (52) _____ disease, which is progressive and irreversible deterioration of neurons, resulting in increasingly impaired mental functioning. Some forms of Alzheimer's disease appear to have a (53) _____ basis. This is supported by the fact that this disorder often recurs in families, and by the finding that individuals with Down Syndrome, a chromosomal disorder, are very likely to develop Alzheimer's disease. (What are some other explanations for Alzheimer's disease?) Another irreversible dementia is (54) _____-_____, which results from cardiovascular problems such as strokes. Some forms of dementia are reversible. (What factors might cause a reversible dementia?)

Treating children and adolescents for disorders is different from treating adults. Adults can initiate their treatment, while children rarely do. Treatment for children is also dependent on parental cooperation. Treatment is also going to differ since children and adults function at different cognitive and emotional levels. Treatment for children is as successful as treatment for adults, and (55) _____ therapies seem to work better for children than "talking" therapies. Treating elderly adults is also challenging, in part because elderly adults are less likely than younger adults to seek treatment. When they do get treatment, elderly adults are responsive and can improve.

REVIEW OF KEY TERMS AND CONCEPTS

Below is a list of terms and concepts from this chapter. Match each one with its appropriate definition. You might also want to try writing definitions in your own words and then checking your definitions with those here in the Study Guide or in the text.

active-behavioral coping strategies
age norm
Alzheimer's disease
anaclitic depression
anorexia nervosa
attention-deficit hyperactivity disorder
avoidance coping strategies
bulimia nervosa
daily hassles
delirium
dementia
developmental psychopathology
diathesis/stress model

echolalia
failure to thrive
infantile autism
juvenile delinquency
learned helplessness
major depression
masked depression
multi-infarct dementia
overcontrolled disorders
social norm
status offense
stress
undercontrolled disorders

_____1. A depression-like state during infancy associated with the loss of an attachment figure.

_____2. Internalizing problems that are disruptive to the individual child and include anxiety disorders, phobias, and severe shyness.

_____3. A state that occurs when we perceive events to tax our coping capacities and threaten our well-being.

_____4. A coping strategy of escaping the problem or failing to take constructive action.

_____5. The study of the origins and course of maladaptive behavior.

_____ 6. An action that is unlawful only if one is a minor.

_____ 7. A group of disorders characterized by progressive deterioration of intellectual functioning and personality.

_____ 8. A condition where infants who are neglected, abused, or otherwise stressed fail to grow normally and become underweight for their age.

_____ 9. Model that proposes that psychopathology results from the interaction of a predisposition to a disorder and the experience of stressful events.

_____ 10. Societal expectation about what behavior is appropriate or normal at various ages.

_____ 11. Progressive and irreversible deterioration of neurons and increasingly impaired mental functioning.

_____ 12. Chronic strains or everyday annoyances of varying magnitude.

_____ 13. Dementia that results from cardiovascular problems such as strokes.

_____ 14. Externalizing problems where children act in ways that disturb other people and conflict with societal expectations.

_____ 15. Expectation about how to behave that exists in a culture or subculture.

_____ 16. An eating disorder characterized by a refusal to maintain a weight that is at least 85% of the expected weight for one's height and age.

_____ 17. A form of language where a child echoes or repeats sounds or words made by someone else.

_____ 18. A condition that results when there is no perceived relationship between one's actions and the outcomes or consequences in a situation.

_____ 19. Depression that is expressed indirectly by symptoms other than those directly associated with depression.

_____ 20. Feeling profoundly depressed, sad, or hopeless, and/or losing interest in activities and not being able to derive pleasure from activities.

_____21. Lawbreaking by a minor.

_____22. A disorder involving inattention, impulsivity, and hyperactivity.

_____23. A reversible condition characterized by periods of disorientation and confusion alternating with periods of coherence.

_____24. An eating disorder characterized by repeated episodes of binging and purging.

_____25. A coping strategy of taking positive action to work out problems.

_____26. A disorder beginning in infancy or early childhood that is characterized by deviant social development, deviant language and communication skills, and repetitive, stereotyped behavior.

RESEARCH SUMMARY AND REVIEW

For each of the following studies, briefly summarize the main point(s) of the research and indicate why the research is important. Don't worry about specific details that are not central to the main points, or memorizing names of researchers. Questions you might ask yourself include: Does the research support or refute a theory or hypothesis presented in the text? How does it further our understanding of some concept? Does it provide an example of a point being made in the text? Use the text to check your understanding.

1. Jessor (1987) and colleagues' research on adolescent drinking (p 522-523): _____

_____

_____

_____

_____

2. Lovaas' (1987) treatment of autism (p 532-533): _____

_____

_____

_____

_____

3. Weisz and colleagues' (1987) review of research on the effectiveness of therapy (p 532): _____

_____

_____

_____

_____

For additional practice, pull out some other research discussed in this chapter or research discussed in class lectures and summarize the main points of the studies.

SELF TEST

For each multiple choice question, read all alternatives and then select the best answer.

1. Age norms are defined as
    a. the ages when it is appropriate to act in a deviant manner
    b. societal expectations about what behavior is appropriate at different ages
    c. societal expectations about how to behave in different contexts
    d. the average ages when people are most susceptible to various disorders

2. Which of the following persons is most likely to be diagnosed as having a psychological disorder?
    a. a child who cannot fall asleep at night because he is worried about goblins under the bed
    b. a woman who can no longer go to work because she is so upset about her appearance
    c. a man who quits his job because it is no longer challenging
    d. a woman who is sobbing because her husband has recently died

3. A disorder that begins in infancy and is characterized by deviant social development and communication skills is
    a. an overcontrolled disorder
    b. infantile dementia
    c. infantile autism
    d. attention-deficit disorder

4. Which of the following is an example of echolalia?
    a. using "you" to refer to one's self
    b. hearing the echo of a phrase after someone has said something
    c. substituting one phrase for another
    d. repeating something that has just been said

5. Autistic children
    a. typically outgrow the disorder as they get older
    b. have a number of physical problems in addition to their deficits
        in social and communication skills
    c. are often mentally retarded
    d. show marked improvement after they enter elementary school

6. Children who act in ways that conflict with rules and other people
    are said to have an
    a. undercontrolled disorder
    b. overcontrolled disorder
    c. internalizing problem
    d. autism

7. Hyperactivity
    a. is a disorder that is diagnosed on the basis of too much motor
        activity
    b. is primarily an attention deficit
    c. is an overcontrolled disorder
    d. is associated with mental retardation

8. Depression
    a. is displayed in similar ways across the life span
    b. is not present until children are old enough to verbally express
        their feelings
    c. is an undercontrolled disorder
    d. can be present throughout the life span but is expressed in
        different behaviors

9. Problems that exist in early childhood
    a. disappear when children enter elementary school
    b. are nonexistent by the time children leave school
    c. are more likely to disappear than persist, although some do
        persist
    d. typically are still present later in life

10. Eating disorders such as anorexia and bulimia
    a. are caused by the body's inability to properly metabolize food
    b. develop, in part, as a result of a genetic predisposition
        interacting with stress and social pressure
    c. are easily controlled with a properly managed diet
    d. are present during adolescence and then disappear

11. Adolescents who engage in delinquent behavior
    a. are seriously disturbed and different from the average
        adolescent
    b. come from low-income, disadvantaged backgrounds
    c. continue to do so once they enter adulthood
    d. often do so to gain the attention and approval of peers

12. Adolescent problem drinkers
    a. are indistinguishable from other adolescents
    b. place less value on academic achievement and more value on independence than other adolescents
    c. typically have just this one area where they have a problem
    d. are generally intolerant of deviant behavior in others

13. With respect to suicide,
    a. adolescents are more likely to attempt suicide than adults but less likely to succeed
    b. adolescents successfully commit suicide at a higher rate than any other age group
    c. males and females are equally likely to end up killing themselves
    d. elderly adults commit suicide at a rate much lower than that of adolescents and younger adults

14. _____ is the term for what can occur when an individual perceives no relationship between one's actions and the consequences in a situation.
    a. learned helplessness
    b. denial
    c. failure to thrive
    d. juvenile delinquency

15. Depression-prone individuals are likely to use a(n) _____ coping strategy.
    a. diathesis/stress
    b. active-behavioral
    c. avoidance
    d. cognitive-behavioral

16. One difference between Alzheimer's disease and delirium is that
    a. Alzheimer's disease affects mental functioning and delirium does not.
    b. Patients with Alzheimer's disease have periods of lucidity, while those with delirium do not.
    c. Alzheimer's disease occurs only in old age, while delirium occurs only at younger ages.
    d. Alzheimer's disease is irreversible, while delirium is reversible.

APPLICATION

Suppose you were an ardent follower of Freud, Piaget, Erikson, or social learning theory. How would you, as a "true believer," explain the development of psychological disorders from the perspective of each of these theories? If necessary, go back and consult earlier chapters to gather information about the theorists that will help you explain or interpret psychological disorders. You might want to pick a specific disorder and systematically apply each theory to this disorder.

Before you leave this chapter, go back and take another look at the
learning objectives presented at the beginning of the chapter. Rephrase
each objective into a question and check to see whether you have
mastered them. A good way to check your understanding of a concept is
to see if you can teach it to someone else. Take turns doing this with
a small group of people. Whenever you are unsure or unclear about a
response, go back to the text and find out what information you are
missing in order to provide a clear and complete response.

ANSWERS

Summary and Guided Review (Fill-in the blank)

1. statistical deviance
2. maladaptiveness
3. personal distress
4. social norms
5. age norms
6. major depression
7. developmental psychopathology
8. infantile autism
9. echolalia
10. mentally retarded
11. poor
12. behavioral
13. anaclitic
14. failure to thrive
15. growth hormone
16. undercontrolled
17. overcontrolled
18. boys
19. girls
20. attention-deficit hyperactivity
21. stimulant
22. cognitive-behavioral
23. masked depression
24. behavioral
25. somatic
26. cognitive
27. environment
28. genetically

29. reciprocal
30. disappear
31. storm and stress
32. anorexia nervosa
33. bulimia nervosa
34. personality
35. family relationships
36. juvenile delinquency
37. status offenses
38. academic achievement
39. social environment
40. suicide
41. stress
42. daily hassles
43. cope
44. diathesis/stress
45. personal resources
46. attribution styles
47. learned helplessness
48. negative
49. active-behavioral
50. avoidance
51. dementia
52. Alzheimer's
53. genetic
54. multi-infarct
55. behavioral

Key Terms

1. anaclitic depression
2. overcontrolled disorders
3. stress
4. avoidance coping strategy
5. developmental psychopathology
6. status offenses
7. dementia
8. failure to thrive
9. diathesis/stress model
10. age norm
11. Alzheimer's disease
12. daily hassles
13. multi-infarct dementia
14. undercontrolled disorders
15. social norm
16. anorexia nervosa
17. echolalia
18. learned helplessness
19. masked depression
20. major depression
21. juvenile delinquency
22. attention-deficit hyperactivity disorder
23. delirium
24. bulimia nervosa
25. active-behavioral coping strategies
26. infantile autism

Self Test

1.	B	9.	C
2.	B	10.	B
3.	C	11.	D
4.	D	12.	B
5.	C	13.	A
6.	A	14.	A
7.	B	15.	C
8.	D	16.	D

Chapter Seventeen
The Final Challenge: Death and Dying

After reading and studying the material in this chapter, you should be able to do the following:

1. Discuss various definitions of biological death and how they lend themselves to different interpretations.

2. Explain euthanasia.

3. Discuss factors that influence life expectancy.

4. Differentiate between programmed theories of aging and damage theories of aging and describe specific examples of each type of theory.

5. Describe Kubler-Ross's stages of dying and evaluate the validity and usefulness of the stages.

6. Describe bereavement, grief, and mourning.

7. Describe the Parkes-Bowlby model of grieving.

8. Discuss the infant's awareness of separation and death.

9. Explain what a "mature" understanding of death consists of in our society and how children's conception of death compares to this mature understanding.

10. Describe factors that might influence a child's understanding of death.

11. Describe dying children's understanding of death and their ability to cope with the prospect of their own death.

12. Discuss children's experience of grief.

13. Discuss death anxiety, including its relationship to age.

14. Describe how family members react and cope with the loss of a spouse, a child, and a parent.

15. Discuss factors that contribute to, or influence, effective and ineffective coping with grief.

16. Discuss what can be done for those who are dying and for those who are bereaved to better understand and face the reality of death.

The following summary provides an overview of the main points contained in this chapter of the text. Fill-in the blanks with terms that appropriately complete the sentence. Although blank spaces are provided, you may want to write your answers on a separate piece of paper, which will make it easier to compare your answers to the correct answers provided at the end of this chapter.

Scattered throughout the summary are questions in parentheses. These are meant to encourage you to think actively as you are reading and connect this summary to the more detailed information provided in the text. You can answer these questions as you are filling in the blanks or you can fill-in all the blanks, then go back and reread the entire summary, addressing the questions in order to provide more depth of understanding.

Biological death is currently viewed as a (1) _____ rather than a single event. The Harvard definition of biological death is that of (2) _____ _____ death. This means an irreversible loss of functioning in the entire brain. To be judged dead by this definition, a person must be totally unresponsive to (3) _____; fail to move for (4) _____ _____ and fail to breathe for (5) _____ minutes after disconnection from life support systems; show no (6) _____; and show no electrical activity in the (7) _____ of the brain. (Why is there debate over when someone is actually dead?)

Hastening someone's death when that person is terminally ill is referred to as (8) _____. Deliberately doing something to bring about a person's death is (9) _____ euthanasia and allowing a person to die by not doing anything is (10) _____ euthanasia. Some people state their desire to not have any extraordinary medical procedures applied in the event that they are hopelessly ill in a document called a (11) _____ _____.

(12) _____ _____, or the average number of years that a person is expected to live, is about 75 years in the United States. This represents a substantial increase over expectancies in earlier centuries. Life expectancies have increased because fewer people are dying young and adults are living longer as a result of better health and medical technology. The leading causes of death in the United States change across the life span. Infants typically die of complications surrounding birth or from congenital abnormalities. Children typically die from (13) _____. Adolescents and young adults are susceptible to (14) _____ deaths while middle-aged adults are more likely to die from (15) _____ diseases.

Theories of aging fall into two main categories. (16) _____ theories of aging focus on the genetic control of

222

aging while (17) _____ theories of aging focus on the
accumulative effects of damage to cells and organs over time. All
species have a (18) _____ life span, or ceiling on the number
of years that any member of that species can live. This figure varies
across species, suggesting that species-specific genes may control how
long one lives. The (19) _____ _____ refers to
the finding that human cells can only divide a certain number of times,
which may limit maximum life span. (20) _____ theories of
aging suggest that genes control aging by triggering
(21) _____ changes that bring about death. The
(22) _____ _____ theory of aging proposes that the
body is less able to defend itself against potentially life-threatening
agents as we age. As the immune system ages, it is more likely to
produce (23) _____ _____, where it produces
antibodies that attack and kill normal body cells.

The (24) _____ _____ theory, a damage theory
of aging, proposes that DNA is damaged over the years and the body's
capacity to repair this damage slows down. Another damage theory of
aging is the (25) _____-_____ theory, which holds
that molecules of the protein collagen become interlinked over time
resulting in visible signs of aging such as wrinkled skin and stiff
joints. A third damage theory of aging focuses on (26) _____
_____, which are molecules that are chemically unstable and
react with other molecules to produce substances that damage normal
cells.

Kubler-Ross proposed that people who are dying progress through a
common sequence of five stages. In the first stage, (27) _____
and (28) _____, a person responds to the news that he or she
is dying by refusing to believe that it is true, a common defense
mechanism to keep anxiety-provoking thoughts out of conscious
awareness. In the second stage, the dying person responds with
(29) _____ or feelings of rage. In the third stage, the
person tries to (30) _____ to gain more time and be given a
second chance. When it becomes apparent that death is really going to
occur, the dying person experiences (31) _____ and if the
person can work through the earlier responses to death, he or she may
come to the final stage, which is (32) _____ of death.
Throughout all the stages, Kubler-Ross believed that people retained a
sense of (33) _____ regarding their death. A major problem
with Kubler-Ross's characterization of death is that dying people really
do not experience these reactions in a stage-like fashion. Shneidman
suggests that dying patients alternate between denial and
(34) _____, rather than moving systematically from one
reaction to another. Another problem with Kubler-Ross's theory is that
it does not account for how the course of an illness affects one's
perceptions. The perceived shape and direction of the path from life to
death is called the (35) _____ _____. A person on
a (36) _____ trajectory slowly gets worse over time, while a
person on an (37) _____ trajectory goes through a series of
ups and downs before dying. A third problem with Kubler-Ross's theory

is that it ignores how a person's (38) _____ affects their
response to dying. (Can you explain how this factor can impact one's
experience of dying?)

     The term (39) _____ is used to refer to a state of loss,
while (40) _____ refers to the emotional response to loss.
Culturally defined ways of displaying reactions to loss are referred to
as (41) _____. Many people experience (42) _____
_____ prior to the actual death of a loved one, unless the
death is quite sudden. Parkes and Bowlby characterize grieving as a
reaction to (43) _____ from a loved one that progresses
through several overlapping phases. The first is (44) _____,
which occurs in the first hours and days following a death. The second
phase is (45) _____, which is most intense about 5 to 14 days
after the death, and is accompanied by restlessness and preoccupation
with thoughts of the loved one. Anger and guilt are also common
reactions during this phase. The third phase (46) is _____
and (47) _____ when the person realizes that the loved one is
gone for always. Finally, in the fourth phase of (48) _____,
a person begins to move on with life by forming new relationships and
getting involved in new activities.

     Infants experience death of a loved one as that person's
(49) _____ from their life, but do not understand death as
the ending of life. Infants separated from their attachment figures
show reactions that are similar to the reactions of bereaved adults.

     Children are curious about death and begin to show some
understanding of death, but have not reached a "mature" understanding.
A mature understanding of death requires understanding that death is:
1) the (50) _____ of life; 2) (51) _____, or
cannot be undone; 3) happens to everyone, or is (52) _____;
and 4) caused by internal or biological factors. Preschool-aged
children tend to think dead people retain some of their living
capabilities and that death is reversible. Between the ages of 5 and 7,
children begin to realize that death involves cessation of life, it is
irreversible, and it is universal. It takes children a few more years,
however, to fully understand that death is caused by biological factors.
Children's understanding of death is affected by their level of
(53) _____ development and by their life experiences. (What
life experiences affect understanding of death?) Terminally ill
children are typically aware that they are dying and experience a
variety of emotions such as anger and depression. (How do terminally
ill children of different ages respond to their situation?) Children
who lose a loved one or a pet grieve, but express their grief
differently than adults do. They may display a variety of problems,
including problems with sleeping, eating, and bedwetting. Because
children are very dependent on their parents, they are particularly
vulnerable to long-term problems following the loss of a parent.

     Adolescents have developed a (54) _____ understanding of
death and may spend time contemplating death and its meaning.

Adolescents grieve similarly to adults. Even adolescents and adults who
fully understand death experience (55) _____ _____,
or concern about death and dying. (What factors influence the degree of
death anxiety that a person experiences?)

Adults who lose a spouse often experience other changes as well and
are at greater risk for illness and physical symptoms. (What effect do
age and gender have on how someone fares following the death of a
spouse?) The loss of a child seems particularly difficult to cope with,
in part because we do not expect children to die before their parents.
The (56) _____ of the child does not really affect the
intensity of a parent's grief. For an adult, the death of a parent may
not be as disruptive as the loss of a spouse or child, because in some
ways, it is expected.

Some people cope more effectively with the loss of a loved one than
others. There are three forms of (57) _____ grief. In one,
people who experience (58) _____ grief spend longer grieving
the loss than is typical. People who show (59) _____ grief
exaggerate some reactions to loss and hardly show other reactions. The
third form of pathological grief is showing an absence or delay of
grief. Several factors affect how capable a person is of coping with
loss. Bowlby argues that early (60) _____ relationships
impact on our later ability to cope with grief. (Can you describe the
relationship between early experience and later coping ability?)
Another factor is how close the bereaved person was to the deceased.
Reactions to death are also affected by the suddenness or unexpectedness
of the death. (61) _____ deaths seem to be somewhat harder
to cope with than deaths that are expected. The (62) _____
of death also influences how a person responds to the loss. Grief at
any age can be positively affected by the presence of
(63) _____ _____. Social support systems for
people who are dying include the (64) _____, a program with a
caring philosophy rather than a curing or prolonging philosophy.

REVIEW OF KEY TERMS AND CONCEPTS

Below is a list of terms and concepts from this chapter. Match each one
with its appropriate definition. You might also want to try writing
definitions in your own words and then checking your definitions with
those here in the Study Guide or in the text.

anticipatory grief   free radicals
autoimmune reactions   grief
bereavement   Hayflick limit
cross-linkage theory   hospice
damage theories of aging   immune system theory
death anxiety   life expectancy
denial   Living Will
DNA repair theory   maximum life span
dying trajectory   mourning

endocrine theory   programmed theories of aging
euthanasia   total brain death

_____1. The limited number of times that a human cell can
                     divide.

_____2. A defense mechanism where anxiety-producing thoughts
                     are kept out of conscious awareness.

_____3. A theory of aging that focuses on age-related changes
                     in the body's ability to defend itself against life-
                     threatening agents.

_____4. The act of killing or allowing a person who is
                     terminally ill to die.

_____5. The emotional response to loss.

_____6. A program that supports dying persons and their
                     families through a caring philosophy.

_____7. Theories of aging that focus on genetic control of
                     aging.

_____8. A theory of aging that proposes that molecules of the
                     protein collagen become intertwined resulting in
                     physical changes associated with aging.

_____9. An irreversible loss of functioning in the entire
                     brain.

_____10. Concern about death and dying.

_____11. The perceived shape and duration of the path that an
                     individual follows from life to death.

_____12. A theory of aging that proposes that DNA is damaged
                     over the years and the body's capacity to repair this
                     damage slows down.

_____13. A ceiling on the number of years that anyone lives.

_____14. Culturally prescribed ways of displaying one's
                     reaction to death.

_____15. Molecules with an extra electron that react with other
                     molecules to produce substances that damage normal
                     cells.

_____16. Theories of aging that propose that damage to cells and organs accumulates over time and eventually causes a person's death.

_____17. The average length of time a person can expect to live.

_____18. The tendency of the immune system to produce antibodies that attack and kill normal body cells as if they were foreign cells.

_____19. A document in which a person indicates that he or she does not want extraordinary medical procedures used to extend life when he or she is hopelessly ill.

_____20. Grieving that begins before a death occurs in anticipation of what will happen.

_____21. A theory of aging that proposes that genes program hormonal changes that bring about death.

_____22. A state of loss.

RESEARCH SUMMARY AND REVIEW

For each of the following studies, briefly summarize the main point(s) of the research and indicate why the research is important. Don't worry about specific details that are not central to the main points, or memorizing names of researchers. Questions you might ask yourself include: Does the research support or refute a theory or hypothesis presented in the text? How does it further our understanding of some concept? Does it provide an example of a point being made in the text? Use the text to check your understanding.

1. Feifel and Branscomb's (1973) research on death anxiety (p 558):

_____

_____

_____

_____

2. Kalish and Reynolds' (1977) surveys about what concerns people most about dying (P 558): _____

_____

_____

_____

_____

3. Lieberman and Videka-Sherman's (1986) evaluation of the THEOS program (p 565): _____

_____

_____

_____

_____

For additional practice, pull out some other research discussed in this chapter or research discussed in class lectures and summarize the main points of the studies.

SELF TEST _____

For each multiple choice question, read all alternatives and then select the best answer.

1. The Harvard definition of biological death is
    a. the point at which the heart stops beating
    b. irreversible loss of functioning in the cerebral cortex
    c. irreversible loss of functioning in the entire brain
    d. failure to breathe without life support systems

2. The average length of time that a person can expect to live is termed
    a. life span
    b. life expectancy
    c. age norm
    d. maximum life span

3. The leading cause of death in childhood is _____ and in middle age, the leading cause of death is _____.
    a. congenital abnormalities; chronic diseases
    b. accidents; suicides
    c. hereditary defects; violent acts such as homicides
    d. accidents; chronic diseases

4. The Hayflick limit is
    a. the number of times that a gene can "turn on" or "turn off" to bring about maturational changes
    b. the ceiling on the number of years that anyone lives
    c. the speed with which the body can repair damaged cells
    d. the limited number times that a human cell can divide

228

5. The theory of aging that holds that genes program hormonal changes that bring about death is the
   a. endocrine theory
   b. immune system theory
   c. cross-linkage theory
   d. DNA repair theory

6. Theories that focus on the genetic control of aging are called _____ theories and those that focus on gradual deterioration of cells are called _____ theories
   a. genetic; environmental
   b. programmed; damage
   c. damage; programmed
   d. biological; psychological

7. According to Kubler-Ross's stages of dying, a person who expresses resentment and criticizes everyone is in the stage of
   a. denial and isolation
   b. anger
   c. bargaining
   d. depression

8. According to Kubler-Ross's stages of dying, a dying person who agrees to stop smoking and drinking in return for a little more time is in the stage of
   a. denial and isolation
   b. anger
   c. bargaining
   d. depression

9. One of the biggest problems with Kubler-Ross's stages of dying is that
   a. dying is not really stage-like
   b. patients go through the stages in order but at different rates
   c. they are focused on a person's cognitive understanding of death rather than the person's affective response
   d. they describe a person's response to death of a spouse or parent but not the response to one's own impending death

10. The emotional response to death is referred to as
    a. bereavement
    b. grief
    c. mourning
    d. depression

11. In the first few days following the death of a loved one, the bereaved person
    a. is usually unable to function
    b. experiences anticipatory grief
    c. experiences the worst despair of the mourning process
    d. is typically in a state of shock and numbness

12. Preschool-aged children are likely to believe that
    a. death is inevitable and will happen to everyone eventually
    b. dead people still experience sensations and perceptions, just not as intensely as live people
    c. people die because of changes in internal bodily functioning
    d. death is irreversible

13. Terminally ill children typically
    a. accept their impending death with equanimity
    b. have no idea that they are dying or what it means to die
    c. go through Kubler-Ross' stages of dying in sequential order
    d. experience a range of negative emotions and express a number of negative behaviors

14. Grief over the loss of a child
    a. is greatest if the child is young
    b. does not differ in intensity as a function of the age of the child
    c. is less intense if the child dies from an accident beyond the parent's control
    d. is more intense for fathers than mothers since mothers in our culture are encouraged to express grief more openly than fathers

15. Children's grief
    a. can be reduced by not talking about death and the deceased
    b. can be reduced if they have a number of other stressors to deal with at the same time
    c. can be reduced if appropriate social support systems are in place
    d. is always expressed openly through behavior such as crying

APPLICATION

Integrate understanding of death with Piaget's stages of cognitive development. How do they apply to the practical situation of coping with the death of a pet and death of a parent? For example, how would you help a child in the preoperational stage cope with death of a parent? How would you explain that the pet dog has died? What cognitive limitations would you need to be aware of? How would your conversations with children in the concrete operational stage and adolescents or adults in the formal operational stage differ from the conversation that you have with the preoperational child? Think back to what you have learned about cognitive and social development across the life span and see whether you can apply any of this information to understanding of death and coping with death.

Before you leave this chapter, go back and take another look at the learning objectives presented at the beginning of the chapter. Rephrase each objective into a question and check to see whether you have mastered them. A good way to check your understanding of a concept is to see if you can teach it to someone else. Take turns doing this with a small group of people. Whenever you are unsure or unclear about a response, go back to the text and find out what information you are missing in order to provide a clear and complete response.

ANSWERS

Summary and Guided Review (Fill-in the blank)

1.	process	33.	hope
2.	total brain	34.	acceptance
3.	stimuli	35.	dying trajectory
4.	one hour	36.	lingering
5.	three	37.	erratic
6.	reflexes	38.	personality
7.	cortex	39.	bereavement
8.	euthanasia	40.	grief
9.	active	41.	mourning
10.	passive	42.	anticipatory grief
11.	Living Will	43.	separation
12.	life expectancy	44.	numbness
13.	accidents	45.	yearning
14.	violent	46.	disorganization
15.	chronic	47.	despair
16.	programmed	48.	reorganization
17.	damage	49.	disappearance
18.	maximum	50.	cessation
19.	Hayflick limit	51.	irreversible
20.	endocrine	52.	universal
21.	hormone	53.	cognitive
22.	immune system	54.	mature
23.	autoimmune reactions	55.	death anxiety
24.	DNA repair	56.	age
25.	cross-linkage	57.	pathological
26.	free radicals	58.	chronic
27.	denial	59.	distorted
28.	isolation	60.	attachment
29.	anger	61.	unexpected
30.	bargain	62.	cause
31.	depression	63.	social support
32.	acceptance	64.	hospice

Key Terms

1. Hayflick limit
2. denial
3. immune system theory
4. euthanasia
5. grief
6. hospice
7. programmed theories of aging
8. cross-linkage theory
9. total brain death
10. death anxiety
11. dying trajectory
12. DNA repair theory
13. maximum life span
14. mourning
15. free radicals
16. damage theories of aging
17. life expectancy
18. autoimmune reactions
19. Living Will
20. anticipatory grief
21. endocrine theory
22. bereavement

Self Test

1.	C	9.	A
2.	B	10.	B
3.	D	11.	D
4.	D	12.	B
5.	A	13.	D
6.	B	14.	B
7.	B	15.	C
8.	C		

Chapter Eighteen
Fitting the Pieces Together

LEARNING OBJECTIVES

There are two major objectives of this chapter. One is to chronologically organize topical information presented in the earlier chapters of the text and briefly summarize developments of each major age or stage of the life span. You should be able to describe the physical-perceptual, cognitive-intellectual, personal, and social developments of infants, preschool children, school-aged children, adolescents, young adults, middle-aged adults, and older adults. A second objective is to pull out and summarize the major developmental themes running throughout the text. These themes help one understand the developmental changes occurring throughout the life span. You should be able to describe the major themes and apply or give examples of each one.

SUMMARY AND GUIDED REVIEW

Infant (birth to age 2) development is remarkably (1) _____. Newborns come equipped with (2) _____ and (3) _____ capabilities that allow them to respond to their environment. Many (4) _____ reflexes disappear as infants mature during the first year and are replaced by voluntary motor behaviors. Infants develop cognitive capabilities through the interaction of (5) _____ and their sensory and motor explorations. According to Piaget, infants are in the (6) _____ period of cognitive development. During this period, they acquire (7) _____ _____, or the understanding that objects exist even when they are not being perceived. They also acquire the (8)_____ _____, which allows them to mentally represent ideas. Along with cognitive developments, infants are developing a sense of self and showing signs of distinct temperaments. According to Erikson, infants face the first (9) _____ conflict of trust vs. mistrust and must somehow resolve this conflict. Infants are also developing affectional ties, or (10) _____ to caregivers.

Preschool children (ages 2 through 5) acquire gross motor control and fine motor skills necessary for many important tasks. According to Piaget, they are in the (11) _____ stage of cognitive development, where they often use perceptually salient features to solve a problem rather than the (12) _____ _____ used by older children. Through application of the (13) _____ _____ acquired at the end of the sensorimotor period, they master the basics of language. Preschool children are notorious for their short (14) _____ _____ and they typically fail to use memory (15) _____. Preschool children are often characterized as (16) _____, since they have difficulty understanding another person's perspective. This might cause them to have trouble communicating since they assume that their listeners know what they know. According to Erikson, preschool children wrestle with two conflicts. In the stage of (17) _____ versus shame and doubt, they must learn to assert themselves and in the stage of (18) _____ versus guilt, they implement bold plans. Although still very close to parents, preschool children begin to spend more time with peers.

School-aged children (ages 6 through 11) are typically more self-controlled, serious, and (19) _____ than younger children. They also have developed better (20) _____ skills, allowing them to participate in a wider range of sports and activities. They are in Piaget's (21) _____ _____ stage, which means they can reason logically about concrete problems. They master the finer points of language and communication, including reading and writing. School-aged children show a greater understanding of self and others. They are faced with Erikson's conflict of (22) _____ versus inferiority, as they struggle to master scholastic and personal tasks. We also see the formation of a more stable (23) _____ during this period. Many school-aged children move from Kohlberg's (24) _____ level of moral reasoning to (25) _____ moral reasoning. The social world expands and (26) _____ of children is increasingly affected by agents outside the home.

Adolescents (ages 12 through 19) undergo dramatic physical changes as they go through (27) _____. As a result, many adolescents are preoccupied with appearance. There are also significant cognitive changes. Adolescents can think more systematically and (28) _____ about hypothetical situations or problems as they progress in Piaget's (29) _____ _____ stage. They are able to think about self and others in more sophisticated ways. According to Erikson, a major developmental task of this period is developing a sense of (30) _____. Adolescents are more serious about preparing for adult roles than younger children and they increasingly participate in making decisions about their lives.

Young adults (ages 20 through 39) are at peak physical capacity and peak (31) _____ _____. Some will move from Kohlberg's level of (32) _____ moral reasoning to (33) _____ reasoning. They face Erikson's conflict of (34) _____ versus isolation and experiment with romantic relationships and marriage. Many become parents and most face a number of family and career responsibilities.

Middle-aged adults (ages 40 through 64) show gradual physical and (35) _____ declines, however, they continue to grow (36) _____. Expertise on the job and at home allows adults to effectively solve everyday problems. Creative achievement is often at its peak during this period. Middle-aged adults struggle with Erikson's conflict of (37) _____ versus stagnation as they

raise their families and make contributions to society. As children
leave home, middle-aged adults often pursue other interests and find
satisfaction in watching their children live adult lives.

Older adults (age 65 and up) experience some losses and declines in
functioning. They take more time to learn things and may experience
some (38) _____ lapses. They have difficulty solving
(39) _____ problems, but experience no big change in
cognitive and linguistic skills that are used everyday. Older adults
face Erikson's conflict of (40) _____ versus despair as they
review their lives and try to find meaning from their accomplishments.
It is difficult to describe a single pattern of development, since there
is immense (41) _____ among capabilities of older adults

This chapter ends with ten major themes in human development that run
throughout the text and these are summarized here.
1. *We are indeed whole beings throughout the life span*. Physical,
    cognitive, personal, and social developments are intertwined during
    each period of the life span.
2. *With age, behavior becomes more complex and organized*, a theme that
    is captured by Werner's orthogenetic principle. Development becomes
    increasingly differentiated and integrated.
3. *Development proceeds in multiple directions*. It involves gains,
    losses, and changes that are simply different but not gains or
    losses. In addition, not everyone moves along the same
    developmental path.
4. *There is both continuity and discontinuity in development*. This
    issue raises questions about whether change is quantitative or
    qualitative; whether we retain the same relative position on traits
    compared to age mates or achieve different positions; and whether
    early experiences have relatively permanent effects on development.
5. *Nature and nurture truly interact*. Multiple forces within and
    outside the person interact to determine human development.
6. *We are individuals, becoming even more diverse with age*. There is
    an incredible amount of diversity among humans, which makes it
    difficult to form generalizations about them. And as we age, human
    development becomes less and less predictable.
7. *We develop in a cultural and historical context*. Development is
    affected by broad cultural and historical contexts, as well as the
    individual's immediate environment.
8. *We are active in our own development*. We actively explore the
    world and create our own understandings of the world rather than
    being passively molded by the world around us.
9. *Development is best viewed from a life-span perspective*.
    Development in any one phase of life is best understood by viewing
    it in a life-span perspective.
10. *Much remains to be learned*. We have just begun to crack the
    surface! In light of the complex nature of human development, more
    developmentalists are turning to the contextual/dialectical models
    of human development.

Summary and Guided Review (Fill-in the blank)

1. rapid
2. reflexes
3. sensory
4. automatic
5. maturation
6. sensorimotor
7. object permanence
8. symbolic capacity
9. psychosocial
10. attachments
11. preoperational
12. logical reasoning
13. symbolic capacity
14. attention spans
15. strategies
16. egocentric
17. autonomy
18. initiative
19. logical
20. motor
21. concrete operations
22. industry
23. personality
24. preconventional
25. conventional
26. socialization
27. puberty
28. abstractly
29. formal operations
30. identity
31. intellectual functioning
32. conventional
33. postconventional
34. intimacy
35. sensory
36. intellectually
37. generativity
38. memory
39. novel
40. integrity
41. diversity